Making Peace with the Earth

Making Peace with the Earth

VANDANA SHIVA

Fernwood Publishing
HALIFAX & WINNIPEG
www.fernwoodpublishing.ca

PlutoPress
www.plutobooks.com

First published 2012 by Women Unlimited (an associate of Kali for Women), New Delhi, India
This edition published 2013 by Pluto Press, 345 Archway Road, London N6 5AA
www.plutobooks.com

Distributed in the United States of America exclusively by
Palgrave Macmillan, a division of St. Martin's Press LLC,
175 Fifth Avenue, New York, NY 10010

Published in Canada by Fernwood Publishing, 32 Oceanvista Lane, Black Point, Nova Scotia,
B0J 1B0 and 748 Broadway Avenue, Winnipeg, Manitoba, R3G 0X3
www.fernwoodpublishing.ca

Fernwood Publishing Company Limited gratefully acknowledges the financial support of the
Government of Canada through the Canada Book Fund and the Canada Council for the Arts,
the Nova Scotia Department of Communities, Culture and Heritage, the Manitoba Department of
Culture, Heritage and Tourism under the Manitoba Publishers Marketing Assistance Program and
the Province of Manitoba, through the Book Publishing Tax Credit, for our publishing program.

 Canadian Heritage Patrimoine canadien  The Canada Council for the Arts / Le Conseil des Arts du Canada  NOVA SCOTIA Manitoba

Library and Archives Canada Cataloguing in Publication
Shiva, Vandana
        Making peace with the earth / Vandana Shiva.
Includes bibliographical references.
ISBN 978-1-55266-566-4
        1. Globalization--Environmental aspects. 2. Industries--
Environmental aspects. 3. Environmental economics. 4. Offenses
against the environment. I. Title.
HC79.E5S434 2013   333.7   C2012-907970-7
Copyright © Vandana Shiva 2012, 2013

The right of Vandana Shiva to be identified as the author of this work has been
asserted by her in accordance with the Copyright, Designs and Patents Act 1988.

British Library Cataloguing in Publication Data
A catalogue record for this book is available from the British Library

ISBN 978 0 7453 3377 9   Hardback   ISBN 978 1 8496 4927 8 PDF eBook
ISBN 978 0 7453 3376 2   Paperback (Pluto Press) ISBN 978 1 8496 4929 2 Kindle eBook
ISBN 978 1 55266 566 4   (Fernwood)   ISBN 978 1 8496 4928 5 EPUB eBook

Library of Congress Cataloging in Publication Data applied for

10   9   8   7   6   5   4   3   2

Typeset at Women Unlimited, New Delhi 110016
Simultaneously printed digitally by CPI Antony Rowe, Chippenham, UK
and Edwards Bros in the United States of America

Contents

Abbreviations

ADB	:	Asian Development Bank
BOOT	:	Build, Own, Operate, Transfer
BOT	:	Build, Operate, Transfer
DJB	:	Delhi Jal (Water) Board
EPZ	:	Export Processing Zone
GDP	:	Gross Domestic Product
GNP	:	Gross National Product
HRV	:	High Responsive Varieties
HYV	:	High Yielding Varieties
IMF	:	International Monetary Fund
IPCC	:	Intergovernmental Panel on Climate Change
LPG	:	Liberalisation, Privatisation, Globalisation
MNC	:	Multinational Corporation
MoEF	:	Ministry of Environment and Forests
MTPA	:	Million Tonnes Per Annum
NGO	:	Non-Governmental Organisation
OECD	:	Organisation for Economic Co-operation and Development
REDD	:	Reducing Emissions from Deforestation and Degradation
SAP	:	Structural Adjustment Programme
SEZ	:	Special Economic Zone
TRIPS	:	Trade Related Aspects of Intellectual Property Rights
WTO	:	World Trade Organisation

Conversions

(Rs.) 1 lakh	=	100,000
(Rs.) 1 crore	=	10 million (10,000,000)
1 hectare (ha.)	=	2.5 acres

Acknowledgements

This book has grown out of my Sydney Peace Prize lecture, "Making Peace with the Earth" in 2010, and from four decades of engagement with movements to protect the earth and people's rights, beginning with Chipko.

I thank the diverse movements in recent times that invited me for support and from whom I learnt both about the wars against the earth, and making peace with the earth – the farmers' movements against the Reliance power plant in Dadri and the Reliance SEZ in Jhajjar; the movement against Salim's SEZ in Nandigram; the movement against Vedanta's bauxite mining in Niyamgiri; the movement against Tata's steel plant in Gopalpur and POSCO's proposed plant in Jagatsinghpur.

I also thank Shreya and Sulakshana for their contributions to the land-grab section.

Over a quarter century, the Navdanya family has practised and articulated a non-violent agriculture. We have shown that it is possible to make peace with the earth and contribute to human well-being.

A human being is a part of the whole called by us the Universe, a part limited in space and time. He experiences himself, his thoughts and feelings, as something separated from the rest, a kind of optical delusion of his consciousness. This delusion is a kind of prison for us, restricting us to our personal desires and to affection for a few persons nearest to us. Our task must be to free ourselves from this prison by widening our circle of compassion to embrace all living creatures and the whole of nature and its beauty.

– *Albert Einstein*

PART I

Wars against the Earth

1 Eco-Apartheid as War

WHEN WE THINK of wars in our times, our minds automatically turn to Iraq and Afghanistan, but the bigger war is the on-going war against the earth. In fact, the wars in Iraq, Afghanistan and Libya can be seen as wars for the earth's resources, especially oil. The war against the earth has its roots in an economy which fails to respect ecological and ethical limits – limits to inequality, to injustice, to greed and to economic concentration. Even though both economy and ecology have their roots in *oikos*, our home, the planet, the economy has separated itself from ecology in our minds, even as the intensity of exploitation and dependence on nature has increased.

The global corporate economy based on the idea of limitless growth has become a permanent war economy against the planet and people. The means are instruments of war; coercive free trade treaties used to organise economies on the basis of trade wars; and technologies of production based on violence and control, such as toxins, genetic engineering, geo-engineering and nano-technologies. Here we have just another form of "weapons of mass destruction" which kill millions in peace-time by robbing them of food and water, and poisoning the web of life. Tools of war have become the tools of economic production. The tragic bombing in Oslo on July 22, 2011 used six tonnes of chemical fertiliser; the serial bomb blasts in Mumbai were fertiliser bombs; the bombings in Afghanistan are, likewise, based on synthetic fertiliser.

The present global "war" is the inevitable next step for economic and corporate globalisation driven by a handful of corporations and powerful countries that seek to control the earth's resources and to transform the planet into a supermarket in which everything is for sale. The continuing wars in Afghanistan, Iraq and onwards are not only about "Blood for Oil"; as they unfold we will see that they will be about "Blood for Land", "Blood for Food", "Blood for Genes and Biodiversity", and "Blood for Water". By extrapolation, the rules of free trade, especially the World Trade Organisation's (WTO) Agreement on Agriculture, are just another kind of weapon in the food wars. Biodiversity and genes have been called the "green oil" of the future; water is frequently referred to as the "oil" of the twenty-first century. Oil has become the metaphor and organising principle for corporate globalisation for all resources in the world. Wars and militarisation are an essential instrument for control over these vital resources, along with free trade treaties and technologies of control.

Every vital, living resource of the planet that maintains the fragile web of life is in the process of being privatised, commodified and appropriated by corporations. Every inch of land that supports the life and livelihoods of tribal and peasant communities is being grabbed, leading to land wars. Every drop of water that flows in our rivers is being appropriated, leading to water wars. Biodiversity is being reduced to "green oil" to extend the fossil fuel age, ignoring the intrinsic worth of life on earth, and ignoring also the rights the poor have to biodiversity to meet their daily needs. Forests were already commoditised by commercial forestry; now their ecological services are being commoditised for a so-called "green economy". Green is supposed to be the colour of life and the biosphere but, increasingly, green symbolises the market and money, and a green economy could well entail the ultimate commodification of the planet. Green is also becoming the colour of the militarisation of the resource-grab taking place in order to fuel limitless growth. Militarisation is the shield for corporate globalisation, both nationally and globally. At the national level, militarisation is becoming the dominant mode of governance, whether through laws regarding Homeland Security in the US or Operation Green Hunt in India. Economic growth is literally flowing through the barrel of a gun. As people resist ecological destruction and appropriation of their resources, the war against the planet also becomes a war against local communities and people struggling for justice and peace. South African writer, David Hallowes, in *Toxic Futures* refers to the Pentagon preparing for "fourth generation war" against "non-state enemies", i.e. ordinary citizens. As he reports, in South Africa, the urban poor have found themselves "under armed assault from the state"[1] (p. 47). As land becomes "real estate", even the polluted dumpsites that the poor make their homes are grabbed by developers. And as people are removed they are told, "You are just people from the dumpsite. You are just scrap."

In his essay, "The Robbery of the Soil", Rabindranath Tagore dramatically describes this war against the earth:

> The temptation of an inordinately high level of living, which was once confined only to a small section of the community, becomes widespread. The blindness is sure to prove fatal to the civilisation which puts no restraint upon the emulation of self-indulgence...
>
> When they had reduced the limited store of material in their immediate surroundings, they proceeded to wage various wars among their different sections, each wanting his own special allotment of the lion's share. In their scramble for the right to self-indulgence, they laughed at moral law and took it to be a sign of superiority to be ruthless in the satisfaction, each of his own desire. They exhausted the water, cut down the trees, reduced the surface of the planet to a desert, riddled it with enormous pits and made its interior a rifled pocket, emptied of its valuables.[2]

Not only is corporate power converging with state power for the great resource grab, corporate-state power is emerging as militarised power to undemocratically impose an unsustainable and unjust agenda on the earth and its people. That is how the war against the earth becomes a war against people, against democracy and against freedom. After two decade of corporate globalisation, we now have evidence of its ecological and social costs. A deregulated financial economy gave us the financial crisis; a deregulated food economy has given us a food crisis; a deregulated mining economy has turned every mineral-rich area into a war zone.

The economic crisis that began in 2008, and still continues, forces us to raise questions about the contradiction between a model based on assumptions of limitless growth and a reality with ecological, social, political and economic limits. Thomas Friedman, till recently a supporter of globalisation and the ideology of limitless growth, asked this question:

> Let's today step out of the normal boundaries of analysis of our economic crisis and ask a radical question – What if the crisis of 2008 represents something much more fundamental than a deep recession? What is it telling us, that the whole growth model we created over the last fifty years is simply unsustainable, economically and ecologically, and that 2008 was when we hit the wall – when Mother Nature and the market both said "no more"?[3]

Despite warnings, the failed model continued to be pushed with trillions of dollars of bail-outs and with further liberalisation, expanding mining for coal and iron ore and bauxite. Protests erupted everywhere – from the coast of Orissa where on June 23, 2011, I met children and women who faced twenty battalions of police sent to clear the land for the mining company, POSCO, to build a giant steel plant, to the squares of Madrid where on July 26, 2011, I met the *indignados* of the M-15 movement. "Who are we? We are the people who have come here freely as volunteers. Why are we here? We are here because we want a new society that gives more priority to life than to economic interest." The M-15 states:

> Today the world is united, both at the level of the forces of destruction of life, and of the defence of life. This contest, taking place in every local globally, has pitted greed for resources and profits against life – in nature and society. There is, of course, the danger that as ecological, economic, cultural and political spaces are robbed from people who become uprooted , they will be

pitted against each other. This is particularly tragic in the case of Africa as her resources and land are grabbed, her people are displaced, and thousands leave their motherland to cross the Mediterranean. Instead of seeing displacement and dispossession of people as a consequence of the economic war against the earth, these refugees are criminalised.

And racist and fascist forces are waiting to capitalise on displacement by making people view immigrants as the cause of their unemployment and economic insecurity, thus diverting attention from the economic structures which work *for* corporations and *against* people and the earth. The political conflicts that are triggered as people lose their resources and livelihoods are converted into markets for arms and militarisation.

Peace with the earth, a survival imperative

Making Peace with the Earth bears witness to the wars taking place in our times against the earth and people. It also tells the stories of struggles to defend the earth and people's rights to land and water, forests, seeds and biodiversity. It outlines how a paradigm shift to earth-centred economics, politics and culture is our only chance of survival. The stories are from India, because India is my home and the ground of my experience. I also focus on it because it is seen as the poster child of the success of economic globalisation, with high growth rates. This book explores what lies beneath the growth – the ecological, economic, social and political costs that are systematically externalised and made invisible. It shows how the growth miracle is based on a kind of war, how it has deepened inequalities and eroded democracy; how it is destroying the rich biodiversity and cultural diversity of our land through ecological destruction and the imposition of monocultures; how millions lose their livelihoods so that a handful of global corporations and billionaires can control markets and resources. "The India Story" is the story of India Inc. and Global Inc., the story of the new Indian oligarchs and billionaires – the

Ambanis, the Lakshmi Mittals, the Anil Agarwals, the Ruias, the Tatas, the Adanis and the Jindals.

However, this story hides two other "India Stories". One is the story of those who have paid the price through the theft of their resources and destruction of their livelihoods to create concentrated wealth in the hands of a few. It is the not-told story of India's seed sector being taken over by Monsanto and of the 250,000 farmers' suicides, of how India's food security system is being dismantled to create markets for Cargill and Walmart. It is also the story of other ways of thinking, of being, of producing and providing that have been subjugated in this war against the earth. The neoliberal model of economic globalisation is based on the assumption that there is no alternative, but there are alternatives everywhere. There are alternatives in indigenous cultures and local economies which people are defending with their lives on the line. Alternatives are emerging as a response to peak oil and climate change, and alternatives are emerging where people face economic closure. Detroit is emerging as a garden city from the ruins of a city where automobiles were produced. I took some seeds to Punjab where indebted farmers are committing suicide today – Navdanya has requests for seeds to start 3,500 more gardens. The story of these alternatives is the story of making peace with the earth.

Humanity's choice: destructive or creative

We have moved out of the Holocene Age that began ten thousand years ago at the end of the Pleistocene. It derives from the Greek words "holos" (whole) and "kainos" (new). This age provided the stable climate which gave us the conditions for our cultural and material evolution as a human species. According to scientists we have entered a new age, the Anthropocene age, in which our species is becoming the most significant force on the planet. Current climate change and species extinction are driven by human activities and our very large ecological footprint.

Climate catastrophes and extreme climate events are already

taking their toll – the floods in Thailand in 2011, in Pakistan and Ladakh in 2010, forest fires in Russia, more frequent and intense cyclones and hurricanes, severe drought and flooding are examples of how humans have destabilised the climate system of our self-regulated planet. Humans have driven 75 per cent of agricultural biodiversity to extinction because of industrial farming, and between three to 300 species are being pushed into extinction every day.

There are planetary wars taking place with geo-engineering – creating artificial volcanoes, fertilising the oceans with iron filings, putting reflectors in the sky to prevent the sun from shining on the earth as if the sun was the problem, not man's violence against the earth, and the arrogant ignorance in dealing with it. In 1997, Edward Teller , a Hungarian-born American theoretical physicist, co-authored a white paper, "Global Warming and Ice Ages: I. Prospects For Physics – Based Modulation of Global Change,"[4] in which he advocated the large – scale introduction of metal particulates into the upper atmosphere to apply an effective "sunscreen". The Pentagon is looking to breed immortal synthetic organisms with the goal of eliminating "the randomness of natural evolutionary advancement". What is being done with the climate is also being done with the evolutionary code of the universe, with total disregard for the consequences. Biodiversity is our living commons – the basis of life and of commons. We are part of nature, not her masters and owners; claiming intellectual property rights on life forms, living resources and living processes is an ethical, ecological and economic perversion.

The destructive Anthropocene need not be the only future, we can shift the paradigm. We can look at the destructive impact our species has had on the planet's biodiversity, ecosystems and climate systems and make that shift. An ecological shift entails not seeing ourselves as outside the ecological web of life, it means seeing ourselves as members of the earth family, with the responsibility of caring for other species and life on earth in all its diversity. It creates the imperative to live, produce and consume within ecological limits and within our share of ecological space, without encroaching on the rights of other species and peoples. It is a shift that recognises that science has already made a paradigm shift from separation to non-separability and interconnectedness, from the mechanistic and reductionist to the relational and holistic.

At the economic level it involves going beyond the artificial and even false categories of perpetual economic growth, so-called free trade, consumerism and competitiveness. It means shifting to a focus on planetary and human well-being, to living economies, to living well rather than having more, to valuing cooperation rather than competitiveness. These are the shifts being made by indigenous communities, peasants, women and young people in the new movements like the Indignants in Europe and Occupy Wall Street in the US. This is the creative and constructive Anthropocene of Earth Democracy, based on ecological humility in place of arrogance, and ecological responsibility instead of the careless and blind exercise of power, control and violence. For humans to protect life on earth and our own future we need to become deeply conscious of the rights of the earth, our duties towards her, our compassion for all her beings. Our world has been structured by capitalist patriarchy around fictions and abstractions like "capital", "corporations" and "growth" which have allowed the unleashing of the negative forces of the destructive Anthropocene. We need to change that. We will either make peace with the earth or face extinction as humans even as we push millions of other species to extinction. Continuing the war against the earth is not an intelligent option.

Paradigm wars: eco-apartheid and wars in the mind

On April 20, 2011, the UN General Assembly organised a conference, "Harmony with Nature", as part of the celebration of Mother Earth Day. I was invited to address the gathering, together with Peter Brown of McGill University; Cormac Cullinan, an environmental attorney from South Africa; Riane Eisler, author of *The Real Wealth of Nations: Creating a Caring Economics;* and Mathis Wackernegal from the Global Footprint Network. The UN Secretary General in his report on the conference has elaborated on the imperative of the "route back to the future" which involves "reconnecting with nature".

Separation is at the root of disharmony with nature and violence against it. As Cormac Cullinan pointed out, "apartheid" means separateness; the world joined the anti-apartheid movement to go beyond the violent assumption of the separation of people on the basis of colour. Tagore, India's national poet, saw in separation the roots of both bondage and poverty. He wrote: "I could understand how great the concrete truth was in any plane of life, the truth that in separation is bondage, in union is liberation ... Poverty lay in separation and wealth in union."[5]

Today, we need to overcome a much wider and deeper apartheid, an eco-apartheid based on the illusion of separateness, of humans from nature, in our minds and lives. This is an illusion because we are *part* of nature and earth, not *apart* from it.

We are made of the same five elements – earth, water, fire, air and space – that constitute the earth. The water that circulates in the biosphere circulates in our bodies; the oxygen that plants produce becomes our breath; the food that is produced by the soil and the sun's energy becomes our cells, our blood, our bones. Biologically and ecologically we are one with the earth. The web of life is woven through interconnectedness. It is the disease of separation and eco-apartheid that denies this and then creates the diseases of loneliness, depression, alienation. As Arthur Robbins has observed in his book, *Paradise Lost, Paradise Regained*:

> To live without a context, to live outside of, rather than within, the community, is to live in a state of *ex statis*, to be out of place, to be without a place. *Ex statis* is to be separated from the stability of forces seeking balance, equilibrium, harmony or stasis. In medieval times the Greek *ex statis* became *alienato mentis*, which is the basis for the English word "alienation". "Lien" is the French for tie; an insane person is known as an aliene, "he who is without ties". Thus insanity and separation have a common origin.[6]

While separation was intrinsic to the old science based on Cartesian,

Baconian and Newtonian assumptions, non-separability is built into the new science of quantum theory and the new biology. The Einstein-Podolsky-Rosen Paradox has shown that when a quantum system is subdivided and the two sub-systems are separated in space and time, their state is non-separable.[7] Physicists like Niels Bohr, Wolfgang Pauli and David Bohm stressed the non-separable wholeness of the universe of physical phenomena.

Even in biology, non-separability is being recognised through fields like epigenetics and gene ecology, a term that was born in Tromso. This is a new interdisciplinary field that is unique in its combination of genetics and biochemistry with bioethics, the philosophy of science, and social studies of science and technology. It builds on innovative work in the area of genomics, proteomics, food science, ecology and evolution, going beyond the reductionist approaches of individual scientific disciplines.[8] Epigenetics shows there is no separation between genes, the organism and the environment. The reductionist view is that the DNA carries all our heritable information and is insulated from the environment. Epigenetics adds new dimensions to the behaviour of genes, it proposes a control system of "switches" that turns genes on or off, and suggests that things people experience, like nutrition and stress, can control these switches and cause heritable effects in humans.[9]

Redefining the economy by embedding it in society and nature is the first step in a paradigm shift. Shifting from GDP and GNP to measures of real wealth, welfare, well-being and happiness is another. Wealth is derived from "weal" (well-being), its original meaning is "condition of well-being". Aristotle distinguished between "chrematistics – the art of money-making – and oikonomia – the art of living. The radical shift that movements around the world are making is the shift from an earth-degrading, human-degrading economic system to earth-centred, human-centred systems which reduce the ecological footprint while increasing well-being. Not only will this shift that is already underway bring harmony with nature, it will sow the seeds of social justice and equity, both in terms of sharing the earth's resources and recognising the work that goes into caring for the planet. It will recognise women's work in sustenance; it will recognise the knowledge creation and production of third world and indigenous communities; it will create space for future generations.

Making peace with the earth involves a shift from fragmentation and reductionism to interconnectedness and holistic thinking, a shift from violence and exploition to non-violence and dialogue with the earth. It involves the inclusion of the biodiversity of knowledge systems. We need other ways of thinking and knowing to overcome our separation from nature. As Tagore reminds us:

> The language of Nature is the eternal language of creation. It penetrates reality to reach the deepest layers of our consciousness, it draws upon a language that has survived thousands of years with the human ... it is the musical instrument of nature; it replicates the rhythm inherent in life itself. If we listen carefully we will be able to trace within it the murmurs of eternity where the spirit of liberation, peace and beauty lurk, it reminds us of the sea that is *santam, shivam, advaitam* ... it reminds us of our bond with the world ... if we can accept this music of the wild within us, we can perceive the great music of oneness ...[10]

Will green be the colour of money or life?

The world order built on the economic fundamentalism of greed, commodification of all life and limitless growth is collapsing. The Wall Street crash of September 2008 and the continuing financial crisis signal the end of the paradigm that put fictitious finance above the real wealth created by nature and humans, profits above people and corporations above citizens. This paradigm can only be kept afloat with endlesss bail-outs that direct public wealth to private rescue instead of using it to rejuvenate nature and economic livelihoods for people. It can only be kept afloat with increasing violence to the earth and people, it can only be kept alive as an economic dictatorship. This is evident in India's heartland, as the unquenchable appetite for steel and aluminium for the global consumer economy is clashing head-on with the rights of tribals to their land and homes, their forests and rivers, their cultures and ways of life. Tribals are saying a loud and clear "no" to their forced uprooting; the only way to get to the minerals and coal in the face of democratic resistance is by the use of militarised violence against them. Operation Green Hunt has been launched in the tribal areas with precisely this objective, even though the proclaimed goal is to clear out the "Maoists". More than 40,000 armed paramilitary forces have been placed in the tribal areas which are rich in minerals and where tribal unrest is growing.

The technological fundamentalism that has externalised costs, both ecological and social, and blinded us to ecological destruction has also reached a dead end. Climate chaos, the externality of technologies based on the use of fossil fuels, is a wake-up call that we cannot continue on the fossil fuel path. The high cost of industrial farming is resulting in the ecological destruction of the natural capital of soil, water, biodiversity and air, as well as in the creation of malnutrition with a billion people denied food and another two billion denied health due to obesity, diabetes and other food-related diseases.

The green economy agenda for Rio+20 can either deepen the privatisation of the earth and, with it, the crisis of ecology and poverty or it can be used to re-embed economies in the ecology of the earth. Green economics needs to be an authentic green, it cannot be the brown of desertification and deforestation. It cannot be the red of violence against nature and people, or the unnecessary conflicts over natural resources.

To be green, economics needs to return to its home, to *oikos*. Ecology is the science of the household, economics is supposed to be the management of the household. When economics works against the science of ecology, it results in the mismanagement of the earth and its resources. We mismanage the earth when we do not recognise nature's capital as the real capital and everything else as derived. If we have no land, we have no economy. When we contribute to the growth of nature's capital, we build green economies.

The Earth Summit in 1992 produced two legally binding treaties – the Convention on Biological Diversity and the United Nations

Framework Convention on Climate Change. We also produced a Women's Action Agenda 21 through Women's Environment and Development Organisation (WEDO), which I co-founded with Bella Abzug and Marilyn Waring.

According to UNEP, "In a green economy, growth in income and employment should be driven by private and public investments that reduce carbon emission and pollution, enhance energy and resource efficiency, and prevent the loss of biodiversity and ecosystem services." This is the old paradigm in green clothes, it is still driven by the flawed laws of financial markets.

Will green be the colour of money or of life?

A green economy can be thought of as one which is low in dead fossil carbon, high in living carbon, resource-efficient and socially inclusive. In a green economy, growth should be measured in terms of the health of ecosystems and communities, not in terms of commercial transactions alone. For this, women should be the drivers since they have shaped economies of care, well-being and happiness for centuries. Growth in incomes and employment should be based on the conservation of natural resources and the equitable sharing of our natural wealth for sustainable livelihoods that reduce carbon emissions and pollution, enhance energy and resource efficiency and prevent the loss of biodiversity and ecosystem services. Public and private investment should support such nature-and-women-centred initiatives. There are two different paradigms for, and approaches to, the green economy. One is the corporate-centred green economy which means:

(*a*) Green Washing – one has just to look at the achievements of Shell and Chevron on how they are "green".

(*b*) Bringing nature into markets and the world of commodification. This includes privatisation of the earth's resources, i.e., patenting seeds, biodiversity and life forms, and commodifying nature. It also includes trading in ecological services which, in effect, is trading in the atmosphere's capacity to recycle carbon.

The UNEP initiative on The Economics of Ecosystems and

Biodiversity (TEEB) can serve as a caution to stop ecological and ecosystem degradation and destruction. For example, according to TEEB, the loss of ecological services from the degradation of forests alone amounts to between $2 trillion and $4.5 trillion a year.[11]

As David Hallowes says, "In the act of costing the loss, however, ecological systems are framed within the market. Ecoservices are monetised, so making them available for sale." Another example is that of a private equity firm that bought the rights to the environmental services generated by a 370,000 ha. rainforest reserve in Guyana, recognising that such services – water storage, biodiversity maintenance and rainfall regulation – will eventually be worth something in international markets.[12]

The commodification and tradability of natural resources and ecological services has been deepening progressively over the last few decades. This commodification is also guiding much of the work of environmental economics; for example, the World Bank policy paper on trade liberalisation for India's agriculture sector recommends the creation of "markets in tradable water rights". It argues that

> If rights to the delivery of water can be freely bought and sold, farmers with new crops or in new areas will be able to obtain water, provided they are willing to pay more than its value to existing users, and established users will take account of its sale value in deciding on what and how much to produce.[13]

The institution of tradable water rights will guarantee the diversion of water from small farmers to large corporate "super farms" and lead to water monopolies, as these tradable rights will be sold to the highest bidder. It will also lead to the over-exploitation and misuse of water, since those who deplete water resources do not suffer the consequences of water scarcity as they can always buy water rights from other farmers and other regions. Tradable water rights will also destroy the social fabric of rural communities, creating discord and disintegration. The social breakdown in Somalia can be traced, in part, to the privatisation of water rights which was based on the assumption that no ecological or social limits should be placed on water use. This policy is, in effect a prescription for social and ecological disaster.

The introduction of tradable land and water rights is often justified on environmental grounds. For example, a World Bank study by Pearce and Warford argues that: "In the absence of rights to sell or transfer land, the land owner may be unable to realise the value of any improvements and thus has little incentive to invest in long-term measures such as soil conservation."[14] This assumption is patently false, since the best examples of soil conservation – the hill terraces of the Himalayas – are based on precisely the opposite: communities not threatened with the possibility of losing their resources and benefits have a long-term interest in conserving resources.

Commodification and privatisation are based and promoted on the flawed belief that price equals value. However, all those working for justice in land and water rights and preventing the ecological abuse of land and water, are asking for the opposite – the inalienable right to resources, and in the case of common property resources like water, the inalienability of common rights.

The second paradigm of the green economy is earth-centred and people-centred. The resources of the earth vital to life – biodiversity, water, air – are a commons for the common good for all, and a green economy is based on a recovery of the commons and the intrinsic value of the earth and all her species. It would put nature's ecological cycles as the drivers and shapers of the economy, it would put people first, not investors, and build on women's core contributions to create economies of sustenance and care that enhance the well-being of all.

The industrial/corporate system of food production uses ten times more units of energy as inputs than it produces as food. It wastes 50 per cent of the food produced; it uses and pollutes 70 per cent of the water on the planet; it has destroyed 75 per cent of the biodiversity in agriculture; and it contributes 40 per cent of the greenhouse gases that are destabilising the climate and further threatening food security. By contrast, earth-centred agriculture produces twice as much food as the inputs it uses; it conserves biodiversity; it mitigates and adapts to climate change; it protects the earth; farmers and public health .

Karl Polanyi in *The Great Transformation: The Political and Economic Origins of Our Times* warned us against commodification and reduction of nature and society to the market.

> A market economy must comprise all elements of industry, including labour, land and money. But labour and land are no other than human beings themselves, of which every society consists, and the natural surroundings in which they exist. To include them in the market mechanism means to subordinate the substance of society itself to the laws of the market.[15]

To this we would add, to include nature and nature's resources and processes in the market mechanism means to subordinate the substance of the earth's living processes to the laws of the market.

Nature has been subjugated to the market as a mere supplier of industrial raw material and dumping ground for waste and pollution. Corporations as the dominant institution shaped by capitalist patriarchy thrive on eco-apartheid and on the Cartesian legacy of dualism which pits nature against humans. Pitting humans against nature is not merely anthropocentric, it is corporate-centric. The earth community has been reduced to humans, and corporations then reshape some part of humanity as consumers of their products, and other parts as disposable. Consumers lose their identity as earth citizens, as co-creators and co-producers with nature. Those rendered disposable lose their very lives and livelihoods.

The false universalism of man as conqueror and owner of the earth has led to the technological hubris of geo-engineering, genetic engineering and nuclear energy. It has led to the ethical outrage of owning life forms through patents, water through privatisation, and air through carbon trading.

The green economy considers it necessary, in the struggle to preserve biodiversity, to put a price on the free services that plants, animals and ecosystems offer humanity – the purification of water, the pollination of plants by bees, the protection of coral reefs, and climate regulation. According to the green economy, we need to identify the specific functions of the ecosystem and biodiversity that can be made subject to a monetary value, evaluate their current state, define the limits of those services, and set out in economic terms the cost of their conservation to develop a market for environmental services. In other words, the transfusion of the rules of the market will save nature.

The climate crisis is a result of releasing pollutants into the atmosphere beyond the recycling capacity of the planet. To continue to add pollutants while letting polluters make money through carbon trading is a deepening of the war against the atmospheric commons. Mathis Wackernagel calculates the ecological footprint of human production and consumption as follows: the ecological footprint of individuals is a measure of the amount of land required to provide for all their resource requirements plus the amount of vegetated land to absorb all carbon dioxide emissions. In 1961, the human demand for resources was 70 per cent of the earth's ability to regenerate. By the 1980s it was equal to the annual supply of resources, and since the 1990s it has exceeded the earth's capacity by 20 per cent. "It takes the biosphere, therefore, at least a year and three months to renew what humanity uses in a single year so that humanity is now eating its capital, Earth's natural capital."[16]

The ecological footprint is not the same for all humans. Not only is corporate-driven consumerism eating into the earth's capital, it is eating into the share of the poor to the earth's capital for sustenance and survival. This is at the root of resource conflicts across the developing world. An equitable ecological footprint is 1.7 ha/person. The average for the US is 10.3 ha. of land, to provide for their consumption and absorb their waste. For the UK, it is 5.2 ha; for Japan 4.3 ha; for Germany 5.3 ha; for China 1.2 ha; for India 0.8 ha; for Australia 7.58 ha.[17]

When seeds, the source of life, are deliberately made non-renewable through technological interventions like hybridisation or genetic engineering to create sterile seed, the abundance of life shrinks, growth is interrupted in evolution and in farmers' fields, but the growth of the profits of corporations like Monsanto increases. In

Part II, I show how farmers' suicides in India are linked to seed monopolies; this is why in Navdanya we defend seed sovereignty and farmers' seed freedom.

If we dam rivers and stop their life-giving flow, we do not have more water, we have less. True, more water goes to cities and commercial farms, but there is much less water for rural communities for drinking and irrigation, and in rivers for keeping the river alive. This is why we have been compelled to start the Save the Ganga Movement to stop large dams and diversions on the Ganges which are killing the river.

Humanity stands at a crossroads. One road continues on the path of eco-apartheid and eco-imperialism, of commodification of the earth, her resources and processes. Ecology movements are resisting the expansion of the market and the commodification of their land, their minerals, their forests and biodiversity. That is why the path of eco-apartheid becomes a path based on a war against people. We witness this in India, today, which is growing at eight per cent, but where violence has become the means for resource appropriation of forests and biodiversity, to fuel that growth. The second road is that of making peace with the earth, beginning with the recognition of earth rights. This is the path of Earth Democracy, based on living within the earth's ecological limits and sharing her resources equitably. It is based on deepening and widening democracy to include all life on earth and all humans who are being excluded by so-called "free market democracy" based on corporate rule and corporate greed. Earth Democracy is the path of caring and sharing, the path to genuine freedom.

Wars against people

The majority of the world's people live in earth-centred biodiversity economies, local economies of sustenance. When ecosystems are destroyed and resources appropriated, people lose their livelihoods and their capacity to provide for their sustenance. The rewriting of rules and laws to perpetrate wars against the earth undermine the rights of communities to co-create and co-produce with the earth and meet their needs for food and water. Laws that make seed the "intellectual property" of corporations undermine the law of the seed to renew, multiply and distribute, and also undermine farmers' rights to save, exchange, and evolve seeds. The transformation of food economies from sustainable, sustenance economies based on small farming into corporate-driven commodity systems is destroying family farms worldwide. In India it has pushed 250,000 farmers to commit suicide. The transformation of food into a commodity has led to India becoming a capital of hunger, with every fourth Indian hungry and every second child "wasted" and severely malnourished.

Rewriting the rules of economy and trade in favour of corporations also rewrites the rules of governance. Governments mutate from welfare states to corporate states as they deregulate corporations and over-regulate citizens. This is then defined as "free-market democracy". Since corporate freedom is based on extinguishing citizen freedom, the enlargement of "free-market democracy" becomes a war against Earth Democracy.

Since the rules of free-markets and free trade aim at disenfranchising citizens and communities of their resources and rights, people resist them. The war against people is carried to the next level with the militarisation of society and the criminalisation of activists and movements. We have seen this on the streets of Seattle and Genoa, we are seeing it in India everywhere.

Geographically, the heart of India is at the centre of resource wars. Bastar, a tribal region rich in forests, biodiversity and minerals in central India is inhabited by the Gonds. The sub-tribes are Maree, Muria and Doria, as well as Raj Gonds. The Marias are further divided into Abhuj Maree, who live in the hills of Abhay Mar, and Bison Horn Maria, who live south of the Indravati river.

Bastar was an independent kingdom under British rule; when they tried to enclose the forests in Bastar in 1910, the tribals revolted. In a confidential letter of March 29, 1910, B.P. Standan, chief secretary to the chief commissioner, Central Provinces, wrote to the secretary,

Government of India, Political Department, listing the grievances of the tribals, which included:

(*i*) inclusion of village land in reserve forests;

(*ii*) high-handed treatment and unjust exactions on the part of forest officials;

(*iii*) maltreatment of pupils and parents by village *mostees* to extract money for tehsildars;

(*iv*) forcible purchase of food at one-fourth the market price by police employees;

(*v*) exaction of excessive *begari* (forced labour); and

(*vi*) interference in brewing local liquor, etc.[18]

The tribal rebellion could only be suppressed by the army.

After Independence, Bastar became part of Madhya Pradesh and is now part of the new state of Chhattisgarh. The tribals of Bastar have always defended their freedom and sovereignty. In the 1980s, they rejected and stopped the World Bank social forestry project which would have replaced 8,000 ha. of natural forests in the Bastar hills with tropical pine for the pulp and paper industry. The indigenous forests provide bamboo for basket-making and weaving, fruits such as tamarind, jackfruit, mango and edible berries for food security. Tribal resistance stopped this Rs 96 million project, a first in the history of the World Bank. Tribal cultures are based on community control of natural resources; the commons are inseparable from ecology and democracy.

The privatisation of the state is most intense in resource-rich tribal areas across the country where it is being undertaken with force and violence. When the state becomes a corporate state and the privatisation of public goods its main objective, then the defence of the commons, the defence of the democratic and constitutional rights of the people, is seen as a threat. Defenders of people's rights are criminalized so as to facilitate criminal takeover of the commons. This is why Dr. Binayak Sen, one of the most courageous defenders of the commons, was sentenced to rigorous life-imprisonment. Dr. Sen, a gold medalist from Christian Medical College, could have become a millionaire through private practice; instead he chose to serve the tribals, practising health care as a public service.

For over thirty years, I have worked with Dr. Sen and his wife, Dr. Ilina Sen, to protect biodiversity and water as a commons. I started Navdanya to protect seeds from privatisation through patents and genetic engineering. The Sens saw our work in biodiversity conservation in Dehradun and they started saving seed in a village outside Raipur to keep alive the legacy of Dr. Richharia who had conserved 22,972 varieties of rice and documented hundreds of thousands in the region that is today's Chhattisgarh. The Richharia collection is with the Raipur-based Indira Gandhi Krishi Vishavidyalaya (Agricultural University), IGAU.

In 2002, Syngenta, the biotech giant, tried to grab these varieties of paddy by signing an MoU with the IGAU for access to Dr. Richharia's priceless collection, painstakingly collected by him from local farmers. Dr. Richharia was the rice sage of India. He is the inspiration behind all agricultural biodiversity conservation movements in India, including Navdanya. Dr. Richharia's vision was to disseminate all appropriate varieties selected from the collection to farmers across Chhattisgarh through decentralised research and extension networks, with rice farmers and scientists as equal partners in development, with ownership of these varieties vesting with farmers.

The International Rice Research Institute (IRRI) was set up in 1960 by the Rockefeller and Ford Foundations, nine years after the establishment of a premier Indian institute, the Central Rice Research Institute (CRRI) in Cuttack. The Cuttack Institute was working on rice research based on indigenous knowledge and genetic resources, a strategy clearly in conflict with the American controlled strategy of IRRI. Under international pressure, Dr. Richharia, then Director of CRRI, was removed when he resisted handing over his collection of rice germplasm to IRRI, and when he called for restraint in the hurried introduction of HYV (High Yield Varieties) from IRRI.

The Madhya Pradesh government gave Dr. Richharia a small

stipend so that he could continue his work at the Madhya Pradesh Rice Research Institute (MPRRI) at Raipur. Later, the MPRRI, which was doing pioneering work in developing a high yielding strategy based on the indigenous knowledge of the Chhattisgarh tribals, was also closed down due to pressure from the World Bank because MPRRI had reservations about sending its collection of germplasm to IRRI.

In 1971, at the initiative of Robert McNamara, then President of the World Bank, a Consultative Group on International Agricultural Research (CGIAR) was formed to finance the network of International Agricultural Centres (IARC). After 1971, nine more IARCS were added to the CGIAR system; the International Crops Research Institute for the Semi-Arid Tropics (ICRISAT) was started in Hyderabad in India in 1971; the International Laboratory for Research on Animal Diseases (ICARD) and the International Livestock Centre for Africa (ILCA) were approved in 1973. This news (*Dainik Bhaskar*, November 9, 2002) came soon after the news that Syngenta was going to be on the board of the CGIAR.

Syngenta's access to Dr. Richharia's collections and control over the World Bank-run International Agricultural Research System, which is obtaining patents on rice, was the MNC's goal for total control over rice, the staple food of most of Asia. Since this news became public, several groups working on people's rights to natural resources, from Chhattisgarh and outside, firmly opposed the deal between Syngenta and IGAU and came together in a mass-based agitation which began on December 3, 2002, the Bhopal gas tragedy day. In addition, the Chhattisgarh Seed Satyagraha was launched on December 10, 2002, International Human Rights Day. Thousands of workers, peasants, women and youth from all over Chhattisgarh courted arrest to protect their sovereignty, fight for survival and sustenance of human community, and to re-assert their rights over rare varieties of rice seeds.

Dr. Binayak Sen played an important role in the seed satyagraha – Syngenta was forced to withdraw from the MOU with IGAU. He also contributed to the defence of water as a commons by resisting the privatisation of the Sheonath river and participating in the movement for water democracy. Villagers have been living beside the semi-perennial Sheonath river near Durg in Chhattisgarh through droughts and floods. They have watered their crops, caught enough fish, and bathed and washed clothes on the ghats along the river. In 2001, a 23.6 km. stretch of the river was sold to Radius Water Ltd. (RWL), a local company, through a BOOT (Build, Own, Operate, Transfer) arrangement for twenty-two years.

The company was contracted to build a dam across the river, with full rights to the reservoir and the water collected in it for supplying water to the industrial estates of Borai, near Durg city. Since the dam has come up, villagers who used to fish in the river and depended on it for their daily needs no longer have any rights to it.

The villages affected on the upper reaches of Sheonath river are: Rasmara, Mohlai, Siloda, Mahmara and Peepar Cheedi, of which the worst-affected are Rasmara and Mohlai. According to the villagers, growing vegetables near the banks is no longer possible as no water supply is available from the river. Some farmers tried to grow vegetables on the small portion of land, but it was washed away due to the excess release of water from the dam. Occasionally, due to a sudden discharge of water, children and women are at risk of being swept away. Farmers' pumps are forcibly taken away by RWL, and they are not even allowed to instal tubewells within a radius of one km from the river. Since no fishing is allowed a large number of families dependent on fish for their livelihood now have no income. Even rearing animals is difficult as animals are allowed in the river only for a few minutes. Bathing and washing clothes at the ghats is totally at the discretion of RWL. Rasmara Gram Panchayat used to get Rs. 90,000 a year from the contract for lifting sand from the river-bank; this has now been monopolised by RWL.

Bastar is not just rich in forests and biodiversity, it is also very rich in minerals. Now, mineral wealth is being privatised in a scam bigger than the recent telecom 2G scam. To mine and export iron ore, a Japanese company built a railway line from Bailadila mines to Vishakhapatnam, a seaport. In February 1995, tribals from different parts of India held an indefinite fast in Delhi to force the government to recognise their demand for 'self-rule'. The National Front for Tribal Self–Rule, a network of organisations of tribal people, started a civil disobedience movement from October 2, 1995 for the establishment of self–rule. They stated:

> We have carried the cross of virtual slavery for much too long in spite of independence. Other rural folks are also in a similar state. Yet, now that everything is clear and there is unanimity in the establishment as also amongst MPs and experts, the change must not be delayed. We will not tolerate this.
>
> Even otherwise, on issues of self-governance we need not be solicitous. It is a natural right. In the hierarchy of democratic institutions gram sabha (village council) is above all, even Parliament. This is what Gandhi preached. We will not obey any law which compromises the position of gram sabhas. In any case we resolve to establish self-rule with effect from October 2, 1995. We will have command over our resources and will manage our affairs thereafter.

In the context of the increasing concentration of power and capital in corporate hands, the space for communities to exercise their right to self-determination and self-rule is rapidly shrinking. The reinvention of the state has to be based on reclaiming sovereignty; sovereignty cannot reside only in centralised state structures, nor does it disappear when the protective functions of the state with respect to its people start to wither away. The new partnership for national sovereignty needs empowered communities which assign functions to the state for their protection. The defence of communities and their resources and livelihoods demands such duties and obligations from state structures.

Such innovation is the basis of the Provisions of the Panchayats (Extension to the Scheduled Areas, PESA) Act which came into effect in December 1996. This Act represents ground-breaking legislation in that, for the first time in India's juridical history, a community of tribals in scheduled areas has been granted legally recognisable collective rights over its own community resources, and the power to manage its own affairs. The Act accepts two important premises: first, that the community is the basic building block of the system; and second, a formal system can be built on the firm foundation of the traditions and customs of the tribal people. The new provisions for the scheduled areas mark a break from the impasse in which the formal system refused to recognise the vibrant tribal community which has been managing its own affairs in accordance with its traditions through the ages, effectively meeting challenges that came its way. The new Act not only formally recognises the community, which is designated as a gram sabha, but treats it as the pivot of the system of self-government in scheduled areas.The new law marks the beginning of a new chapter in the history of democracy in our country, and demonstrates the existence of juridical innovation for the recognition and protection of indigenous knowledge. What must follow from this is an expansion of such rights to cover all communities within India. Further juridical innovation is therefore needed, which would achieve three tasks simultaneously:

- Protect the biodiversity and cultural integrity of indigenous communities, and allow them to continue to use their resources and knowledge freely as they have done from time immemorial;
- Prevent the piracy and privatisation of indigenous biodiversity and indigenous knowledge through IPRs, nationally and internationally;
- Carve out a public domain of commons in the area of biodiversity and knowledge.

Self-rule of communities is the basis for indigenous self-determination, for sustainable agriculture, and for democratic pluralism. This concept has already been accepted by the Indian Constitution through its 72nd and 73rd Constitutional Amendments which have recognised the panchayat as the basic unit of self-rule and democratic functioning at the level of the community. When the panchayat in Kerim in Goa did not give DuPont permission to set up its industry on the ground that it would be detrimental to the environment, the community was exercising its right to self-determination and self-rule.

I was invited twice to be a witness to the democratic decision-making of the tribals, once each in Mavlibhata and Nagarnar in Bastar. At the end of the three-day meeting in Mavlibhata, with day-long discussions and night-long dancing, the tribals decided not to allow a German steel plant – for them the forests, the land, the biodiversity, could not be exchanged for "compensation" money. Later, when Dr. B.D. Sharma, Siddharaj Dhadda and I were travelling to Nagarnar, the local Inspector General of Police arrested us on grounds that our lives were in danger. We were prevented from reaching the gram sabha meeting. The decision of the gram sabha to say "no" to a steel plant was nullified by the district administration and the tribals were arrested for protesting. As the democratic rights of tribals were undermined, the influence of the Naxalites or "Maoists" grew – today, one-third of India is controlled by the Maoists.

Violence intensified in 2005 when the Salwa Judum, the government-created tribal militias, was set upon to kill tribals. Never in India's history had such intra–tribal killings taken place. In the Maria dialect, "salwa" means sprinkling of holy water over a sick person to make him healthy; "judum" means the community. Thus "Salwa Judum" means sprinkling holy water over a community which has been infected by the "disease of Naxalism". However, the new "holy water" is arms and bullets. The violence between Salwa Judum and Naxalites has displaced more than 46,000 people to roadside refugee camps. Thirty-five thousand special police officers are part of Salwa Judum, and Mahendra Karma, a Congress leader, is known to be its leader. Even though Chhattisgarh is ruled by the Bharatiya Janata Party, the Congress and the BJP are clearly unified in their commitment to alienate tribals from their resources.

This is eco-apartheid.

References

[1] David Hallowes, *Toxic Futures*, Durban: Kwazulu Natal Press, forthcoming.

[2] Sisir Kumar (ed.), *English Language Writings of Rabindranath Tagore*, "The Robbery of the Soil" in EWRT, Vol. III, 866 (870), Delhi: Sahitya Akademi, 1966.

[3] *The New York Times*, March 8, 2009.

[4] DOE Technical Report, August 1996.

[5] Sabyasachi Bhattarcharya, *The Mahatma and the Poet*, Delhi: National Book Trust, 2008, p. 108.

[6] Arthur Robbins, *Paradise Lost, Paradise Regained: The True Meaning of Democracy*, New York: Acropolis Books, forthcoming.

[7] A. Einstein, B. Podolsky and N. Rosen, "Can Quantum Mechanical Description of Physical Reality be Considered Complete"? *Physics Review* 47, 999 (1935).

[8] http://www.genok.com//gene-ecology

[9] Epigenetics: DNA isn't everything, www.sciencedaily.com/releases/2009/04/ 090412081315.htm

[10] Rabindranath Tagore,"Introduction" to *Bonobani*, Rabindra Rachanavali, Vol. 8, 87.

[11] UNEP, "The Economics of Ecosystems and Biodiversity" (TEEB), Nairobi: 2009.

[12] David Hallowes, *Toxic Futures*, op.cit., p. 40.

[13] Internal World Bank document, source protected.

[14] David W. Pearce and Jeremy J. Warford, World Bank Environment Department Working Paper No. 58, March 1993. TOPIC 3: Issues in Resource and Environmental Analysis.

[15] Karl Polanyi, *The Great Transformation: The Political and Economic Origins of Our Times*, Boston: Beacon Press, 1944.

[16] Mathis Wackernagel "Tracking the Ecological Overshoot of the Human Economy", Proceedings of the National Academy of Science, Vol. 99, No. 14, 2002.

[17] Mathis Wackernagel, "Ecological footprints of nations: how much nature do they use? How much nature do they have?" www.ecouncil.ac.cr/rio/focus/report/english/footprint.1997

[18] http://www.scribe.com/doc/33817/Bastar- Peace-Dialogue

2 The Great Land-Grab

The earth upon which the sea, and the rivers and waters, upon which food and the tribes of man have arisen, upon which this breathing, moving life exists.

— Prithvi Sukta, Atharva Veda

LAND IS LIFE. It is the basis of livelihoods for peasants and indigenous people across the third world, and is also becoming the most vital asset in the global economy. As the resource demands of globalisation increase, land has emerged as a key site of conflict. In India, 65 per cent of the people are dependent on land. At the same time a global economy, driven by speculative finance and unbridled consumerism, needs land for mining and industry, for towns, highways, and biofuel plantations. The speculative economy of global finance is hundreds of times larger than the value of real goods and services produced in the world. Financial capital is hungry for investment and returns on investment. It must commodify everything on the planet – land and water, plants and genes, microbes and mammals. The commodification of land is fuelling corporate land-grab in India, both through the creation of special economic zones and through foreign direct investment in real estate. Land, for most people in the world, is people's identity; it is the ground of culture and economy. Seventy-five per cent of people in the third world live on the land and are supported by it – the earth is the biggest employer on the planet.

In India, land-grab is facilitated by a toxic mixture of the colonial Land Acquisition Act of 1894, the deregulation of investment and commerce through neoliberal policies, and the emergence of the rule of uncontrolled greed and exploitation. The World Bank has worked for many years to commodify land, and in 1991 structural adjustment programmes reversed land reform and deregulated mining, roads and ports in India. Whereas the laws of independent India to keep land in the hands of the tiller were reversed, the 1894 Land Acquisition Act was untouched; the state could forcibly acquire land from peasants and tribals and hand it over to private speculators, real estate corporations, mining companies and industry. Across the length and breadth of India, from Bhatta in Uttar Pradesh to Jagatsinghpur in Orissa and Jaitapur in Maharashtra, the government has declared war on our farmers in order to grab their fertile farmland, by enforcing the Land Acquisition Act of 1984 for the benefit of Jai Prakash Associates in UP, for the Yamuna expressway; the Korean steel giant, POSCO in Orissa; and the French company, Areva, in Jaitapur. While the Orissa government prepares to take over land in Jagatsinghpur, Rahul Gandhi makes it known that in a similar case in Bhatta Parsaul he stands against forcible land acquisition. The then Minister of Environment, Jairam Ramesh, admitted in 2001 that he gave the green signal to POSCO under great pressure. One may ask, pressure from whom?

In Bhatta Parsaul, Greater Noida (UP) about 6,000 acres of land are being acquired by the infrastructure company, Jai Prakash Associates, to build luxury townships and sports cities, including a Formula 1 race track, in the garb of the Yamuna Expressway. In all, the land of 1,225 villages will be acquired for the Expressway. Farmers have been protesting this unjust land acquisition, four people have died and many were injured during a clash between protestors and the police on May 7, 2011.

Money cannot compensate for the alienation of land. As 80-year old Parshuram, who lost his land to the Yamuna Expressway, said, "You will never understand how it feels to become landless."[1] Land that has been taken from farmers at Rs. 300 a sq.metre by the government is sold by developers at Rs. 600,000 a sq.metre – a 200,000 per cent increase in price and, hence, profits. In Maharashtra, police opened fire on peaceful protestors demonstrating against the proposed nuclear power park at Jaitapur in Ratnagiri. One person died and about eight were seriously injured on April 18, 2011. The Jaitapur nuclear plant being built by Areva will be the biggest in the world. Protest has intensified after the Fukushima disaster, as has government obduracy. A similar crisis is brewing in Jagatsinghpur (Orissa) where 20 battalions have been deployed to assist in the anti-constitutional land acquisition to protect the stake of India's largest Foreign Direct Investment (FDI) to date – the POSCO steel project. The government has set a target of destroying 40 betel farms a day to facilitate the land-grab. The betel farms bring the farmers an income of Rs 400,000 per acre. The anti-POSCO movement, in its five years of peaceful protest, has faced state violence numerous times and is now gearing up for another, perhaps final, non-violent and democratic resistance.

While the Constitution recognises the rights of the people and of the panchayats to democratically decide the issues of land and development, the government is giving these a go-by; on the POSCO project three panchayats have refused to give up their land. The use of violence and destruction of livelihoods that the current trend is reflecting is not only dangerous for the future of Indian democracy but for the survival of the Indian nation-state itself.

Handing over fertile land to private corporations who are the new zamindars, cannot be defined as public purpose. Creating multiple, privatised, super highways and expressways does not qualify as necessary infrastructure; the real infrastructure India needs is an ecological infrastructure for food security and water security. Burying our fertile food-producing soils under concrete and factories is burying the country's future. While the country democratically debates the future of land we call on the government to: freeze all land-grab; stop police action against farmers defending their land rights; shift the policy discussion from land acquisition to land conservation; identify "no-go areas" regarding land use change for ecologically rich and fertile farmland.

One of the biggest land-grabs taking place in India is for special economic zones (SEZs). The Union Government, after prolonged deliberations, notified SEZ Rules in February 2006, operationalising the SEZ Act (2005). Since then the government has cleared hundreds of SEZs and applications of several other developers are pending. SEZs are specially demarcated zones where the normal rules and regulations of the country do not apply. The emphasis is on enhancing exports and creating an environment for attracting FDI by offering tax sops. While units in the zone have to be net foreign exhange earners, they are not subjected to any pre-determined value addition or minimum export performance requirements. Nor are they bound bye-laws governing labour relations and terms of employment. Any private, public, joint sector or state government or its agencies can set up SEZs. Foreign companies are also eligible.

SEZ units are eligible for 100 per cent tax exemption for the first five years, 50 per cent for the next two, and 50 per cent of the ploughed-back export profits for the following five years. Losses are allowed to be carried forward; the finance ministry has stated that this will lead to losses of nearly Rs. 2 trillion. Developers may import or procure goods without payment of duty for the development, operation and maintenance of SEZs. They enjoy income tax exemption for ten years, with a block period of fifteen years. They also have the authority to allocate developed plots to approved SEZ units on a purely commercial basis, and to provide services like water, electricity, security, restaurants, recreation centres, etc., on commercial lines. Moreover, they are exempt from paying service tax. Within one year of the Central Act, and less than six months after the enactment of the legislation, Haryana started setting up the country's largest multi-product SEZ, stretching over 25,000 ha. between Gurgaon and Jhajjar, off the Delhi-Jaipur highway. It is being set up jointly by Reliance Industries Limited (RIL, with a 90 per cent stake) and the Haryana State Industrial and Infrastructure Development Corporation (HSIIDC, with a 10 per cent share); RIL alone will invest Rs. 25,000 crores, while Rs. 15,000 crores will be put up by companies interested in investing in the SEZ.

It is claimed that the SEZ has provision for a cargo airport and a 2,000 megawatt power plant, that it will generate 500,000 jobs, and that the state government will earn revenues up to Rs. 10,000 crores.

On December 31, 2006, 22 panchayats in the district outlined a strategy to fight Reliance's land-grab.

Reliance has also acquired about 10,000 hectares of land for an SEZ in Pen Tehsil of Raigad district in Maharashtra. The villagers now know that they are pitted against a formidable adversary – the giant Reliance spreading its wings in textiles, power, contract farming, medicinal herbs, sugar industries and retail. They realise that the company has enormous influence on the political and bureaucratic establishment and on the media. Yet in Raigad, too, farmers have declared that they will not allow their land to be appropriated.

Average land holdings in India are two acres or less; to rob small peasants of what little they have and put it into the hands of mega companies like Reliance with Rs. 100,000 crore wealth is to create a country of dispossessed paupers.

At a national convention on "Corporate Land-Grab" organised by Navdanya on February 7-8, 2007, movements from across the country, from Dadri, Gurgaon, Raigad, Nandigram, Singur, Kalinga Nagar, Paradip and Barnala, demanded that the SEZ Act be scrapped. Other demands were that the government not use the Land Acquisition Act for forcefully acquiring farmland for corporations, and that all corporate projects be subjected to a land ceiling.

At a later meeting on April 5, two of the demands of the movements seemed to have been met. The government decided not to use the Land Acquisition Act to acquire land for SEZs, and although a ceiling has been placed on land for them, at 5,000 ha. the ceiling is too high. Corporations have already decided to split up their SEZs; thus Reliance plans to divide its 25,000 ha. SEZ in Gurgaon into five SEZs – this is still corporate "zamindari".

The government not acquiring land for SEZs on behalf of private companies is only a partial step, it is far from adequate to protect the interests of small farmers. After all, the government is already acting against the farmers and favouring corporations by passing the SEZ Act and handing out approvals. If the government means to stop injustice to farmers, scrapping the SEZ Act is necessary, because as long as it exists it will be used as a legal instrument to dispossess farmers and peasants and destroy agriculture, in favour of privileged corporate enclaves, which pay no taxes but burden the entire society with increased fossil fuel use and greenhouse gas emissions. SEZs are tax havens and also pollution havens.

According to the finance ministry, rules regarding SEZs were issued without consulting them; though a Board of Approvals (BoA) was set up comprising two finance ministry representatives (one each from the Central Board of Direct Taxes and Central Board of Excise and Customs), proposals for SEZs were cleared with a free hand by the commerce ministry in spite of the objections raised by finance ministry nominees. The then finance minister himself consistently raised the issue of loss of taxes, which he estimated at almost Rs. 1,70,000 crores by 2010, due to tax sops.[2] This amount only accounts for loss accruing from processing units – be it manufacturing, trading or services. But SEZ developers are not just exempted from income tax for such units, but also from ancillary activities. It stands to reason that they get exemptions or tax breaks for activities that range from running golf courses to spas, multiplexes and shopping arcades. They can import the best, from cobblestones to Italian marble, and not pay customs duties – every fitting in the zone comes minus excise duties and all services are exempt from tax. Even the International Monetary Fund, one of the major proponents of globalisation, says that foregoing such huge revenue is something India cannot afford to do, as we are already foregoing revenue to the tune of Rs. 158,000 crores for industries; exports account for just Rs.35,000 crores. As for revenue generation, the 1998 Comptroller and Auditor General (CAG) Report on EPZs (export processing zones) stated that customs duty amounting to Rs. 7,500 crores was foregone for achieving net foreign exchange earnings of Rs. 4,700 crores. Even that money goes to the accounts of the corporates. Thus, while the government is cutting subsidies on agriculture, it has opened its basket for corporate subsidies.

There are no provisions for monitoring the cumulative environmental impact of all the units under one SEZ; they have been exempted from public hearings under the Environment Impact

Assessment notification. Environmental clearance, particularly the clearance required by state pollution control boards, is vested in the development commissioner appointed for the administrative coordination of the SEZ.

Local governments have no authority over SEZs. When there is a crying need to distribute scarce water and electricity equitably between urban and rural, rich and poor, there is apprehension about how much water SEZs will use. Who will own the water and electricity? How will it be regulated when there is no environmental law applicable to the SEZ? And what will be the impact on the climate by increased emissions from SEZs? With SEZs, environmental impact assessments, if any, can only be made after the project starts functioning.

During the SEZ debate, P. Chidambaram, the then finance minister said, "There is a sacred tie between the tiller and the land. Any attempt to snap the relationship is bound to face opposition." The government often acquired land at a fraction of the market price, thus creating a massive subsidy for rich corporations. This led to a major peasant resistance in Dadri against the Reliance Power Plant; in Aligarh against the Yamuna Expressway (Uttar Pradesh); in Jhajjar against the Reliance SEZ (Haryana); in Singur against the Tata Nano factory; and in Nandigram against Salim's chemical SEZ (both, West Bengal); and in Puri-Konarak against the Vedanta University (Orissa).

In remote forested tribal regions of India where rich mineral deposits lie underground, land-grab is part of mineral-grab. Deregulation of mining released thirteen minerals for exploitation, including iron, manganese, chrome, sulphur, gold, diamond, copper, lead, zinc, molybdenum, tungsten, nickel and platinum, and increased the mine area for a single prospecting licence from 25 sq. kms. to 5,000 sq. kms., a 20,000 per cent increase.

In many cases, tribal and peasant struggles against land-grab have been victorious; the Dadri power plant, the Singur car factory, the Nandigram SEZ, the Vedanta bauxite mine in Niyamgiri, have been cancelled, and villages in coastal Orissa have so far prevented the setting up of a steel plant by POSCO.

Across the world, two worlds and world views are clashing –

that of *terra nullius* which has justified the takeover of other people's land and resources, and that of *terra madre*. This clash of civilisations is intense in India. The world of the earth is the world of two-thirds of India – her land and her rivers, her peasants and tribals, her artisans and small producers, and her hawkers, street vendors and petty shopkeepers. The other is the world of the global corporations, including those which started in India, who seek to grab the land of India's 650 million peasants, and corner the markets where more than 100 million hawkers and vendors make a living. The Reliances and the Cargills, the Bhartis and the Walmarts, the Tatas and Vedantas are a handful, but their appetites are enormous. But resistance is growing. The National Movement for Retail Democracy, a broad coalition of farmers and hawkers, traders and consumers, is organising to prevent Walmart and Reliance from destroying the livelihoods of millions in India's diverse and decentralised, vibrant and self-organised retailers. While farmers defend their land in their villages, corporate CEOs held a "cook-out" at Delhi's Maurya Sheraton hotel in 2010. The theme was "No Man's Land – Getting Real about Real Estate". The 650 million peasants who had disappeared became "no man", their land became "no man's land". And in the "Menu of Ideas" offered on the land question, Sunil Mittal of Bharti, India's Walmart partner, said: "Be it West Bengal, Kerala or Punjab, no state can prevent industrialisation from taking place."

Industrialisation has become an amoeba word. When Sunil Mittal takes over land in Punjab to export vegetables under his partnership with Rothschild, called Field Fresh, agriculture becomes an industry. When he grabs millions of square feet of land for its retail partnership with Walmart, selling Chinese goods that destroy India's domestic industry, retail becomes an industry. When Reliance grabs land outside Mumbai in Raigad or outside Delhi in Gurgaon and Jhajjar, luxury houses and supermarkets become an industry.

SEZs have become the most potent symbol of globalisation and corporate rule run amok. We have mapped the SEZs so far approved in our report, "The Corporate Hijack of Land."[3] They are concentrated around big cities because this is where land speculation and real estate development are most profitable. The fact that the corporations were grabbing more land than required became clear when the government was forced to limit the size of SEZs. This is now happening in non-SEZ projects as well – Vedanta has been asked to scale down its land demands by about 1,800 acres from the original estimated 8,000 acres of its proposed mega Rs. 15,000 crore university in Puri. Arcelor Mittal has been asked to reduce land demands of 8,000 acres for its 12 million tonne per annum steel mill, captive power plant and civil township to be built for Rs. 40,000 crores.

Biofuels

More and more land and food are being diverted to industrial biofuels. Corn prices have doubled because of the diversion of corn to ethanol. Mexico, which was first made dependent on US corn through NAFTA, is now a victim of food scarcity – there have been tortilla riots in the land where corn originated. There could soon be rice and wheat riots in India if we allow more and more fertile land to be diverted to SEZs and corporate farming. India's large population of small farmers is a result of policies of land reform, of support to agriculture and to agricultural producers. Small farmers are the backbone of India's economy and democracy. Today, under the tsunami of corporate globalisation, an attempt is under way to render India's small farmers dispensable, using the argument that the small farmer has become economically unviable. It is not the small farm that is unviable; small farmers have had a secure livelihood on small holdings before globalisation when they received just prices and public policy support. Even today, small farms not caught in the corporate trap, such as those in the Navdanya network, have secure production and secure incomes. The problem is corporate globalisation, not agriculture, small farms or small farmers.

On January 28, 2007 Prime Minister Dr. Manmohan Singh announced a ten-year Automotive Mission with the objective of making India the global hub of vehicle manufacturing, designing and component-making, achieving a turnover of $145 billion by the year

2016. Special automotive zones, like special economic zones, will be set up in Chennai, Mumbai and Kolkata. The Indian automobile industry currently produces 10 million vehicles per annum of the 66.46 million produced worldwide.

The aim of the Automotive Mission is to produce 50 million vehicles per year. At a time of climate change and peak oil, when we need to look at options beyond oil and motorisation, globalisation is driving India headlong into being a hub for the production of cars and automobiles. If the mines and steel plants in Orissa and car factories in Kolkata and Chennai are already triggering major land conflicts and ecological havoc, how many more conflicts will emerge when India increases its automobile production, five-fold, in the next decade? Why is India poised to adopt the non-sustainabile, obsolete model of production and consumption in the industrial West and make it our future, instead of building sustainable and equitable models that respond to the ecological imperative of limited natural resources and impending climate catastrophe?

For those who avoid the core issue of land-grab and deflect it into a debate on "industrialisation", it is important to recognise that if the world were to consume resources and energy at US levels, we would need five planets. India's small peasants cannot possibly carry the ecological footprint of a non-sustainable model of global manufacture and consumption.

How much bauxite and iron can we mine for the insatiable appetite of global markets? How many more cars can we put on the roads before climate chaos disrupts the planetary processes that allow us to inherit the earth as our home?

MOVEMENTS FOR LAND SOVEREIGNTY

Stronger than steel: people's movement against the Gopalpur steel plant

One of the characteristics of globalisation is the relocation of capital-intensive and polluting industries to Third World countries. This "environmental apartheid" was justified by Lawrence Summers when he was vice-president of the World Bank, as being economically "efficient". After all, life is cheap in the Third World. At a time when steel plants are closing in the US, UK, Germany and Australia, new plants are being commissioned in India. One such steel plant was planned for Gopalpur in Orissa in 1995. This 100 per cent export-oriented steel plant was cleared with unprecedented speed by the government of Orissa, but the people of Gopalpur refused to move, refused to allow their sustainable economic prosperity, based on a biodiversity economy, to be destroyed to subsidise a globalised steel industry.

The Gopalpur steel plant is a product not of the "development" era but of the globalisation era. Globalisation demands that local communities sacrifice their lives and livelihoods for corporate profit; development demanded that local communities give up their claim to resources and their sovereignty for national sovereignty. Globalisation demands that local communities and the country should both give up their sovereign rights for the benefit of global free trade.

The Gopalpur plant was being built to produce steel not for the domestic market but for export, *when global steel capacity exceeded demand by 20 per cent*. At a time when steel manufacturing was becoming unviable in most parts of the world, a ten-million tonne integrated steel plant was being planned in Orissa on the basis of major environmental and social subsidies extracted forcefully from the people. When the mantra of globalisation is that governments should play a reduced role in economic affairs, the government of Orissa was most active in appropriating resources from people against their will and handing them over to global commerce. An artificial competitiveness is created because the real costs of production are not internalised in the export price.

Gopalpur: a profile

Since August 1995, the environmental threat from liberalisation and globalisation has been haunting the peaceful communities of twenty-five villages in the Chhatarpur-Berhampur tehsils, and about twelve villages at Pipalapanka Reserve Forest in Saroda block, Ganjam district. The former is the proposed site for the Rs. 7,000 crores (cost of the first two phases) Gopalpur Steel Project of Tata Iron and Steel Company Ltd (TISCO), while the latter was the proposed site for the construction of a dam across the Rushikulya river for pumping water to the steel plant. The people's response to being systematically displaced from and deprived of 'ownership' and control over their traditional source of sustenance is to put up a resistance which is stronger than steel, against the forceful acquisition of their land for the Tatas and their global partners.

Eight decades after Tatas established their first steel works at Jamshedpur in Bihar, they decided to put up a second integrated steel plant at a greenfield site in Ganjam district in Orissa. TISCO signed an MoU with the Orissa governemnt on August 28, 1995, to set up a Rs. 20,000 crores integrated steel plant, for export purposes. In the first phase, cold-rolled strips in a capacity of 1.20 million tonnes per annum would be installed by using hot-rolled coils produced in its Jamshedpur plant; in the second phase a hot-rolled capacity of 2.5 million tonnes per annum would be installed. The total cost of both phases was estimated at Rs. 7,000 crores. The plant capacity was to be expanded to five million tonnes per annum by March 2006, and finally to ten million tonnes in the third phase, expected to be completed by 2012. The steel unit would consist of two blast furnaces, an LD shop, and a Hot-Rolled (HR) and Cold-Rolled (CR) Mill Complex. The technology chosen is the blast furnace-basic oxygen furnace continuous slab caster, hot-strip mill, cold-rolling mill route. However, TISCO itself will have full control only over the core iron and steel making facilities; other aspects, such as the oxygen plant, coke-ovens, the port, power plant and iron-ore mines, will be the responsibility of joint ventures in which TISCO will only be one of the partners.

TISCO had planned to acquire 5,000 acres of private land for the plant site in the Chamakhandi area of the Chhatarpur-Berhampur tehsils, apart from 1,000 acres of private land for a township for its workforce in Aruapalli and Dura villages in Berhampur tehsil. Besides these, TISCO had already acquired about 538 acres of land through Orissa Industrial Infrastructure Development Corporation (OIDCO) in Sitalapalli and Luharjhar villages in Berhampur tehsil, where a rehabilitation colony for people displaced by the proposed steel plant would be built.

In addition, the government of Orissa had promised to make available land required for the dam in the Pipalapanka and surrounding villages; for mining iron ore in Mankadnacha and Baliapahar; for laying roads and constructing a township for the TISCO workforce at the mine site; for the Banspani-Daitari railway line for the transport of iron ore to the plant site; for power transmission lines; roads from National Highway-5 to the plant site; railway line from the plant to the South-Eastern Railway mainline; water pipelines from Pipalapanka dam to the Gopalpur plant; corridor from the Gopalpur port; approach roads to mines and convoy or corridor from mines. Taken together, this integrated steel plant at Gopalpur would require thousands of acres of land and displace many thousands of people in the state in the name of development.

In addition to TISCO, Larsen & Toubro were also acquiring land for their proposed steel plant. It had signed an MoU with the government of Orissa in December 1995 for establishing a Rs. 7,000 crores mega steel plant of 2.60 million tonnes near the rail tracks, parallel to the northern side of the proposed plant site, a couple of miles from the TISCO site across the NH-5, and about 15 kms. from the Gopalpur port, in Chhatarpur-Berhampur tehsil. For this, L&T required 6,300 acres of land for its plant and township, further affecting seventeen villages and displacing about 17,000 people. It is curious that Tata needs only 6,538 acres of land for its plant, township and rehabilitation sites for a ten-million tonne steel plant, while L&T requires 6,300 acres, though its proposed capacity is only 2.60 million tonnes. The district administration of Ganjam has already issued notifications for acquiring 6,300 acres of land in seventeen villages for L&T.

Though TISCO, as promised in the MoU, is ready to pay for land acquired for its steel plant and related activities the questions that arise here are: (a) is the compensation adequate to substitute the livelihood and biodiversity economy that is being destroyed; and (*b*) how valid is an economic growth based on the destruction of existing economic prosperity, irrespective of the compensation paid?

There is strong opposition to TISCO setting up its plant at the present site. Villagers are not opposed to the steel industry in Ganjam district – if only TISCO moves a few kilometres away and spares the present site. At stake is the livelihood and habitat of approximately 25,000 people who will be uprooted and displaced. The 5,000 acres of land earmarked for the plant site is a lush, green, coastal area full of coconut groves, jackfruit trees, plantations of banana, mango, cashew-nut, pineapple, date, blackberry, guava, roseberry, sapeta, papeta, laxman and sita fruits, tamarind, palang, drumstick, casuarinas, lemon, achu, and other trees, but above all, it provides the most precious and perennial source of income for the local people – the kewra plant (*Pandanus Fascicularis*), a rare species, which has been the primary means of sustenance to the people of this area for generations.

The unique feature of this land is the multi-cropping system, where people are dependent on horticultural as well as agricultural produce for sustenance and survival. They grow paddy and pulses which they store and consume, after selling the surplus, for the whole year and also sell horticultural produce; kewra is their money-bank which gives them sufficient income in each flowering season. Even though rain is sometimes scarce, people are not worried because their daily needs are met by selling coconuts, cashew-nuts, bananas and jackfruit in the nearby Gopalpur and Berhampur markets. Besides the seasonal cultivation of rabi and kharif crops and vegetables, this area is known for its kewra plantations.

The kewra economy

Kewra (ketaki or kia) is the basis of wealth for the local community, a perennial and lucrative source of income requiring hardly any investment. It is a bushy plant with thorny leaves that grows wild in the coastal belt, planted mostly as fencing on the boundaries of agricultural and orchid fields. The aromatic scent distilled and extracted from kewra flowers is in great demand. A study by the Regional Research Laboratories, Bhubaneswar, shows that 95 per cent of kewra flowers produced in the country come from the Chhatarpur-Rangeilunda block of Ganjam district. About five per cent is found in Andhra Pradesh, on the border of this district, but its fragrance is not as good as that obtained from here.

Products generally extracted from the kewra flowers are kewra absolute (*rhoo*), kewra essence, absorbed in sandalwood oil or in a paraffin base. The yield of the kewra absolute varies from 15 to 20 grams per 1,000 flowers and commands a market price of Rs. 300,000 per kg. Kewra essence has a huge demand in the domestic and export markets and is used for flavouring chewing tobacco, paan masala, sarda, sherbats, sweets, incense sticks, medicines, etc., and the distilled spirit is exported to West Asian countries for use in perfumes. The export potential to Europe and America is very high, as it is used as a natural ingredient in packaged food items.

What is interesting about kewra cultivation is that it hardly needs any investment or any specific attention, other than watering for a few months in the beginning. That is why it is planted only during the rainy season because of sporadic rain in this area. Kewra does not need any manure, but the old plants (five years and above) need trimming annually to help them grow straight. It flowers thrice a year, in April-May, July-September and December-February, but its best flowering is in August and September. It starts flowering from its fifth year, lasts for years, and each plant is capable of bearing around 200 flowers per plant every year. They are generally plucked by women, early in the morning, so that the least amount of essence is lost.

Kewra is the backbone of all economic activities in this region. There are a total of 65 distillation units (bhattis) in the Chhatarpur Block Kewra Union, of which 62 are currently operational. Of these 62 units, 56 are located in the proposed TISCO plant area. The demand for flowers is rising phenomenally, as are prices; distillers, flower vendors and some growers have formed an association which determines the prices. The entire village economy in this area revolves around kewra, which the locals call 'gold'. During flowering season almost every villager is involved due to increasing demand. There is hardly any wastage as all the blooms are bought by distillers; distillation units are generally owned by traders and businessmen from Kanauj in UP.

Kewra absolute is very expensive because only 10-12 grams of *rhoo* can be extracted from 400-500 buds. About 500 flowers yield 12 litres of kewra water, but the quality is determined by the quantity of flowers – more flowers make for better quality. The kewra plant itself is a story of commercial success that involves local villagers, and is based on the sustainable use of biodiversity and the environment. According to a report by the National Agricultural Bank for Rural Development (NABARD), kewra farmers make a net profit of almost Rs 40,000 per acre of plantation every year.

Assuming that 56 working distillation units can process around five lakh kewra flowers each, on average, annually, the total production value of flowers on the TISCO plant site is approximately Rs. 2.80 crores. It fetches around Rs. 12.60 crores at the present rate of Rs. 4.50 per flower, which goes directly to the people of the region. Moreover, the distillation charges give an additional Rs. 1.68 crores from kewra. Further, the bhatti owners earn money even out of the waste produced from distilled flowers since it is used as manure and can sell for Rs. 1,68,000. Hence, the total money generated only from kewra flowers is Rs. 14,29,68,000 (Rs 142.96 million), per annum.

An independent study indicated that about 200 kewra plants can be planted per acre, besides about 100 on the bunds. According to the Kewra Survey Report conducted on behalf of TISCO by the Regional Research Laboratory (RRL), Bhubaneshwar, the proposed TISCO plant site consists of eleven revenue villages of the Chhatarpur-Berhampur tehsil, covering an area of 2,200 hectares, of which 477 hectares are covered by dense kewra plantation. (In fact, kewra plantations cover a much bigger area, but in keeping with the underestimation by Tatas, the RRL report does likewise.) Even if we accept their figure of 477 hectares – or approximately 1,190 acres of land with about 119,000 kewra plants, at 100 plants per acre, growing only on the bunds – the yield will be around 2.38 crore flowers annually at 200 flowers per plant. At current rates this works out to Rs. 10.71 crores as net profit to the people from flowers alone, besides distillation charges and waste. The RRL report, however, says that the TISCO plant would cause a loss of about 36 lakh flowers annually, valued at Rs. 1.8 crores, besides Rs. 12-13 lakhs as distillation charges.

The entire kewra plant – flowers, branches, roots and leaves – has equal economic value. The fibre extracted from the aerial stilt roots is used for making ropes, sold mainly in the states of Andhra Pradesh and Tamil Nadu, sustaining the livelihoods of more than 2,000 people, especially old dalit women who earn at least Rs. 40 a day. The branches are used as pillars in small huts for cattle; leaves are used in making durable nets, mattresses, hats, flower baskets, money purses, handbags and file folders, among other household articles. The kewra bushes help check soil erosion from agricultural land, stabilising sand-dunes along the seashore, and act as barriers to cyclones and heavy rain. The report also describes kewra as a perennial monocat aerial creeper, and its fleshy, stout stems can sustain water stress for long periods.

What underlies people's resistance to TISCO is not the sheer sentimental attachment of villagers to their homes, but the fear of losing their perennial and lucrative source of income. The proposed acquisition of their land would not only affect kewra-growers, but the local labour force involved in its processing.

TISCO, attracted by the kewra economy and the potential for foreign exchange earnings from it, has prepared a plan to protect and develop kewra in its proposed plant area, with the help of RRL. It proposes to rehabilitate kewra plantations inside the proposed area after identifying 477 hectares of cultivable fallow land; and have decided not to damage a single kewra plant growing within the TISCO area, to take phase-wise plant improvement work in the surrounding kewra plantations, and to engage local people in plant rehabilitation and improvement. However, this proposal by TISCO throws a doubt on its actual plan; is it interested in steel or in kewra? It may even have planned to patent kewra essence, and if it succeeds it would have the monopoly on the kewra plantation and its products.

The perennial coconut economy

If kewra is gold, coconut is the king of this region. Each part of the coconut, like kewra, has commercial value. The kernel of the unripe nut is full of coconut water, considered a health drink; the ripened nut and dried nut are eaten and also used to extract coconut oil; the dry spines of the leaves are used for making brooms; the leaves are used as thatching and also for mats and hats, etc., and the trunk of the tree is generally used as a rafter or beam in houses. An important commercial use is the coir made from its husk, used for string, ropes and cushioned mats. Coir dust produced while ratting the husk is used in manure, and coir and leaves as fuel.

To protect their land and environment from the threat of destruction by Tata Steel, 25,000 people from 25 villages have been protesting against the state government's decision to hand over their land to TISCO without their consent. Their slogans are, "We will rather die than leave our place of birth," and "We will give our blood and life but will not leave our land." On August 7, 1995, they formed the Gana Sangram Samiti (GSS) with an executive body of 11 and a council of 70 members to resist the entry of any government or steel plant officials into the proposed plant site area, which led to several sporadic clashes between the police and the villagers. In frustration, the district administration began a reign of terror in August 1996, on the pretext of doing survey work, and deployed six platoons of armed police (about 6,000 men), who used all means to harass the people. During the four days of protest, the police mercilessly beat the villagers and used tear gas shells to suppress the peaceful protest. Women and children were badly injured, and two, D. Laxamma (Badaputti village) and S. Iramma (Laxmipur village) died. Despite this, the people did not allow the police to enter the villages. Frustrated, the district administration booked several people under different false charges. The chairman of the GSS, N. Narayan Reddy, was booked under the National Security Act (NSA) and jailed twice, with 60 other people from this area.

These atrocities forced the people to install 14 "people's gates" at all possible entry points to the border villages of the proposed site. They erected two pillars, one at the entry to Badaputti and the other at Sindhigaon, which said, "Water, land and environment belong to us and no one else has any rights over them. NO ONE dare enter without our permission." The GSS is very clear in its opposition to the steel plant – the main issue is not environment *vs.* development but extinction *vs.* survival.

Despite continuous resistance by local people against the steel plant, the response from the Orissa government has been, in effect: "We will not protect the environment or the people, we will only protect Tata and provide them the full support of the state machinery to be free to do whatever they can to the people and ecology of the region."

The people of the proposed site suggested three alternative sites to the state government and Tata. These were:

1. Chandipadar, 13-14 kms. from Gopalpur port where 12,000 acres of land are available, with the displacement of only 500 houses.
2. Two kms. north-east from Gopalpur port where 8,000 acres of mostly government land are available, with only 300 houses displaced.
3. Pallur, 25 kms. from Gopalpur, with 13,000 acres of land near the beach.

None of the available sites suggested, that will cause less ecological damage, has been accepted by Tatas, or the government. The people's movement has stopped the Gopalpur steel plant, but Tatas have now applied for SEZ status. The struggle continues.

POSCO-INDIA in Orissa

In 2005, the government of Orissa entered into an MoU with South

Korean steel giant, POSCO, for the creation of a 12 million tonnes/year steel plant in Jagatsinghpur with a captive port, requiring 4,004 acres of land (of this 3,000 acres are forest land); captive mines in Kandhadar; a captive power plant; and captive railway lines. The total land-grab for the POSCO project is over 13,000 acres. Proposed as the largest FDI in India ever, at $12 billion, the project has been hailed by the government of Orissa as a boon for the local and national economy in terms of foreign exchange earnings, employment generation and returns to the state and central governments. Orissa is going through a boom in steel production; in the past three years, the state government has signed more than 40 MoUs with companies, both domestic and foreign.

POSCO was to first construct the steel works from 2007 to 2010 on about 4,500 acres of land at Kujang tehsil near Paradip. Of the total land only 20 per cent is individually owned, the rest comes under government/community land; and of this POSCO has been given prospecting licences or direct lease for mining over a total area of about 2,000 acres. The production capacity will first be expanded to six million tonnes, and ultimately to 12 million tonnes. Construction will require US $3 billion in the first stage, and is expected to go up to US $12 billion. The 12 million tonne capacity of the POSCO steel plant is equal to the total production of the top six steel plants in India – Bhilai, Bokaro, Durgapur, Rourkela, Burnpur and Salem. The project has a captive power plant with an initial capacity of 400 MW, to be increased to 1100 MW; the 200 acre captive port has a capacity of handling 170,000 DTW (Dead Tonne Weightage) cargo ships. In addition, POSCO needs 1,000 acres for dumping fly ash, and 2,000 acres for an integrated township to house its workforce. Water will be diverted from the Mahanadi river. The Orissa state government has promised to provide a total of 0.6 billion tonnes of iron sources, and will allow POSCO to use iron ore from these sources over the next thirty years to ensure its competitiveness. The government will also provide infrastructure such as railroads, road systems, water supply and electricity as scheduled, to assist POSCO in the construction process.

With the coming in of the company, three panchayats – Dhinkia, Nuagaon and Gadakujanga, comprising 11 villages/hamlets with about 22,000 people (3,500 families) – will be directly affected. The estimates of only those whose agricultural land will be compromised are the ones who get recognised in terms of loss of livelihood; there is no estimate of those who will be indirectly affected, such as people engaged in grazing, collecting firewood, forest produce, fishing, etc. Kujang block is also unique since the best quality betel leaf (paan) is grown in the area; with the plant coming up the whole paan belt will be ruined and the livelihood of those engaged in paan-leaf cultivation destroyed.

The POSCO Company is proposing to build a captive port at Jatadhari, which evoked concern regarding damage to the coastline and to the nesting habitat of the endangered Olive Ridley turtles, giving rise to intense opposition. It will likely also destroy the complex system of myriad natural creeks, nalas and waterways that are the vast backwater of the Mahanadi and its tributaries, especially during the rainy season and floods. The proposed plant is near the Bhitarakanika mangrove forest (which now has the status of a sanctuary); there are fears that the plant will encroach upon the mangroves and draw water from a watershed that also feeds the sanctuary. Mangroves act as natural protection against super cyclones and coastal cyclones; destroying these forests will leave Orissa's coastline very vulnerable. All this has raised fundamental questions regarding industry-induced displacement on the one hand, and the government's commitment to promote the interests of the corporate world on the other.

A global boom in the steel market, which is growing at the rate of more than four per cent, and the race for cheap labour and raw materials are two significant factors which led POSCO-India to enter this territory. In addition, according to recent developments, the government of Orissa has recommended a special economic zone for this project, claiming an investment of Rs. 45,000 crores and net foreign exchange earnings of $42 billion over thirty years; claiming also, that about 25,600 direct jobs and more than 30,000 indirect employment opportunities will be created.

In addition to the 22,000 villagers who will be displaced by the steel plant, a further 20,000-25,000 people from around 30 neighbouring villages will lose their livelihoods as fisherfolk because of the new port that POSCO will build. Furthermore, 6,100 acres have been earmarked for POSCO's captive mines. The extraction of coal and iron ore for the steel plant will cause 116 villages – 32 in Keonjhar and 84 in Sundergarh, comprising mostly tribal households – to lose access to the forests on which they are dependent. The mining alone will bring POSCO $1.5 billion in profits, annually. In other words, POSCO would recoup its $12 billion investment in eight years. As documented in *Iron and Steal,* and contrary to the state government's inflated claim of hundreds of thousands of jobs, the POSCO project will generate a maximum of about 17,000 permanent jobs, completely unsuited to the skills of the affected populations, and thus inaccessible to them.[4]

Six years on, the MoU has expired and the project is at the centre of intense controversy, just like Vedanta: while the government, in the person of chief minister, Naveen Patnaik, is lobbying relentlessly on behalf of POSCO, the local population and civil society organisations are strongly campaigning for it to be dropped on grounds of considerable threats to residents and the environment, regulatory violations and deliberate manipulation of data. The eight villages – Dhinkia, Govindpur, Noliasahi, Bhuyanpal, Polanga, Bayana-Lakanda, Nuagaon, Jatadhar – in the three gram panchayats (Dhinkia, Nuagaon, Gadakujanga) that will be affected by the project are stoutly resisting state violence and repression in a fight for survival, for their livelihoods and their homes. The Orissa government has failed to abide by the Forest Regulation Act which clearly states:

> *Sec.4(5): No member of a forest-dwelling scheduled tribe or other traditional forest-dweller shall be evicted or removed from forest land under his occupation till the recognition of rights and verification procedure is complete.*

The local administration has failed to recognise that these tracts of land are, in fact, inhabited, claiming the absence of forest-dwellers, while rejecting all claims filed by locals and ignoring their clear disapproval of the project. Despite such open violation of the democratic laws of the country and the deliberate misrepresentation of costs and benefits, POSCO was granted in-principle approval, while the local affected population is subjected to violent repression and intimidation. Two ministry of environment and forests committees have since been appointed to look into the matter: the Saxena Committee (July/August 2010) and the Meena Gupta Committee (September/October 2010) both indicated evidence of gross violation of laws, government procedures and rules: [5]

- FRA 2006 not implemented, tribal dwellers not duly acknowledged, gram sabha resolutions deliberately ignored.
- Environmental Impact Assessment to be extensive and comprehensive, not partial and brief.
- Coastal Regulation Zone Notification, 1991, violated.
- Forest Conservation Act (impact of deforestation/mitigation measures) violated.
- Environmental Protection Act not complied with.
- Deliberate misuse of information.

Despite the findings of the two MoEF appointed committees exposing serious irregularities, the ministry has not yet revoked or rejected the project; simultaneously, the CM of Orissa is moving the Supreme Court in a desperate attempt to attract the POSCO FDI.

Navdanya has joined hands with the anti-POSCO movement, POSCO Pratirodh Sangram Samiti (PPSS), to stop this anti-people, anti-environment project in an effort to protect the local residents and their land, and to uphold the rights guaranteed in Indian laws and the Constitution, when citizens supposed to be protected are subjected to state violence. On May 18, 2011, 20 police battalions arrived in coastal Jagatsinghpur to uproot the people and the biodiversity economy.

If approved, the POSCO project will displace over 22,000 people, destroy the local economy, causing a huge loss of livelihoods, environmental damage and resource exhaustion. It will also entail substantial losses to the country in potential revenue, be it by granting SEZ status or because of the loot of an expensive resource by a foreign company at throwaway prices.

There is no explanation why India should hand over iron ore at dirt-cheap prices – the revised royalty is a meagre 10 per cent - instead of charging market rates. The price of iron ore has shot up from around Rs 300 to over Rs 5,000 per tonne, and was expected to rise to Rs 10,000 per tonne by 2011. Also, why allow a foreign company to mine the precious resource for export – according to the MoU the state government is committed to providing 600 MT of iron ore for use in its Indian plant and 400 MT for the South Korea plant. When increased demand for steel has escalated the price of iron ore exponentially – being in short supply – why should India make it over to foreign companies? It would make more economic sense to charge market rates for the raw material or generate more returns by domestic value addition, i.e., for Indian companies to use the iron ore for domestic steel production.

It is noteworthy that POSCO *was given precedence over more than 200 applicants, both Indian and foreign, some of which are public sector corporations!*

The government of Orissa is also lobbying for POSCO to be granted SEZ status: this, of course, means a considerably lower potential revenue to the state and the government as SEZs are exempted from customs/excise duties and all taxes.[6]

The National Council of Applied Economic Research (NCAER) cost-opportunity analysis used by the government to justify its claims of unprecedented benefits to the people and the country, has been openly discredited; figures are inconsistent and based on flawed assumptions (such as the calculation of tax revenue from SEZs, not accounting for any SEZ exemption); costs are minimised while benefits are maximised; and there appears to be an inherent conflict of interest given that POSCO is among NCAER's sponsors.

While there seems to be no plausible justification for government support to POSCO, it is actively lobbying for the company, to the extent of moving the Supreme Court on its behalf. What is striking about the MoU is the role assumed by the state as facilitator, spokesperson and promoter of POSCO. Imposing environmentally and socially destructive projects in the name of attracting foreign capital is not development, nor is this a growth story. What we are witnessing is the demise of a democratic state committed to equality and inclusion, and the simultaneous rise of what can almost be seen as a corporate lobbyist, knight in shining armour for multinationals greedy for undivided, unfair profits.

Who is set to benefit from this mammoth project? The intuitive answer is POSCO, but it doesn't end here. At the time of the Asian financial crisis, South Korea, suffering from strong devaluation of its currency, found itself near financial collapse and was forced to approach the IMF for stabilisation loans; the IMF agreed on condition that South Korea undertake structural reforms of the economy and privatise government-owned companies, one of which was POSCO. The majority sold-off shares of POSCO went to foreign investors, with a fair amount to American interests.

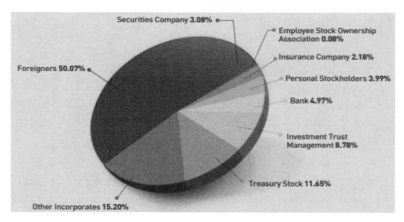

POSCO foreign ownership
(*Source*: POSCO website)

Renowned US investor and millionaire Warren Buffet's company, Berkshire Hathaway, owns at least 5.2 per cent of POSCO; also holding POSCO shares are top American investment banks that were bailed out by Buffet's Berkshire Hathaway's POSCO holdings. Their report for the year 2009 listed their investments as below:

12/03/09

Shares	Company	Percentage of company owned	Cost* (in millions)	Market (in millions)
151,610,700	American Express Company	12.7	$1,287	$6,143
225,000,000	BYD Company, Ltd	9.9	232	1,986
200,000,000	The Coca-Cola Company	8.6	1,299	11,400
37,711,330	ConocoPhilips	2.5	2,741	1,926
28,530,467	Johnson & Johnson	1.0	1,724	1,838
130,272,500	Kraft Foods Inc	8.8	4,330	3,541
3,947,554	POSCO	5.2	768	2,092
83,128,411	The Procter & Gamble Company	2.9	533	5,040
25,108,967	Sanofi-Aventis	1.9	2,027	1,979
234,247,373	Tesco Plc	3.0	1,367	1,620
76,633,426	U.S. Bancorp	4.0	2,371	1,725
39,037,142	Wal-Mart Stores, Inc	1.0	1,893	2,087
334,235,585	Wells Fargo & Company	6.5	7,394	9,021
	Others		6,680	8,636
	Total Common Stocks Carried at Market		$34,646	$59,034

Source: Berkshire Hathaway Corporate Performance Report, 2009.

POSCO's ownership pattern leads to a number of considerations and possible reflections, as POSCO India is neither Korean nor Indian – it is owned by global investors.

- Foreign ownership constitutes the main holdings, with American investment banks topping the list (Citigroup, JP Morgan, Transamerica, etc.)
- Citigroup and JP Morgan are two of the "Big Four Banks" in the US – Citigroup was bailed out by the US government during the 2008 financial crisis, which in turn gave Washington $27 billion of preferred shares and warrants to acquire stocks and exercise wide powers over its banking operations.
- As of July 2009, the US government owned one-third of Citi.
- Citigroup is the sixteenth largest US political campaign contributor of all organisations (Centre for Responsive Politics)

- Citigroup, JP Morgan and the American Bankers' Association spent the most on political lobbying in 2008, an amount totalling $21.4 million.
- JP Morgan was associated with Enron and subject to fines because of its involvement in the scandal.
- In December 2002, Chase paid fines totalling $80 million towards state and federal governments as part of a settlement involving charges that ten banks, including Chase, deceived investors with biased research.
- The Treasury Department invested about $200 billion in hundreds of banks through its Capital Purchase Program.[7]

In the five years since POSCO signed an MoU with the Orissa government, and even as the project met with strong opposition from the thousands whose lives would be uprooted by the steel plant, Berkshire Hathaway's POSCO stock has more than doubled in value and yielded millions of dollars in dividends. Buffett has held onto POSCO's shares at a time when the company has been complicit in violence against villagers in Orissa, and when its dealings have been mired in corruption and are deeply subversive of the democratic process.

Open Letter to Mr. Buffet on his visit to India in March, 2011 to promote the "Art of Giving"

Dear Mr Buffet,

Charity begins at home!!! First grabbing, then giving, is not an option!!!

In 2006, your company, Berkshire Hathway, bought five per cent shares of the Korean Steel Company, POSCO, which is setting up a steel plant in Orissa's Jagatsinghpura district, robbing over 50,000 villagers of their lands and livelihoods.

Investing in the POSCO project is not only unethical but is robbery of land, livelihood and dignity of the coast of Orissa. Giving the money stolen from the poor and marginalised in the name of charity and using it as an example to encourage more people to "give back to society" what they have stolen in the first place, is a sham and hypocrisy.

There is no justification for the large-scale devastation that the POSCO project would cause given that it is:

Creating food insecurity: the destruction and appropriation of fertile farmland for industrial projects at a time when the country is facing a severe food security crisis is criminal. The project would destroy the local economy that is not only sustainable but also ensures livelihoods and food security to the local community in times when fertile land is more precious than ever.

Subverting democracy and human rights by not respecting the rights of the local community enshrined in the Constitution and recognised by FRA. The three gram panchayats that would be affected by the project have already rejected it, and they are staunchly resisting state violence and repression in a fight for survival, for their livelihoods and their homes, exercising democracy and their constitutional rights.

Encouraging predatory investment: While the local population and civil society are strongly campaigning for the project to be dropped on grounds of innumerable violations, manipulation of data and considerable threat to local communities and the environment, the GoO is lobbying relentlessly on behalf of POSCO to attract FDI for accruing profits only to POSCO and its foreign stakeholders – mostly US financial institutions! Given that the MoU has expired, to revisit the POSCO project shows that the government is committed to promoting corporations' interests over its people.

Government committees have rejected the project on grounds of gross violations of regulatory procedures and deliberate misuse of information. Two committees have been appointed to assess the project: the first was the MoEF N.C. Saxena committee which recommended the withdrawal of the forest clearance and stopping illegal land acquisition in this area. The second was the Meena Gupta committee's majority recommendation which called for cancellation of the CRZ clearance, forest clearance and environmental clearance for this project.

We urge you not to make a mockery of human values by masking the gross human rights violations that your investments are causing. Good deeds are not auctioned out in life, they have to be earned by doing what is right, not that which is convenient. We hope that before you urge others to straighten up their act you will put your house in order and disinvest in projects which violate the very humanity that you wish to save by your act of charity. We appeal to your moral compass to do the right thing.

Warm regards,
Vandana Shiva

Reliance power plant at Dadri

In 2004, the world's largest gas-based 3,500 MW power plant was to be set up in the country's most fertile land – Dadri, Ghaziabad, about 40 kms. from Delhi – by the Reliance group, at a cost of Rs. 10,000 crores. Taking the help of Mulayam Singh Yadav, then chief minister of Uttar Pradesh, they acquired 2,700 acres of farmers' land – an act the farmers were totally unaware of till the plant's foundation stone was unveiled.

I visited the protesting farmers regularly and was to accompany former prime minister, V.P. Singh, for a rally on July 8, 2006, but we were prevented from doing so. On the night of July 7-8, 2006, police battalions and the private security force of Reliance invaded the village of Bhejera Khurd, Ghaziabad, beat up women, children and the aged, shot young boys, looted the jewellery of all the women, stole cash and other expensive belongings, broke every vehicle and seized every mobile. Villagers have been protesting the unlawful and unjust acquisition of their land by the Uttar Pradesh government for Reliance, which allegedly finalised the deal by agreeing to a mere Rs.150/sq. mt. as compensation. But at the launch of the project on February 22, 2004, the chief minister, Mulayam Singh Yadav, had announced that the rate would be Rs.350/sq. mt. – market prices are around Rs.13,500/sq. mt. Besides this, the state government has waived stamp fees and other related costs for buying the land for Reliance, along with providing a subsidy by which Reliance would pay only 40 per cent of the costs, the government paying the rest. This deal was struck under the Land Acquisition Act, by which governments can acquire the land of farmers and villagers but only for public development projects. Reliance was reportedly planning to use 2,700 acres of land for the project, when experts maintained that 700-800 acres would be sufficient. This is prime agricultural land in northern India, one of the most fertile in the world, with the alluvial layer being deeper than 300 metres. It also has abundant water, and is just a few kilometers away from the main Ganga canal. Reliance had fenced off the land with barbed wire.

Affected farmers, local leaders and villagers planned a peaceful protest on July 8, 2006. Big tents were erected and food was being cooked. Former prime minister, V.P. Singh, Bollywood actor-turned-MP, Raj Babbar, and the dalit leader, Udit Raj, were on their way to support the villagers, when they were arrested at the UP-Delhi border, banned from entering the area under threat of arrest.

On December 5, 2010, the Dadri land-grab was stopped by the Allahabad High Court which quashed the state government notification for use of emergency powers to buy land for the Reliance power project; the Court ordered that the land be returned to the farmers.

Land-grab in Nandigram

Nandigram, a little known corner of Bengal near the mouth of the Ganges, suddenly entered the nation's consciousness in early 2007. The fertile land of Nandigram had been identified as an SEZ for a chemical hub to be run by the Salim Group of Indonesia, named after its founder, Liem Sioe Liong, alias Sordono Salim. Liem Sioe Liong was born in Haikou in Fujian province of China in 1916. When he was 15, he started a noodle-soup shop and five years later, his father died. At the time both the Red Army and the Kuomintang were conscripting all young men and Sioe Liong, alias Salim, fled to join an uncle who had a provision store in Indonesia.

Salim's real break came in 1965, when Suharto overthrew Soekarno in a counter-coup. Suharto was reputedly the world's most corrupt ruler of his time; when he abdicated in 1998, he was ranked the world's sixth richest person, with assets estimated at $16 billion. He was also the most nepotistic of men. Almost all his cronies were from his family – his half-brother, cousin, sons and daughters were all direct beneficiaries – but two were outsiders: Liem and Mohamed Hasan.

Indonesia saw a big oil-driven boom in the 1980s and 1990s. Like India in recent years, Indonesia then had a big payments surplus. It increased money supply at home, and one of the most lucrative businesses in those circumstances was to open a bank. Liong set up

Bank Central Asia and gave a son and daughter of Suharto's a 30 per cent share of the capital. In 1997, the bank had 788 branches and eight million customers. The bank gave Liem money to play with, so he set up noodle, flour and bread businesses; Indomobil Sukses Internasional to make cars; Indocement Tunggal Prakasa to make cement; and a resort in suburban Jakarta; altogether he had about 500 companies in Indonesia. He also bought into QAF, a company that owned a supermarket in Singapore, and First Pacific Co. in Hong Kong, that took a 49 per cent share in the Nandas' telephone company, Escotel, in the 1990s. He also invested in Smart Communications, a telephone company in the Philippines.

Liem was not as rich as Suharto, but was far ahead of any other Indonesian; his business assets were estimated to be $10 billion, but his plans were even grander than his empire. He wanted to take half a million acres of swamp in Kalimantan, drain it and grow rice there.

With the East Asian crisis of 1998, capital flew out of Indonesia and the rupiah collapsed; from 2,400 to the US dollar in July 1997, it went down to 11,500 a year later. There was a run on Bank Central Asia; mobs destroyed 122 branches and 150 ATMs. There were terrible anti-Chinese riots all over Indonesia; Liong's villa in Jakarta was attacked. Indofood had $1billion in overseas loans; Indocement, $830 million. The empire could not come out of the crisis unscathed, but the Liem family managed it with aplomb. Liem Sieo Liong moved to Singapore; his son, Anthoni, took over the reins. The government took over Bank Central Asia; and since 90 per cent of its loans were to Salim companies, it now effectively owned them. The Indonesian Bank Restructuring Authority took over 107 Salim Group companies, including 25 property firms, 24 plantations, 10 food and consumer product firms, nine petrochemical firms, five coal and granite firms, four sugar firms, and one communications company.[8]

It is difficult to get an accurate picture of the Salim Group today. Of the companies that went into the hands of IBRA, some were sold, some reverted to the Salim Group or were rumoured to have been sold to their frontmen, while others continue to be in limbo; it is impossible to work out which belongs where. In the meanwhile, a new generation of entrepreneurs has occupied the business space in Indonesia. The Salim Group's petrochemical plant was taken over by the Wings group of Hanny Sutanto. Buddhadeb Bhattacharjee, the former chief minister of West Bengal, is right when he says that money knows no colour and that Salim's connection with Suharto is history. Nobody knows how much financial resources the Salim Group commands, but the state government should have done due diligence and some homework before signing an MoU with them.

The SEZ at Nandigram

Haldia is a city and a municipality in Purba Medinipur in West Bengal, a major seaport, approximately 50 kms. southwest of Kolkata, near the mouth of the Hooghly river, one of the tributaries of the Ganges. It is being developed as a major trade port for Kolkata, intended mainly for bulk cargo. It has now become an industrial city with several factories – Indian Oil Corporation Limited (IOCL), Exide, Shaw-Wallace, Tata Chemicals, Hindustan Lever, various light industries; the Haldia Petrochemical complex has attracted foreign companies like Mitsubishi Chemical Company (MCC), as well.

Haldia will be the biggest and most important SEZ in the state as it is near the seaport. It has been chosen as the location for one of the petrochemicals, chemicals, petroleum investment regions (PCPIRS) in the country, which will bring in more central funds and benefits. The PCPIRS is to have a minimum area of 250 sq. kms. The state government proposes three SEZs, each a different model for Haldia – one for chemicals; another, a multi-product one, to be set up by Indonesia's Salim Group. All existing industries, and even the Nandigram map villages, were to be included to meet the minimum size of 250 sq. kms. or 62,500 acres. It was the attempt to acquire 14,200 acres of land which resulted in people protesting and the resultant killing of eleven villagers.

Problems began when letters of acquisition were pasted on the Nandigram Block Development Office (BDO) and the District Magistrate's office on January 2, 2006. The next day angry villagers marched into the Garchakraberia panchayat office; panchayat members called the police, resulting in a lathi charge. The villagers retaliated by torching two police vehicles and attacking the panchayat office. The situation worsened when eleven people were killed in the clashes between them and the CPI(M) (Communist Party of India, Marxist) cadres.

Some youths claimed to have been branded with hot iron rods so that they could be identified as CPI(M) opponents. A member of the Krishi Bhumi Ucched Pratirodh Committee said, "We are being tortured by the CPI(M) every day. We are confused, whether to approach the police for assistance as we know the police might take their side." But the local CPI(M) leader, Sadhin Pramanick, said the charges were false.

A party that distributed land to the landless and grew from strength to strength on the support of 'empowered' peasants was now accused of grabbing the same land to hand it over to industrialists. This land acquisition had the blessings of the CPI(M) central leadership which, though critical of the central government's SEZ policy, was united in its support to the West Bengal government. The CPI(M) general secretary, Prakash Karat, stated that, "We will continue to oppose farmland acquisition for SEZs in other states," but he welcomed SEZs in West Bengal because, "here farmers are getting much better prices for their land". The then chief minister justified his policies in a different way – he said that the state's success in agriculture should form the base for transformation in industry. "If a society has to move forward it has to move from agriculture to industry. Further employment is not possible in agriculture. Opportunities therefore have to be created in industry, business and commerce." However, in 2007, due to a public outcry against the methods of the state and the killings in Nandigram, the SEZ had to be scrapped.

I was in Nandigram on April 28-29, 2007, to pay tribute to the martyrs and to give farmers Navdanya seeds for setting up seed banks and starting organic farming. I felt it was appropriate that we work together to make Nandigram a chemical-free organic zone; we sat together all day and made plans while shoot-outs were taking place a few miles away. Nandigram is rich in soil, water and biodiversity, the real capital of communities. Each village has its ponds, making for water sovereignty. Each farm is a multi-functional unit, producing paan, coconut, rice, bananas, papaya, drumstick and a rich diversity of vegetables. The village square blossoms into a farmers' market – selling four kinds of potatoes, eight kinds of bananas, gur (sugar) made from date-palm and palmyra palm. Farmers' markets like these need no oil, no Walmart, no Reliance, no middlemen. Farmers are traders, sellers and buyers. The community organises itself for trade. There is no government licence raj, no corporate control; this is the real free market, the real economic democracy.

The rich biodiversity of Nandigram supports a rich productivity. In conventional measurements based on monocultures, industrial agriculture is presented as being more productive because inputs are not counted, nor is the destruction of biodiverse outputs in the soil, water and air. In a biodiversity assessment, the dense small farms of Nandigram are much more productive than the most chemical-and-energy-intensive industrial farms. Nandigram is a post-oil economy: cycles and cycle rickshaws are the main mode of transport. When the government unleashed violence against the people, they dug up the roads so that no police or government vehicle could enter. Their freedom from oil allowed them to defend their land freedom; their living economy allowed them to have a living democracy.

There has been an attempt to present the land conflict as an inter-party conflict, but the Land Sovereignty Movement in Nandigram was totally self-organised and transcended party lines. However, it could be seen as a conflict between global capital and local peasants, and defending land is not a new issue in Nandigram. Peasants of the region participated in the revolt against the East India Company in 1857; Nandigram was also the site of the Tebhaga movement for land rights after the great Bengal famine of 1942-43. One could only enter Nandigram as a guest of the community, with their consent. There is a high level of self-organisation with women and children, old and young, all involved in keeping watch for unwanted outsiders.

I left Nandigram, humbled and inspired. These are the elements of Earth Democracy we need to defend and protect from the violence and greed of corporate globalisation. The people's movement for bhu-swaraj (land sovereignty) in Nandigram changed West Bengal politics irreversibly. In May 2011, Mamata Banerjee's Trinamool Congress won a thumping majority in the state, largely because of her party's support to the rights of local farmers with the slogan, "Ma, Maati, Manush" (Mother, Earth and Humanity).

Niyamgiri: mining as war

The Government of India, through the ministry of mines and the ministry of steel, applauds mining and metallurgy as the backbone of industrial development, and is committed to an increase in mineral exploration, extraction and exploitation. India is set to pace up mining and related industries to become the world's second largest steel producer by 2015-16; the total value of mineral production in India (excluding atomic minerals) increased by 11.83 per cent in 2010-11 over the previous year. Global aluminium output reached its peak in 1999: rising market prices are pushing producers to raise capacity manifold. In India too, minister for mines, B.K. Handique, promised increased production by 2015, as all major primary metal producers are expanding capacity. Foreign and domestic private investment has been flowing into the industry, with 222 MoUs for planned capacity of around 276 MT signed between investors and various state governments, mostly in Orissa, Jharkhand, Chhattisgarh and West Bengal. The Indian government has thus made it clear that it sees mining as a direct propeller of growth and development, and that it is set to push it forward.

This has led to an explosive growth in the extraction of bauxite, coal and iron ore. Mining for bauxite jumped from 6.1 million tonnes in 1997-98 to 15.25 million tonnes in 2008-09; coal mining increased from 297 million tonnes in 1997-98 to 493 million tonnes in 2008-09; extraction of ore increased to 75 million tonnes in 2008-09.[9] Between 1991 and 2004, the value of mineral production increased four-fold, while employment dropped by 30 per cent. Policies of trade liberalisation led to an increase in prospecting licences from 25 sq. kms. to 5,000 sq. kms – about 14 per cent of India's land mass, 466,556 sq. kms., is today covered by prospecting licences.

Most mineral reserves also happen to be demarcated on tracts of pristine forest land inhabited by scheduled castes and tribes, adivasis and agricultural and fishing communities: in the first four-and-a-half decades of India's independence, mining displaced 25,00,000 (2.5 million) people, with hardly 25 per cent of them rehabilitated. Industrialisation has displaced around 60 million people, two million in Orissa alone, 75 per cent of whom are adivasis and dalits. Over 16.4 million hectares of forest land have been diverted and 77 million tonnes of water used for iron ore mining in 2005-06 alone – enough to satisfy the daily needs of three million people. Mining of major minerals generated about 1.84 tonnes of waste in 2003.[10]

Orissa is at the top for diversion of forest land to mining with a whopping 15,386 hectares, and prone to increasingly violent land and resource wars. The Patnaik-led government was asked by the Supreme Court in May 2010 to explain why 215 of 341 working mines were allowed to operate without government clearance or a mining plan. But Orissa is one amongst many: across the country there are 15,000 illegal mines compared to 8,700 legal ones. Mega projects are cleared by government ministries, disregarding existing legislation and norms. Political patronage and corruption make the legal and illegal go hand in hand in a business that is generating huge profits for corporations and bureaucrats, while costing the country the displacement of millions, loss of lives, environmental degradation and depletion of resources.

Against the usual claims of linkages to the economy and employment generation, mining activities are mostly closed in themselves, a model known as "enclave economies": localised, capital-intensive, non-renewable clusters with hardly any backward linkage to the broader economy. As far as employment is concerned, several factors deserve consideration: (*i*) the claims have always been countered by evidence of abysmal job creation; (*ii*) jobs are of a casual, contractual nature violating all minimum standards of workers' and human rights; (*iii*) overall, because of mechanisation, computerisation and consolidation, the rate of employment in the mining sector has seen a 30 per cent decrease between 1991 and 2004, while the value of mineral production has risen manifold; (*iv*) forced industrialisation ultimately translates into an involuntary shift from traditional sustainable primary occupations to lowly industrial work; it is imposed on the displaced to train them in one or more technical skills in a top-down manner, at a point where locals' bargaining power has been reduced to zero.

Mining represents the "non-inclusive" growth model par excellence, as its costs are widespread and its benefits extremely concentrated in a small constituency. Contrary to general perception, the relationship between mining and economic growth and development is highly controversial. First, the contribution of the mining sector to GDP is minimal (2010-11: 2.6 per cent).[11] Second, for every one per cent contribution to GDP, mining activity displaces three to four times more people than all other development projects put together.[12] Third, being born through illegality, it leads to more corruption than its contribution to the general economy by way of returns. Furthermore, many mining-related projects have recently been promoted in the form of foreign direct investment which totalled Rs 3,416.62 crores between 2000-2011. To attract investments from abroad state governments are bending over backwards, actively facilitating and promoting mega projects.

I have witnessed the blood of red mud being squeezed from mountains of bauxite to be transformed into aluminium at Vedanta's aluminium refinery in Orissa. Most people would never connect toxic red sludge with the shiny white metal or to the green hills of Niyamgiri. Vedanta must not be allowed to mine Niyamgiri at any cost. This is an epic contest between the rights of the earth and earth democracy on the one hand, and the illegitimate self-assured rights of a corrupt and greedy corporation on the other. The most significant contribution of bauxite hills like Niyamgiri is the provisioning of water by one river, Indravati, and 32 streams and tributaries of the Mahanadi. It takes two tonnes of bauxite and it needs 250 kilowatt tonnes of electricity to make one tonne of alumina. The rest accumulates as pollution. Smelting one tonne of aluminium consumes 13,500 kilowatt tonnes of electricity emitting, on average, 13.1 tonnes of carbon dioxide and other greenhouse gases such as fluorocarbons. One tonne of aluminium uses 1,200 tonnes of water which destroys its very sources in the bauxite hills.

Vedanta is destroying water at three levels. First, if bauxite is mined 32 streams will run dry, ruining the agriculture and food security of millions. Second, the aluminium refinery and smelter are already diverting millions of litres from agriculture; the 30 kms. long Upper Indravati dam has diverted its water to the Hati Tel river through a four kilometer tunnel at Mukhiguda – the water is then pumped from the Tel river to its refinery in Lanjigarh. Vedanta's Burkhamunda smelter in Jharsuguda is getting water from the Hirakud dam on the Mahanadi. Groundwater levels are falling and double-crop land is being converted to single crop due to a decline in availability of irrigation water. Third, water released by the refinery and smelter is toxic, destroying what remains of the rivers and groundwater. This scale of mining, industrial production and dumping of waste can only take place by violating the rights of citizens and communities. This is why the Dongria have been resisting the mining of Niyamgiri.

I celebrated World Environment Day with 7,000 tribals and peasants of Niyamgiri and surrounding areas. Niyamgiri means the mountain (giri) that upholds the laws (niyam) of the earth and the universe. It is sacred to the Dongria Kond who live in its upper reaches and protect its biodiversity. The tribals had organised a mango festival to celebrate, roads and villages were dense with mango trees and mango groves which are hundreds of years old. The forests provide food and fibre and medicine. As Lavanya Gowda said, "The earth and forest give us everything. All we have to get from outside the forest is salt." While the biodiversity supports the economy of the mountain, water from the bauxite hills supports the economy for miles around. Bauxite, like limestone, holds water in its cavities and is therefore a vital aquifer.

On April 1, 2003, Lingaraj Azad, a local activist, was arrested; on March 27, Suren Majhi was run over by a truck while walking back from a meeting; on June 5, 15 Dongria Kond were arrested for a few hours to prevent them from attending a rally. Two tribals were arrested while coming to Delhi to attend a conference we had organised. On January 23, 2004, police forced the Konds of Kinaru, Borabhats, Sindhaballi and Kotduar out of their houses. They now live in a concentration camp called Vedanta Nagar. Bulldozers wiped out the ancient villages for Vedanta's refinery. The alumina from the refinery is taken to Vedanta's smelter at Jharsuguda and both are already creating massive pollution, killing animals and people. Vedanta is illegally spreading its red mud ponds into villages and forest land. Rivers are dying, and with them the communities that the rivers support. If the destruction of water and biodiversity is internalised, bauxite mining and aluminium smelters would be uneconomic – it is far more beneficial to leave the bauxite in the mountain to produce water and biodiversity.

The world's biggest mining company, BHP Billiton, is Australian; it would have been even bigger if its acquisition of Rio Tinto and Potash Corporation had gone through. Rio Tinto's Ok Tedi Copper Mines had already devastated Papua-New Guinea, but the indigenous communities forced the mine to close. BHP Billiton is in Brazil, Mozambique and Indonesia. Vedanta is a UK company, owned by an Indian, and an Indian company, Gujarat NRI, is mining coal in the Murray Darling Basin (Australia), which is already suffering severe water stress. For the communities in the Murray Darling Basin, this is "coal mining on steroids", and as they say, "coal companies are stealing our rivers". Where does this hubris come from? Who gives the licence for a war against the earth?

Unfortunately, not many have grasped the philosophy that guides forest-dwelling communities' lifestyle; in fact, the debate over upholding tribal and community rights in forest land is a very controversial one. In India, it is erroneously claimed that it is the tribals and other forest-dwellers who have destroyed forests; they have come to be seen as encroachers, enemies of the state and of wildlife, responsible for deforestation and the killing of endangered species like tigers. In fact, it is precisely the tribals and forest-dwellers who have preserved, conserved and protected the forest in its entirety, and maintained an ecosystem for the survival of all the species living within it, tribal communities included: that is the true spirit of sustainable livelihoods.

We, the forest people of the world – living in the woods, surviving on the fruits and crops, farming on the jhoom land, re-cultivating the forest land, roaming around with our herds – have occupied this land since ages. We announce loudly, in unity and solidarity, let there be no doubt on the future: we are the forests and the forests are us, and our existence is mutually dependent. The crisis faced by our forests and environment today will only intensify without us.
—Excerpt from the Declaration of National Forum for Forest People and Forest Workers

The indigenous people in India understand their relationship with the earth, land and resources quite differently from the modern nation state's understanding of private ownership. They understand land in the traditional framework of community ownership and individual use. According to Alex Ekka, eminent social scientist and director of the Xavier Institute of Social Sciences (Ranchi),

> If I own a plot (of land) the understanding is that I have trusteeship of the land, but that it really belongs to the community. The understanding that we have equal access to the use of forest, water bodies and mineral systems is very strong. Our political system is based on this – all have access to land, hence all are equal. Everyone has a voice in the panchayat and everyone is heard.

Our indigenous traditions have been based on diversity, interdependence, pluralism, multifunctionality, non-exclusivity. We have sometimes had more trees on our farms than in forests, and forests have co-existed with farming, as in the shifting cultivation practised in tribal areas. While tribals and forest-dwellers created an economy of subsistence centuries ago – which means the environment itself is their source of livelihood, home, income, food – problems arise when this is subverted by an economy of profits by the private sector, industries and the state apparatus itself.

Jaitapur: land-grab for nuclear power

Fukushima in Japan has once again raised the perennial questions about human fallibility and human frailty. It has raised questions about mankind's hubris, about man's arrogance in thinking he can control nature. It also raises questions about the so-called "nuclear renaissance" as an answer to the climate and energy crises. The International Energy Agency has stated that,

> A nuclear renaissance is possible but cannot occur overnight. Nuclear projects face significant hurdles, including extended construction periods and related risks, long licencing processes and manpower shortages, plus long-standing issues related to waste disposal, proliferation and local opposition. The financing of new nuclear power plants, especially in liberalised markets, has always been difficult and the financial crisis seems almost certain to have made it even more so. The huge capital requirements, combined with risks of cost overruns and regulatory uncertainties make investors and lenders very cautious, even when demand growth is robust.[13]

A nuclear renaissance would need 300 reactors every week and two to three uranium enrichment plants every year. The spent fuel would contain 90,000 bombs of plutonium per year if separated; the water required would be 10–20 million litres per day.[14] China, Germany, Switzerland, Israel, Malaysia, Thailand and Philippines are reviewing their nuclear power programmes. As Alexander Glaser observed,

> It will take time to grasp the full impact of the unimaginable human tragedy unfolding after the earthquake and tsunami in Japan, but it is already clear that the proposition of a global nuclear renaissance ended on that day.[15]

Across India, movements are growing against old and new nuclear power plants. New plants are proposed at Haripur (West Bengal), Mithi Virdi (Gujarat), Madban (Maharashtra), Pitti Sonapur (Orissa), Chutka (Madhya Pradesh) and Kavada (Andhra Pradesh). The 9,900 MW Jaitapur nuclear power plant consisting of six nuclear reactors in Madban village of Ratnagiri district in Maharashtra will be the world's largest, if built. French state-owned nuclear engineering firm, Areva S.A., and Indian state-owned operator, Nuclear Power Corporation of India, signed the $22 billion agreement to build six nuclear reactors in December 2010, in the presence of Nicolas Sarkozy, then French president, and Dr. Manmohan Singh, the Indian prime minister. In the light of an expected surge in orders following the France–India agreement, Areva started hiring one thousand people a month. The project foresees the installation of six European Pressurised Reactors (EPRs) based on new technologies, so far unused in the world. While the Indian government and Areva push this forward as enough justification for safety, the same premise raises serious concerns in the minds of the public and eminent scientists. Being unused and untested, the reactors pose obvious safety problems.

Jaitapur is a seismically sensitive area and earthquake risks are high. There is no plan for the disposal of the 300 tonnes of nuclear waste that the plant will generate each year. Jaitapur is one of many nuclear power plants proposed in a thin strip of the fertile coastland of Raigad, Ratnagiri and Sindhudurg districts. The combined power generated would be 33,000 MW. (This is a region for which the government of India applied to UNESCO to be declared a world heritage site under its Man and Biosphere programme.) While the broader debate over the direction India should take to meet its energy requirements plays out between misleading claims and hard facts, resistance to the nuclear plant has intensified with the government's recourse to land acquisition at the proposed site. Local villagers, farmers and members of civil society are protesting the forcible acquisition of 968 hectares of fertile land from five villages of Madban, Niveli, Karel, Mithgavane and Varliwada, directly affecting over 2,400 families and more than 40,000 overall livelihoods. Strongly opposing the displacement which would cause them loss of land, livelihood and substantial income from agriculture and horticulture, hardly a hundred families have accepted compensation, and many of them are rethinking that, too.

The acquisition process was announced in 2007 when the government first offered a compensation of Rs 1 to 1.5 lakhs per acre. Later, because of the controversy and the land, in fact, being cultivated and not barren, compensation has been revised to Rs 10 lakhs per acre, plus one job per displaced family. What the government fails to understand when offering higher cash handouts and relief packages is that farmers and other local communities are not protesting to get more money, they are protesting the possible loss of their land and livelihood, on which no price tag can be placed.

The people have created a Konkan Bachao Samiti and Janahit Seva Samiti; when the government authorities went to distribute cheques for the forced land acquisition on December 29, 2009, January 12, 2010 and January 22, 2010, people refused to accept them. On January 22, 1,972 people were arrested and on December 4, 1,500 were detained during protests.

Experts on nuclear power and activists resisting new nuclear power plants gathered on April 9, 2011 in Delhi, at a conference titled, "Learning from the Fukushima Disaster." As Dr Surender Gadakar, a physicist and anti-nuclear activist explained, nuclear power is a technology for boiling water that produces large quantities of poisons that need to be isolated from the environment for long periods of time. Plutonium, produced as nuclear waste, has a half life of 240,000 years, while the average life of nuclear reactors is twenty-one years. So far no proven, safe system for nuclear waste disposal exists. Spent nuclear fuel has to be constantly cooled, and when cooling systems fail we have a nuclear disaster – as happened at nuclear reactor 4 at Fukushima, which was off-line for maintenance work but whose spent fuel leaked. Plutonium is not just nuclear waste; it is also a strategic resource for nuclear weapons. The world's "civil" plutonium stockpile exceeds 230 tonnes – a few kilograms are sufficient to produce a nuclear weapon.

As a technology, nuclear power consumes more energy than it generates, if the energy required for cooling spent fuel for thousands of years is taken into account. In India, the costs of nuclear energy become even higher because nuclear power plants must grab land and displace people. The Narora nuclear plant in Uttar Pradesh, 125 kms. from Delhi, displaced five villages but 22 villages lie in the 5 km. control area. In 1993, there was a major fire and near meltdown in Narora. The 2,800 MW nuclear plant planned at Fatehbad, Haryana, involves the acquisition of 1,503 acres of fertile farmland; 80 villages are protesting, two farmers have died during protests. They have taken a pledge, *"Jaan denge, zameen nahi denge"* (we will give up our lives, not our land). The people of Mithi Virdi, Gujarat, and Kovvada in Srikakulam in Andhra Pradesh, speak in the same voice. A nuclear power plant is planned at Chutkah in Madhya Pradesh, but 44 villages have resisted it. Here, 162 villages were earlier displaced by the Bargi dam. When the government went for land acquisition, a tribal woman said, "You displaced us for the Bargi dam, promising electricity. We still have no electricity. We do not want your nuclear plant. Take it where people use the electricity." At Jaitapur, activists like Vaishali Patel have 3,000 court cases against them for resisting the land-grab. Jaitapur is under prohibitory orders, where more than five people cannot gather. Ten gram panchayats have resigned to protest the violation of the 73rd Amendment. The anti-nuclear movement is a democratic imperative, a health imperative, an ecological imperative. That is why a Tarapur-to-Jaitapur anti-nuclear march was planned from April 23-25, 2011; activists on the march were arrested and prevented from reaching Jaitapur.

As physicist Sowmya Dutta reminds us, the world has potential for 17 terra watt nuclear energy, 700 terra watt wind energy and 86,000 terra watt of solar energy. Alternatives to nuclear energy are a thousand times more abundant and a million times less risky. To push nuclear plants after Fukushima is pure insanity. The problem with hazardous technologies like nuclear power for energy production is that regulators are committed to promoting the technology. They are not independent. There is a history of collusion between the regulators and the industry; both believe in the viability of nuclear power and neither wants to tell the whole truth to a public that is uneasy about it because of the gruesome effects of radiation in Hiroshima and Nagasaki. A. Gopalkrishna, a former chairman of India's Atomic Energy Regulatory Board has accused "the administration of Manmohan Singh, the Prime Minister, of recklessly rushing to embrace untried foreign nuclear technology". He added that India's nuclear regulator "operates like a lapdog of the department of atomic energy and the Prime Minister's Office".[16]

If it was "madness" for Japan to build the Fukushima nuclear plant in a seismic zone, it is doubly so for India to build the Jaitapur nuclear plant in a similar zone. As Jonathan Schell has so sensitively observed in "From Hiroshima to Fukushima",

> Nuclear power is a complex, high technology. But the things that endemically malfunction are of a humble kind. The art of nuclear power is to boil water with the incredible heat generated by a nuclear chain reaction. But such temperatures necessitate continuous cooling. Cooling requires pumps. Pumps require conventional power. These are the things that habitually go wrong – and have gone wrong in Japan. A back-up generator shuts down. A battery runs out. The pump grinds to a halt.
>
> The problem is not that another back-up generator is needed, or that the safety rules aren't tight enough, or that the pit for nuclear waste is in the wrong geological location, it is that a stumbling, imperfect, probably imperfectable creature like ourselves is unfit to wield the stellar fire released by the split or fused atom.
>
> *International Herald Tribune*, March 17, 2011.

Movements for land sovereignty and Operation Green Hunt

The land wars are testing every aspect of India, an agrarian economy based on small farmers and peasants, a decentralised democracy which, through the 73rd and 74th Amendments, has entrusted local communities with making decisions on natural resources. For the first time, after fifty years of India's independence, a significant step was taken by the introduction of the Provisions of the Panchayats (Extension to the Scheduled Areas) (PESA) Act, 1996, whereby village communities (gram sabhas) were granted legal recognition as a community entity; it also recognised their control over their commons. This new law (which provides an extension to the provisions of Part IX of the Constitution of India) for scheduled areas came into force on December 24, 1996. According to Section 4(b): "A village shall ordinarily consist of a habitation or group of habitations, or a hamlet or group of hamlets comprising a community and managing its affairs in accordance with tradition and custom."

It is the village community which has been been endowed with specific powers, including management of community resources, resolution of disputes, approval of plans and programmes, and also mandatory consultation before the acquisition of land. Conferral of certain other powers on the gram sabha, such as ownership of minor forest produce, enforcement of prohibition, restoration of unlawfully alienated lands, control over moneylending and marketing, etc. have been made mandatory under this Act. In 2006, India also passed The Scheduled Tribes and Other Traditional Forest Dwellers (Recognition of Forest Rights) Act to correct the historic wrong of violating the rights of tribals.

As tribals have exercised their constitutional, democratic, resource rights and human rights, they have been met with violence. They are being hunted down in their homelands by paramilitary forces called Cobra Commando Battalion for Resolute Action, and militias like Salwa Judum, now renamed Koya Commandos, to clear the way for mines and factories. This war against India's "green" capital – the forest regions – and against India's original inhabitants is being called the "green hunt".

In one sense it is a hunt for "green", the rich natural resources in tribal lands, but like the earlier green revolution, this war against nature and people is using "green" to counter "red". The justification for Operation Green Hunt is hunting out the Maoists, the red threat. Its reality is terrorising the tribals, treating every tribal as a Maoist so that they leave their homes in the forest, and mining corporations and steel and aluminium giants have direct, uninterrupted access to the minerals that lie beneath the soil. "Green Hunt" is not just a war against the tribals, it is a war against India's forests and rivers that support all of us. It is therefore also a war against the people of India. It is a war against nature and our future. And it is a war against the real "green" agenda of peace, justice and sustainability.

However, there are no Maoists in the coastal areas of Orissa where POSCO wants to set up its plant. The POSCO Pratirodh Sangram Samiti (PPSS) has been peacefully continuing its day-and-night dharna at Balitutha since January 26, 2010, when I joined them. Every day thousands of women, men, children from families of peasants, fisherfolk, landless labourers and dalits participate in the sit-in. On May 11, 25 platoons of heavily armed police arrived in Dhutiria Chreidesh and Balitutha to attack the peaceful protestors. This is a militarised land-grab, not a control of Maoists. On May 12, police fired at and killed 50-year old Lokima Jamuda and injured twenty people in Chandra village, Jagpur district, where Tata wants to set up its steel plant and where earlier, thirteen people had been killed in January 2006. These were not Maoists, they are innocent tribals defending their land sovereignty.

Home Minister, P. Chidambaram, instead of condemning the killings, said there is a "trust deficit" in Red Areas. Does he expect people to start trusting their killers? Green areas such as coastal Orissa where 40 platoons have been sent, or Niyamgiri or Kalinganagar which are rich in forests and farming, are being falsely coloured and called "Naxal areas". The deficit is not just of trust, there is a "democracy deficit" because the government is refusing to listen to the democratic voices of the people in defence of their democratic rights, using violence to uproot them. There is a "peace deficit" because the government is using force to facilitate the land-grab by corporations. There is a "justice deficit" because it is unjust to rob the poor of their resources and livelihoods. There is a "sustainability deficit" because the green areas being hijacked through Green Hunt will become black and brown areas of polluted wastelands. If India is to survive, this land-grab must stop.

Central India is home to the adivasis and dalits, India's original inhabitants. It is also home to the richest concentration of natural resources in the country. Today, as powerful Indian and global corporations race each other to gain control of the land, water, forest and mineral wealth of the region, this natural wealth has become a curse for these indigenous but marginalised communities. Coming between corporate greed and natural resources are the tribals asserting their customary rights, right to life and livelihood, and their constitutional rights over the same natural resources. A virtual information blockade prevents information from coming out of states like Chhattisgarh which are bearing the brunt of the violence.

To address the above concerns, Citizens Against Forced Displacement and War on People (of which Navdanya is a founding member) held the Independent Peoples' Tribunal on Land Acquisition, Resource Grab and Operation Green Hunt at the Constitution Club, New Delhi, on April 9, 10 and 11, 2010. The Tribunal focused on the states of Chhattisgarh, Jharkhand, Orissa, West Bengal and Andhra Pradesh, where Operation Green Hunt is most active. A jury of six eminent persons comprising Justice P.B. Sawant (former judge, Supreme Court of India); Justice H. Suresh (former judge, Mumbai High Court); Professor Yashpal (educationist and former chairman, University Grants Commission); Dr. P.M. Bhargava (founder of Centre for Cellular and Molecular Biology and former vice-chairman, Knowledge Commission); Dr. Mohini Giri (former chairperson, National Commission of Women); and Dr. K.S. Subramanian (former director-general, police) presided. Over three days, testimonies of a large number of witnesses from the states of Chhattisgarh, Jharkhand, West Bengal and Orissa, as well as expert witnesses on land acquisition, mining and human rights violations were presented to the jury. After hearing them the following statement was issued by them.

Tribal communities represent a substantial and important proportion of India's population and heritage. Not even ten countries in the world have more people than we have tribals in

India. Not only are they crucial components of the country's human biodiversity, which is greater than in the rest of the world put together, but they are also an important source of social, political and economic wisdom that would be currently relevant and can give India an edge. In addition, they understand the language of nature better than anyone else, and have been the most successful custodians of our environment, including forests. There is also a great deal to learn from them in areas as diverse as art, culture, resource management, waste management, medicine and metallurgy. They have also been far more humane and committed to universally accepted values than our urban society. It is clear that the country has been witnessing gross violations of the rights of the poor, particularly tribal rights, which have reached unprecedented levels since the new economic policies of the 1990s. The Fifth Schedule rights of the tribals, in particular the Panchayat Extension to Scheduled Areas (PESA) Act and the Forest Rights Act have been grossly violated. These violations have now gone to the extent where fully tribal villages have been declared to be non-tribal. The entire executive and judicial administrations appear to have been totally apathetic to their plight. The development model which has been adopted and which is sharply embodied in the new economic policies of liberalisation, privatisation and globalisation, has led in recent years to a huge drive by the state to transfer resources, particularly land and forests, which are critical for the livelihood and the survival of the tribal people, to corporations for exploitation of mineral resources, SEZs and other industries, most of which have been enormously destructive to the environment. These industries have critically polluted water bodies, land, trees, plants, and have had a devastating impact on the health and livelihoods of the people. The consultation with the gram sabhas required by the PESA Act has been rendered a farce as has the process of environment impact assessment of these industries. This has resulted in leaving the tribals in a state of acute malnutrition and hunger which has pushed them to the very brink of survival. It could well be the severest indictment of the state in the history of democracy anywhere, on account of the sheer number of people (tribals) affected and the diabolic nature of the atrocities committed on them by the state, especially the police, leave aside the enormous and irreversible damage to the environment. It is also a glaring example of corruption – financial, intellectual and moral – sponsored and/or abetted by the state, that characterises today's India, cutting across all party lines.

Peaceful resistance movements of tribal communities against their forced displacement and the corporate grab of their resources is being sought to be violently crushed by the use of police and security forces and state and corporate-funded and armed militias. The state violence has been accentuated by Operation Green Hunt in which a huge number of paramilitary forces are being used mostly on the tribals. The militarisation of the state has reached a level where schools are occupied by security forces.

Even peaceful activists opposing these violent actions of the state against the tribals are being targeted by the state and victimised. This has led to a total alienation of the people from the state as well as their loss of faith in the government and the security forces. The government – both at the Centre and in the states – must realise that the above-mentioned actions, combined with total apathy, could very well be sowing the seeds of a violent revolution, demanding justice and rule of law, that would engulf the entire country. We should not forget French, Russian and American history, leave aside our own.

Recommendations

- Stop Operation Green Hunt and start a dialogue with the local people.
- Immediately stop all compulsory acquisition of agricultural or forest land and the forced displacement of the tribal people.
- Declare the details of all MoUs, industrial and infrastructural projects proposed in these areas and freeze all MoUs and

leases for non-agricultural use of such land, which the home minister has proposed.

- Rehabilitate and reinstate the tribals forcibly displaced back to their land and forests.
- Stop all environmentally destructive industries as well as those on land acquired without the consent of the gram sabhas in these areas.
- Withdraw the paramilitary and police forces from schools and health centres, which must be effectuated with adequate teachers and infrastructure.
- Stop victimising dissenters and those who question the actions of the state.
- Replace the model of development which is exploitative, environmentally destructive, iniquitous and not suitable for the country by a completely different model which is participatory, gives importance to agriculture and the rural sector, and respects equity and the environment.
- It must be ensured that all development, especially use of land and natural resources, is with the consent and participation of the tribal communities as guaranteed by the Constitution. Credible citizens' commissions must be constituted to monitor and ensure this.
- Constitute an empowered citizens' commission to investigate and recommend action against persons responsible for human rights violations of the tribal communities. This commission must also be empowered to ensure that tribals actually receive the benefit of whatever government schemes exist for them.

A decision was taken at the IPT to undertake a Citizens' Peace March to call for an end to violence. A coalition of groups, led by Azadi Bachao Andolan and supported by Navdanya, started the peace march from Raipur on April 5, 2010. After the march the government invited Swami Agnivesh, a Right Livelihood Awardee, to be an interlocutor between it and the Maoists for a peace initiative. However, the government used his communication with the Maoists to track and kill one of their major leaders, Azad.

One year later, on March 11, 2011, the Salwa Judum (reincarnated as Koya Commandos) and the Central Reserve Police Force's elite Cobra Battalion burnt 300 huts, sexually assaulted three women and seized three men whose bodies were later found dumped in the forest. Following this genocide, Swami Agnivesh went to Dantewada on March 26, 2011, with police protection; he reported:

> The reality of what was happening dawned at 6.30 a.m. when we reached Dornapal and I saw a mob of hundreds of people waiting for us. They started shouting slogans against our visit, demanding we turn back. When we got closer, they *gheraoed* (encircled) the Scorpio I was travelling in and dragged me out. They hurled stones and eggs at us. We had to run to our rest house.
>
> At 10.30 am I called Chief Minister Raman Singh, informing him about the incident and my desire to return to the capital, Raipur. But he wanted me to take the relief material to the violence-hit villages and promised tight security. I agreed to do that.
>
> The security came at 3.30 pm. This time, when we reached the same spot, the crowd had swelled to more than 3,000. Salwa Judum cadres and SPOs brandishing guns, lathis, stones and iron rods had positioned themselves to attack us. In a span of six hours, another attack was to be mounted on me. They beat up all of us. One of the stones they threw hit my head from behind and I fell down. They also took off my turban and pushed me around. Colleagues and media personnel rushing to rescue me were also roughed up. The relief material was looted. The information that the SSP, S.R.P. Kalluri – who has now been transferred – had been instigating the mob against us for many days, turned out to be accurate. It was all pre-planned.
>
> More than the humiliation, what irks me is the police going back on their word. When I had helped in the release of five policemen from Maoist custody recently, the CM had promised that talks would be held with the Maoists. But he did nothing.

I may be the Centre's interlocutor for peace talks with the Maoists, but what is the use of this effort when I know that the state orchestrated a murderous plot against me? I have no animosity towards the state government but I want a judicial inquiry by a retired Supreme Court judge into the violence meted out to poor villagers since March 11. And I want the CM to assume moral responsibility for these events.[17]

Chhattisgarh and other mineral-rich tribal areas have been transformed into a war zone where peace and democracy are facing total closure.

References

[1]   Quoted in "Road to Disaster," *Down to Earth*, June 1-15, 2011, p. 39.

[2]   http://infochangeindia.org/governance/analysis/five-years-after sezs-chronicle-of-revenues-foregone. html

[3]   Navdanya/RFSTE report, "The Corporate Hijack of Land", Delhi: 2007.

[4]   Miningzone.org/wp-content/uploads/2010/10/Iron-and Steal.pdf

[5]   Unanimously, but for Meena Gupta herself who was MoEF Secretary at the time of the original POSCO environmental clearance approval.

[6]   For a detailed list of incentives and facilities to SEZs visit http: www.sezindia.nic.in/about-fi.asp

[7]   http://money.cnn.com/news/specials/storysupplement bankbailout/

[8]   See movement literature from Nandigram or the Salim Group website.

[9]   Ministry of Coal and Mines Annual Reports, 2001-02 and 2008-09.

[10] http://www.mmpindia.org/Multinationals.htm

[11] Ministry of Mines and Minerals, Annual Reports, 1999-2000.

[12] http://www.mmpindia.org/Multinationals.htm

[13] IEA, "World Energy, Outlook," 2009, p.160.

[14] Arjun Makhijani, a leading nuclear expert, at the Public Interest Environmental Law Conference, Oregon, 2011.

[15] Alexander Glaser, "After the Nuclear Renaissance, the Age of Discovery," *Bulletin of Atomic Scientists*, March 17, 2011.

[16] Amy Kazmin and James Lamot, "Former Watchdog Attacks Delhi Over Expansion Plans," *Financial Times*, March 19/20, 2011.

[17] http://www.tehelka.com/story_main49.asp?filename= Ne090411It_was.asp#

3 Water Wars and Water Peace

THE EARTH IS 70 per cent water, and we could have water in perpetuity because it renews itself through the water cycle; yet today we have a severe water scarcity. The water crisis is a result of excessive water withdrawal from the ground and from rivers, as well as of dumping waste and pollution into our rivers and water bodies.

India is a land of major rivers and abundant monsoon rain in most regions but it is facing a serious water crisis. Rivers are dying as their waters are dammed and diverted, groundwater is disappearing as it is mined, and World Bank loans have had a major role in creating India's water crisis. The Bank has driven intensive irrigation projects which have wasted water and created water-logged and saline deserts. It has promoted groundwater mining with its tubewell irrigation loans. During the 1950s-1980s the World Bank assisted the creation of a water crisis in India by financing dams and diversion of river waters; from the 1990s on the Bank has used the financial and hydrological crises it created to force Indian states and public utilities to privatise water services and assets.

Water privatisation projects are a major World Bank-mediated political and financial scam, locking public utilities and citizens into a system where the public pays a global corporation super-high tariffs for water that has been provided through the services to our public utilities. First, the World Bank uses its loans as a conditionality for privatisation. Second, it reduces the universal access system of public utilities to a privileged access to industry and 24x7 supply to rich urban areas. Third, it diverts limited and scarce groundwater from rural areas to urban areas, thus undermining the Millennium

Development Goal(s) to reduce by half the proportion of people without sustainable access to safe drinking water. Fourth, it is forcing governments and public utilities to increase water tariffs and to commodify water, subverting people's fundamental right to water as part of the right to life. Fifth, since World Bank projects are based on non-sustainable water use, they are failing, as is clear in the case of the Sonia Vihar plant in Delhi and the Veeranam project in Tamil Nadu. World Bank loans are failing to bring water to people; they are successful only in guaranteeing contracts and profits for water corporations like Suez, Vivendi, Bechtel.

World Bank loan conditionalities have many paradigm shifts built into them – the shift from "water for life" to "water for profits"; from "water democracy" to "water apartheid"; from "some for all" to "all for some".

"Privatisation" was launched as the core of the globalisation and trade liberalisation paradigm, based on the crude ideology that public is bad, private is good; domestic is bad, multinational is good. As movements emerged against water privatisation, the World Bank rhetoric shifted to "private sector participation", and an attempt was made to define the privatisation of services and management contracts as not being privatisation.

The World Bank loan of $2.5 million was used to privatise the Sonia Vihar Project to Suez Degremont, as well as to privatise the study on Delhi's water supply to PriceWaterhouse, and was even being used to privatise law-making by global corporations by having PriceWaterhouse draft the law for a water regulatory authority, thus bypassing our elected representatives. This privatisation of the water system by the government was at the heart of the debate between the Delhi Jal Board and the Citizens' Front for Water Democracy.

The latest semantic shift is to refer to privatisation as "outsourcing". As Delhi chief minister Sheila Dikshit has stated, "The Planning Commission has asked us to make the entire procedure for outsourcing the management of water supply more transparent." ("Water Supply Outsourcing to be an Open Book: CM" *Express*

Newsline, New Delhi, August 17, 2005.). We see a number of problems in the way the government has handled this issue. First, changing the terms does not change the substance. Second, the chief minister should have gone to the citizens of Delhi or their elected representatives to resolve the issue – the Planning Commission has no executive function in issues of governance. It is a different matter that the deputy chairman of the Commission, Montek Singh Ahluwalia, is taking the initiative in executive decisions related to water. The government's priority for commodification and privatisation of water was clearly stated by him in his opening remarks at the National Development Council (NDC) that farmers should pay for water. While Mr. Ahluwalia argued that rich farmers are the real beneficiaries of free water, the reality is that when water is commodified, it is only the rich who can afford to pay. The poor peasants, already struggling under the burden of debt, driven to suicide, will be wiped out if they are denied access to water and made to pay for a resource that is their common property. If poor peasants are pitted against rich agribusinesses in competition for water, agribusinesses will monopolise irrigation and the rich will win.

The problem of water waste is not agriculture, per se, but chemical industrial farming mistakenly referred to as the Green Revolution. It is possible to produce more nutrition per acre growing millets that need only 200 mm. of water; we can increase food availability two hundredfold through simultaneously conserving our biodiversity and scarce water resources by shifting from chemical farming to organic farming. However, these water conservation strategies were not what Mr. Ahluwalia proposed; he proposed more water-intensive cultivation of fruits, vegetables, shrimps for export. In other words, while India is gripped by a severe water crisis and even more severe water conflicts, the Planning Commission is recommending that we export water as a "virtual water" subsidy to the rich consumers of the North. Instead of calling for water conservation through organic farming, he wants the impoverished peasantry to finance insane schemes like the $200 billion River Linking Scheme. The deputy chairman stated that "chasing short-term benefits that accrue from vote bank politics instead of seeking long-term gains that flow from prudent economic policies, has become the bane of our decision-making process."[1]

What Mr. Ahluwalia calls "vote bank politics" others call democracy; what he refers to as "prudent economic policies" are the World Bank/IMF/ADB paradigm of water privatisation which has already led to the killing of farmers in Tonk and could lead to many more water wars.

The problem of privatisation cannot be reduced simply to a matter of transparency. It is more crucially an issue of who will own and manage water resources and services – the public, or private corporations. Transparency alone cannot settle the basic issue of law and governance, of rights and ownership. While the government talking transparency is the success of people's movements against Delhi's water privatisation that began in 2002, the real issue is not just citizens' access to information on privatisation processes, but their participation in deciding whether the water supply should be privatised or outsourced in the first place.

The alternatives we have proposed in the form of public-public partnership show that water privatisation is neither necessary nor desirable. Affordable water for all can only be provided when water is managed as a public good, with strong public utilities and vital public participation. This is the agenda of water democracy, which we are committed to building, as an alternative to the water dictatorship that the World Bank is trying to establish through its loan conditionalities imposing corrupt, greedy, unaccountable water corporations on Indian citizens.

Water Privatisation in Delhi and Peoples' Movements that Stalled It

Dry Run 1998	World Bank's entry into Delhi and restructuring of public utility, creation of Delhi Jal Board.
2000	Project Preparation Facility Advance of $2.5 million by World Bank.
2001	World Bank consultants PriceWaterhouseCoopers draws up proposals for privatisation, including

	contracts for Sonia Vihar, Water Tariffs, 24x7 scheme and water legislation.
June 21, 2002	Sonia Vihar Plant inaugurated by Delhi's chief minister.
August 2002	"Ganga Yatra" - Peoples' movements against diversion of Ganga water to Delhi, declares "Mother Ganga is not for sale." Pressure built up on Uttarakhand and Uttar Pradesh governments not to supply water.
2003	Sonia Vihar Plant is not commissioned – people's first victory.
March 22, 2003 (World Water Day)	Citizens' Front for Water Democracy launched, to stop Delhi's water privatisation.
November 30, 2003	Delhi Jal Board announces increase in water tariffs. Citizens' Front for Water Democracy calls for non-co-operation movement against increased tariffs.
March 15-22, 2004	Jal Swaraj Yatra against water privatisation – 1.5 million people participate.
Mid-2004	Delhi Jal Board tries to run 24x7 scheme without Sonia Vihar supply by diverting water from the poor to the rich.
Late 2004	Time-table prepared for implementation; target date mid-2005, scheme to spread to five other zones by October 2006 and the whole of Delhi by 2015.
Early 2005	DJB shortlists firms for project. Criticism from several quarters, especially NGOs and Water Workers' Alliance, alleging 24x7 was a move towards "privatisation" of DJB. Civic body shifts target date to September 2005, then to year-end.
September 2005	Delhi government writes to World Bank that they have put the 24x7 project on hold "for the time being".
November 23, 2005	Delhi government writes to the Centre that they are withdrawing the World Bank loan application.

In India, the privatisation of water supply utilities and the irrigation sector is taking place aggressively, with water resource management being transferred to private corporations through BOT/BOOT projects or management contracts. The interlinking of rivers is another large and even more insidious privatisation project – camouflaged under water sector restructuring in various states – which will have a profound and far-reaching impact. Together the two processes will hand over complete control of water resources to multinational private corporations. This privatisation of water in major towns in India is a natural corollary to India becoming a member-nation of WTO, whose basic requirement was to transform the existing 1987 policy by enacting the 2002 Water Policy with a special section on private sector participation. This opened the floodgates – Bhopal, Gwalior, Jabalpur, Indore, Dewas, Maksi (all in Madhya Pradesh); Hyderabad, Visakhapatnam (Andhra Pradesh); Borai (Chhattisgarh); Bangalore (Karnataka); Chennai, Tirapur (Tamil Nadu); Rajkot, Ahmedabad (Gujarat); Pune, Sangli-Miraj (Maharashtra); Haldia (West Bengal); Jamshedpur (Jharkhand); Noida (Uttar Pradesh); Delhi, and other cities fell into the net.

In order to privatise the urban water supply, concerned states must undertake the restructuring of water resources within their territories; accordingly, many states have entered into loan agreements either with the World Bank or the Asian Development Bank (ADB) for this restructuring. These loan agreements go beyond privatising of the urban water supply, making deep encroachments in the area of water tariffs in irrigation. To justify the sharp increase in water tariffs, the loan agreements increase property tax, in some cases by as much as 200 per cent. In addition, new taxes are also envisaged – for sewer drainage, sanitation and investment return. These agreements may eventually prove to be a death-knell for small and marginal farmers (those with less than two acres of land), who constitute 82 per cent of farmers. The total quantum of loans taken in these eighteen water sector projects (barring the 2004 Karnataka Coastal Area Water Management Project) is a staggering US $3,027.70 million or Rs. 14,475.20 crores. Besides these, a contract for the Kerala Urban

Water Supply Project has also been signed, under which water supply systems in large and medium towns will be privatised. Another project, SWAJAL (with a World Bank loan), is being implemented in Uttarakhand for the last few years. On March 29, 2004, the ADB also granted a loan of US $46.1 million to Chhattisgarh for water sector reforms.

The clause on private sector participation was incorporated in the water policy document of various states; in Maharashtra this clause was reproduced verbatim. Worse still, the entire structure of the state water policy was an exact replica of the 2002 Water Policy. The water policy of the government of Karnataka has more or less used the same words in the paragraph relating to privatisation. The government of Andhra Pradesh has also begun the water privatisation process. Already, some thirty cities in Maharashtra, Karnataka, Andhra Pradesh and Rajasthan are bidding their respective municipal water supply to a handful of powerful MNCs, even though the experiences of cities in other developing countries have shown that the privatised and commercialised supply of water often deprives the poorer and marginalised sections of society of their basic right to it. Tirupur in Tamil Nadu and Hubli-Dharwad in Karnataka have moved closer to privatising their water utilities; New Delhi's water supply will soon be in the hands of Vivendi.

These policies have the underlying thrust of converting the whole sector into a market. The reform agenda ensures full cost recovery, elimination of subsidies, public-private partnerships, allocation of water to highest value use through market mechanisms.

On October 28, 2004, agitating farmers set ablaze a police station and staged protests in Sriganganagar district (Rajasthan) where four persons were killed in police firing on October 27, prompting authorities to extend curfew to more areas like Gharsana, Rawala and Anoopgarh in Rajasthan. In 2005, farmers in Tonk protested against the diversion of their river Banas to urban areas, leaving their fields and wells dry. On August 26, five people were killed when the police shot at them during a peaceful protest for water rights. The promotion and spread of water-intensive green revolution farming has led to water conflicts and an acute water crisis; in Punjab and Haryana, groundwater levels are falling by three feet every year. Two-thirds of India's surface and groundwater is polluted with agricultural pesticide and fertiliser run-off, industrial discharge and urban waste.

The water crisis embodies a gender-equality dimension that should not be underestimated. In developing countries, fetching water is the job of women and children; women are the world's water carriers. Walking for hours, they carry home as much as 60 litres of water, day after day, for their families. Most women and girl children in Rajasthan find themselves looking for water for much of the year. They trudge in the hot sun for hours over wastelands, across thorny fields or rough terrain in search of water, often brackish and like the colour of mud, but still welcome for parched throats at home. On average, a rural woman walks more than 14,000 kms. a year just to fetch water. Their urban sisters are only slightly better off – they may not walk such distances, but they stand in long queues for hours on end to collect water from roadside taps or water lorries.

Chronic health problems result from carrying this heavy load. After such an expenditure of energy and time, there is no room left for education and, by extension, for development and economic independence. Whereas women are carriers of water, men are makers of policy. It is the men who make up the water authorities and decide about pumps, the location of wells and the distribution of water, and water privatisation is further exacerbating social discrimination against women.

Women are also the world's bread-winners – water and food go together; this has always been so. Women produce more than half the world's total food supply – 80 per cent in Africa. Their role as those responsible for the entire food chain contrasts starkly with their lack of rights when it comes to land acquisition and ownership, as well as the provision of loans, seeds and technical assistance. Numerous action plans from UN conferences (e.g. Cairo, Beijing, Copenhagen, Rome) ascribe capital importance to the principle that "women's rights are human rights". Equal access for women to water and land are key factors in the fight against poverty and hunger. Equal rights for women means a secure nutritional base. An international water convention would give women of all countries a binding powerful instrument with which to enforce and demand fulfilment of their rights – even vis-à-vis their own (passive) governments.

Water rights are at the heart of earth rights. The right to water is also a human right. On July 28, 2010, the UN General Assembly adopted a resolution recognising access to clean water and sanitation as a human right. The resolution was adopted by a vote of 122 in favour, and none against, with 41 abstentions.[2]

When the Italian government passed a law to privatise water, Italian citizens organised as the Forum Italiano del Movimenti per l'Acqua, a network of national associations and local communities, and mobilised 1.4 million people for a referendum on water. The law under referendum had proposed that water supply be managed exclusively by private enterprises with the private investor holding at least 40 per cent, and local authorities reducing their shareholding to 30 per cent by 2015.

The referendum was held in June 2011. Students, families and workers mobilised everywhere in spite of a holiday weekend. Italians voted 'No' to water privatisation and 'Yes' to water as a public common good to which all citizens have a universal right. As Alex Zanotelli, an Italian priest said to the Naples celebration rally,

> All life comes from water, water is the mother of our existence and it must not be the multinationals that decide how it should be managed and distributed, but the people of the world. We must join together to build human relationships and to create a network of direct democracy to protect water and other public goods from exploitation.[3]

If the Ganga lives, India lives

India is the land through which the Ganga flows – where the Bhagirathi, the Bhilangana, the Mandakini and Alakananda join to form the river which has supported our culture and civilisation, our agriculture and economy, from time immemorial.

This region in the Himalaya used to be called Dev Bhoomi, divine and sacred land; today it has been defined as "Urja Pradesh", the land of hydroelectric power. The Ganga is also threatened at its very source, the Gangotri glacier, with climate change, which is leading to a decline in snowfall and an increase in the rate of melting snow. From 1935 to 1956 the retreat of the Gangotri glacier was 4.35 m/yr; during the period 1990-96 it was 28.33 m/yr. The average rate of retreat is 20–38 m/yr. If this retreat continues, the Ganga will become a seasonal river, with major ecological and economic consequences for the entire Ganges basin. This is why we need climate justice for water justice.

Planners do not see our rivers as rivers of life, they see them as 20,000 megawatts of hydro-power. In 1916, Rai Patiram Bahadur in his book, *Garhwal, Ancient and Modern* wrote:

> We may say that there is no country in the world of the dimension of Garhwal which has so many rivers as a traveller will find in this land. The district has sixty rivers of different size; besides these there are rivulets, rills, springs and fountains in hundreds, showing that nature has been especially bountiful to this land in the matter of its water supply.

Five hundred dams are planned in this region on the Ganga system. Among thirty-seven hydroelectric projects on the Alakananda, one in Srinagar is being constructed by GVK, a South Indian corporation. Other dams proposed on the Alakananda and Mandakini rivers are:

1. Alakananda (Badrinath)   (300 MW)
2. Bagoli   (72 MW)
3. Bowla Nandprayag   (132 MW)
4. Chuni Senu   (24 MW)
5. Deodi   (60 MW)
6. Devsari   (255 MW)
7. Gauribund   (18.6 MW)
8. Gohana Tal   (60 MW)
9. Jelam Tameh   (60 MW)

10.	Kalnaprayag	(160 MW)
11.	Lakshmanganga	(4.4 MW)
12.	Lata Tapovan	(310 MW)
13.	Maleri Jalam	(55 MW)
14.	Nand Prayag Langasn	(141 MW)
15.	Padli dam	(27 MW)
16.	Phata Bying	(108 MW)
17.	Rambara	(24 MW)
18.	Rishi Ganga I	(70 MW)
19.	Rishi Ganga II	(35 MW)
20.	Simgoli Bhatwari	(99 MW)
21.	Tamak Lata	(280 MW)
22.	Urgam – II	(3.8 MW)
23.	Utyasu Dam	(860 MW)
24.	Vishnugad Pipalkata	(444 MW)

Source: "Hydroelectric Projects on Alakananda River Basin" by South Asia Network on Dams, Rivers and People. www.sandrp.in.

The 99 MW power project at Singoli–Bhatwari near Augustmuni, being constructed by Larson & Toubro, which will affect 60 villages is one of the twelve hydroelectric projects coming up on the Mandakini. The Ganga's tributaries are threatened by dams and diversions in the upper reaches. The 260.5 m. high Tehri dam built on the confluence of the Bhagirathi and Bhilangana has been an unmitigated disaster. It submerged the ancient capital of Tehri Garhwal, destroyed the lush and fertile fields of Bhilangana and Bhagirathi valleys, and displaced 100,000 people from 125 villages of which 33 were completely submerged. But the displacement due to the dam continues. A hundred new landslides have been triggered by the dam, threatening another 100,000 people, and in the heavy monsoon of 2010, the disasters intensified.

At the shore of the reservoir people were flooded from below and above, simultaneously. Fields and homes by the dam shore were submerged as the water level rose from 820 to 835 metres. The Tehri hydro-power plant authorities did not want to release excess water from the dam, even though the water levels were affecting the surrounding villages, because they consider release through the slush gates is spillage. Mooni Devi, who lives at water level, says, "This used to be such a great place with great farms, the dam builders have turned us all into beggars."

The government of India has been proposing hydroelectric projects on Loharinag-Pala, Pala-Maneri and Bhaironghati on the Bhagirathi in addition to the already built Tehri dam and Maneri Bhali-2 dam, a series of dams between Gangotri and Uttarakashi. In 2008, it took the penance and fasting by 76-year old Prof. G.D. Aggarwal, a former professor of IIT Kanpur, to stop the string of dams on the Bhagirathi, including the 600 MW Loharinag Pala, being built by National Thermal Power Corporation. The Ganga would be channeled into a 17 km. tunnel to generate electricity. Other dams on the Bhagirathi include the 480 MW Pala Maneri, and 381 MW Bharan Ghati.[4]

Projects under construction on the Bhagirathi include:

1.	Loharinag Pala	600 MW
2.	Kateshwar	400 MW
3.	Kotli Bhel 1A	195 MW
4.	Kotli Bhel 1B	320 MW
5.	Kotli Bhel 2	530 MW
6.	Maneri Bhali 2	304 MW
7.	Pala Maneri 1	480 MW

Projects planned on the Bhagirathi and Bhilangana are:

1.	Bhaironghati 1	380 MW
2.	Bhaironghati 2	65 MW
3.	Bhilangana 1	22.5 MW
4.	Bhilangana 2	11 MW
5.	Gangotri	55 MW
6.	Harsil	210 MW
7.	Jadhganga	50 MW
8.	Karmoli	140 MW
9.	Tehri PSS	1000 MW

Projects under operation are:

| Maneri Bhali 1 | 90 MW |
| Tehri | 1000 MW |

Source: "The Disappearing Ganga: Is There any Hope for this River?" in *Dams, Rivers, People* SANDP, August 2008.

On January 14, 2009, Prof. Aggarwal again undertook a fast because the government failed to stop the dam, following which the Lohan Nappala dam was stopped. In addition the government announced the setting up of the National Ganga River Basin Authority, (NGRBA) whose objectives are:

- To generate basic ecological data required by NGRBA for short-and long-term planning of sustainable development of the Ganges river basin.
- To investigate the hydrology and pollution problems along the river basin.
- To study social, cultural and religious dimensions and develop eco-friendly technologies for sustainable development and for collection and analysis of all relevant data regarding the Ganges basin.
- To develop long-term models for future planning to maintain water quality and its sustainable valued use.

Announcing the stopping of dams on the Bhagirathi, then union minister of environment, Jairam Ramesh, said,

> I have said in Parliament that India is a civilisation of rivers, that it should not become a land of tunnels ... There are no two opinions. There is just one mass opinion that the projects proposed on the river Bhagirathi, named Pala Maneri and Bhaironghati projects, will not be entertained any further by the government.

In the plains a big threat to the Ganga and Yamuna is pollution, both from industry and from sewage. And even as billions are poured into cleaning the Ganga and Yamuna through the Ganga Action Plan and the Yamuna Action Plan, the pollution of our rivers increases because of a combination of corruption and inappropriate technologies. The Yamuna is clean before it enters Delhi; in 22 kms. of its journey through Delhi, it picks up 70 per cent of all the pollution of the river along its entire length. All that the action plans have done is to set up centralised Sewage Treatment Plants (STPs) that do not work – 70 per cent of all sewage is dumped untreated into the river. The river dies because of pollution; the land dies because it is deprived of rich nutrients. Intelligent zero-waste sewage treatment systems like those evolved at IIT, Kanpur, by Dr. Vinod Tare would both clean the Ganga and fertilise the soil; we would not be wasting Rs. 130,000 crores on fertiliser subsidies and thousands of crores on river action plans. Organic farming can be a major action for cleaning the Ganga.

The Save the Ganga Movement has organised yatras (pilgrimages) seminars, protests to keep the Ganga *aviral* (free-flowing) and *nirmal* (clean and pure). On August 9, 2002, on the eve of Quit India Day, more than 5,000 farmers from Muradnagar and adjoining areas of western Uttar Pradesh gathered in a rally at village Bhanera to protest the laying of a giant 3.25 metre diameter pipeline to supply water from the river Ganga to the Sonia Vihar water treatment plant in Delhi. The project, which has been contracted to Suez Degremont of France by the government of Delhi, will deprive the richest farmlands in India of irrigation water. Such a rally was part of a Ganga Yatra organised by the Research Foundation for Science, Technology and Environment (RFSTE)/Navdanya over three consecutive years – 2002, 2003, 2004. Organisations which participated in the yatras included Kalp Vikas Sansthan, Lupin Human Welfare Research Foundation, Bharat Jagriti Mission Nyas, Janhit Foundation, Ganga Mahasamiti, Akhil Bharatiya Tirth Purohit Mahasabha, Ganga Raksha Samiti, Yuva Shakti, Ganga Mukti Aandolan, Taj Mission and Bharat Seva Ashram Sangh.

More than 300 people from across the country, representing over a hundred grassroots' groups, intellectuals, writers and lawyers joined the rallyists at the three-day convention organised by Navdanya from August 10-12, 2002 at the Indian Social Institute, New Delhi. The convention sought to provide evidence of the state's violent appropriation of people's land, water and biodiversity, and evolve common action plans and strategies to defend collective community rights to resources.

The final threat to the Ganga is privatisation of its water, make giant corporations its owners and sellers, and ordinary citizens, buyers and consumers. The role of citizens and communities as conservers and caretakers will be destroyed. The human right to water which was recognised by the UN in April 2010 will be undermined. That is why, when the Ganges water which was brought to Delhi from Tehri was being privatised to Suez through a World Bank project, we formed a Citizens' Alliance for Water Democracy and told the World Bank and the Delhi government that our "Mother Ganga is not for sale". The World Bank project was withdrawn.

References

[1] Editorial, *The Pioneer*, June 29, 2005.
[2] http://www.un.org/new/press/docs/2010/ga10927.doc.htm
[3] http://the globalrealm.com/2011/06/19 huge-victory inItalianreferendum-no-to-nuclear-power-and-privatised water
[4] http://www.asiantribune.com

4 Climate Wars and Climate Peace

THE UN CLIMATE Summit in Copenhagen (2009) was probably the largest gathering of citizens and governments on climate change. The numbers were huge because the issue is urgent; climate chaos is already costing millions of lives and billions of dollars. The world had gathered to get legally binding cuts in emissions by the rich North in the post-Kyoto phase, i.e., after 2012. Science tells us that to keep temperature rise within 2°C, an 80 per cent cut in emissions is needed by 2020. Without a legally binding treaty, the emission of greenhouse gases will not be reduced, polluters will continue to pollute, and life on earth will be increasingly threatened. There were multiple contests at Copenhagen, reflecting the myriad dimensions of climate wars.

1 Between the earth's ecological limits and limitless growth (with its associated limitless pollution and limitless resource exploitation).
2 Between the need for legally binding commitments and the US-led initiative to dismantle the international framework of obligations to reduce greenhouse gas emissions.
3 Between the economically powerful historical polluters of the North and economically weak countries of the South who are the victims of climate change, with the BASIC countries (Brazil, South Africa, India, China) negotiating with the South but finally signing the Copenhagen Accord with the US.
4 Between corporate rule based on greed and profits and military power, and earth democracy based on sustainability, justice and peace.

The hundreds of thousands of people who gathered at Klimaforum and on the streets of Copenhagen came as earth citizens. Danes and Africans, Americans and Latin Americans, Canadians and Indians were one in their concern for the earth, for climate justice, for the rights of the poor and the vulnerable, and for the rights of future generations. Never before had there been such a large presence of citizens at a UN conference. Never before had climate negotiations seen such a large people's participation.

Ever since the Earth Summit of 1992 in Rio de Janeiro, the US has been unwilling to be part of the UN framework of international law – it refused to sign the Kyoto Protocol. During his visit to China, President Obama, with Prime Minster Rasmussen of Denmark, had already announced that there would only be a political declaration in Copenhagen, not a legally binding outcome. And this is exactly what the world got – a non-binding Copenhagen Accord, initially signed by five countries, the US and the Basic Four, and then supported by twenty-six others, with the rest of the 192 UN member states left out of the process. Most countries came to know that an "accord" had been reached when President Obama announced it to the US press corps. Many excluded countries refused to sign, it remained an agreement between the countries that chose to declare their adherence. The United Nations Framework Convention on Climate Change (UNFCC) only "noted" the Accord, it did not adopt it. In the language of the UN, "taking note" gives a low or neutral status to the document being referred to and indicates that it is not approved by the meeting (in which case the word "adopts" would be used). Thus no member of the Convention is obliged to implement the Accord. When the full membership of the Conference of Parties was summoned to the closing plenary, and the bottom-up membership of the Conference of Parties met at 3 a.m. on December 19 with the top-down group of twenty-six who had endorsed the Accord of the group of five, the consequences had to be explosive. The Venezuelan delegate, Claudia Caldera, said, "Until you tell us where the text has come from and we hold consultations on it, we should not suspend the session. Even if we have to cut our hands and draw blood to make you allow us to speak, we will do so."

Sudan's Ambassador, Lumumba Di Aping, said the 2°C increase accepted in the document would result in a 3° to 5° rise in temperatures in Africa. He saw the pact as a suicide pact to maintain the economic dominance of a few countries.

Ian Fry of the small island of Tavalu said, "We are given respect under the UN, whether big or small countries, and matters are decided collectively in the Conference of Parties. But I saw on TV that a leader of a developed country said he had a deal. This is disrespectful of the UN." On the money that had been offered in the Accord he said, "We are offered thirty pieces of silver to betray our people and our future. Our future is not for sale. Tavalu cannot accept this document."

The thirty pieces of silver are the $30 billion that are supposed to address the mitigation and adaptation needs of the entire Third World. India alone lost $30 billion in 2009 as a result of the failure of the monsoon and the post-monsoon floods in south India. The money being talked about is inadequate for the challenge being faced by climate change, nor is it clear how this money will be mobilised. It could be through carbon trading, which has promoted polluting sponge-iron plants and HCFC plants in India as part of the "clean development mechanism".

Even though the intention of the accord was to dismantle the UN process, the reports of the two ad hoc working groups on the Kyoto Protocol (AWG-KP) and the long-term cooperative action (AWG-LCA) which have been negotiating for four and two years, respectively, were adopted in the closing plenary.

The Copenhagen Accord will undoubtedly interfere with the official UNFCC process in future negotiations as it did in Copenhagen. Like the earth's future, the future of the UN now hangs in the balance. There has been repeated reference to the emergence of a new world order in Copenhagen, but this is the world order shaped by corporate globalisation and the WTO, not by the UN Climate Treaty. It is a world order based on the outsourcing of pollution from the rich industrialised North to countries like China and India. It is a world order based on the rights of polluters.

Climate change today is global in cause and global in effect. Globalisation of the economy has outsourced energy-intensive production to countries like China, which is flooding the shelves of supermarkets with cheap products. Corporations and consumers of the North thus bear responsibility for the increased emissions in the countries of the South. In fact, the rural poor in China and India are losing their land and livelihood to make way for an energy-intensive industrialisation: to count them as polluters would be doubly criminal. Ten years after citizens' movements and African governments shut down the WTO Ministerial Meeting in Seattle, the same contest between corporate power and citizens' power, between limitless profits and growth and the limits of a fragile earth, was played out in Copenhagen. The only difference was that in trade negotiations the commercial interests of corporations stand revealed, whereas in climate negotiations corporate power hides behind corporate states. The Copenhagen Accord is in reality the accord of global corporations to continue to pollute globally by attempting to dismantle the UN Climate Treaty. It should really be called the "Right to Pollute Accord".

The COP 15 talks in Copenhagen and COP 16 in Cançun did not show much promise of an outcome that would reduce greenhouse gas emissions and avoid catastrophic climate change, because a series of false assumptions were driving the negotiations, or rather, blocking them.

False assumption 1 : GNP measures quality of life
False assumption 2 : Growth in GNP and improvement in quality of life is based on increased use of fossil fuel
False assumption 3 : Growth and fossil fuel use have no limits
False assumption 4 : Polluters have no responsibility, only rights

Assumption 1 is false because even as India's GNP has risen, the number of hungry people has grown — in fact, India is now the capital of hunger — and it has concentrated wealth in the hands of a few hundred billionaires who now control 25 per cent of India's economy.

Assumption 2 is false because there are alternatives to fossil fuels, such as renewable energy. Further, reduction in fossil fuel use can actually improve the quality of food and quality of life. Industrial agriculture based on fossil fuels uses ten units of energy to produce one unit of food; ecological systems based on internal inputs produce two to three units out of every unit of energy used. We can therefore produce more and better quality of food by reducing fossil fuel use.

Assumption 3 is false because the financial collapse of 2008 showed that growth is not limitless, and peak oil shows that fossil fuels will become more difficult and costlier to access.

Assumption 4 formed the basis of carbon trading and emissions trading under the Kyoto Protocol, which allowed polluters to get paid billions of dollars instead of making them pay. Thus Arcelor Mittal has walked away with £ 1 billion in the form of carbon credits. It was given the right to emit 90 m tonnes of CO_2 each year from its plants in EU from 2008 to 2012. As Jonathan Leake said in "Carbon Credits Bring Mittal £ 1 billion Bonanza":

> Arcelor Mittal is now free to sell its surplus permits in the market or to hoard them for future use. The latter would allow it to avoid cutting greenhouse gas emissions for years, effectively undermining the point of the scheme. Either way, the company will have gained assets worth around £ 1 billion by 2012. The eventual value could be much greater. Each carbon permit is currently worth about £ 12.70, but the EU has said it wants to drive this price above £ 30.

Times of India, December 7, 2009

To protect the planet, to prevent climate catastrophe through continued pollution, we will have to continue to work beyond Copenhagen, by building Earth Democracy based on principles of justice and sustainability. The struggle for climate justice and trade justice are one struggle, not two. The climate crisis is the result of an economic model based on fossil fuel energy and resource-intensive production and consumption systems. The Copenhagen Accord was designed to extend the life of this obsolete model for living on earth. Earth Democracy can help us build another future for the human species – a future in which we recognise we are members of the earth family and that protecting the earth and her living processes is part of our species identity and meaning. The polluters of the world united in Copenhagen to prevent a legally-binding accord to cut emissions and prevent disastrous climate change – they extended the climate war. Now citizens of the earth must unite to pressurise governments and corporations to obey the laws of the earth and make clilmate peace. And for this we will have to be the change we want to see.

As I have written in *Soil Not Oil*, food is where we can begin. Forty per cent emissions are produced by fossil-fuel-based chemical, globalised food and agriculture systems which are also pushing our farmers to suicide and destroying our health; 40 per cent reduction in emissions can take place through biodiverse organic farming which sequesters carbon while enriching our soils and our diets.

Climate change at the third pole

The year 2010 witnessed some extreme and tragic impacts of climate change. The floods in the Indus basin, in which over 2,000 people died in Pakistan, were the worst in its history.

In the high altitude desert of Ladakh, intense rain and floods washed away homes and villages and killed 200 people. While deserts received too much rain, the monsoon failed in eastern India – Bihar, Jharkhand, Orissa and Bengal were declared drought-affected.

The melting of snow in the Arctic and Antarctic due to global warming and climate change is reported frequently. However, the melting of the Himalayan glaciers goes largely unreported, even though more people are impacted. Presently ten per cent of the earth's landmass is covered with snow, with 84.16 per cent in the Antarctic, 13.9 per cent in Greenland, 0.77 per cent in the Himalaya, 0.51 per cent in North America, 0.37 per cent in Africa, 0.15 per cent in South America, 0.06 per cent in Europe. Outside the polar region, the

Himalaya has the maximum concentration of glaciers with 9.04 per cent covered with glaciers, and 30-40 per cent additional area covered with snow. The glaciers of the Himalaya are the Third Pole, they feed the giant rivers of Asia and support half of humanity.

The Gangotri glacier, the source of the Ganga, is receding at 20-23 miles per year; Millam glacier is receding at 30m/yr; Dokrani is retreating at 15-20m/yr. The rate of retreat of the Gangotri glacier has tripled in the last three years. Some of the most devastating effects of glacial meltdown occur when glacial lakes overflow and the phenomenon of Glacial Lake Outburst Floods (GLOFs) takes place. Climate change thus initially leads to widespread flooding, but over time, as the snow disappears, there will be drought in the summer. In the Ganga, the loss of glacier meltdown will reduce July-September flows by two-thirds, causing water shortages for 500 million people and 37 per cent of India's irrigated land. Glacial run-off in the Himalaya is the largest source of fresh water for northern India and provides more than half the water to the Ganga. Glacial run-off is also the source of the Indus, the Brahmaputra, the Mekong, the Irrawady and the Yellow and Yangtze rivers. According to the Intergovernmental Panel on Climate Change (IPCC),

> Glaciers in the Himayalas are receding faster than in any other part of the world, and if the present rate continues, the likelihood of them disappearing by the year 2035, and perhaps sooner, is very high if the earth keeps getting warmer at the current rate.

According to the IPCC report the total area of glaciers in the Himalaya will shrink from 193,051 square miles to 38,000 square miles by 2035.

The lives of billions are at stake. That is why we have started a participatory process for Himalayan communities to engage in the discussion on climate change, including issues of climate justice, adaptation and disaster preparedness. In terms of numbers of people impacted, climate change at the Third Pole is the most far-reaching, and no climate change policy or treaty will be complete without including the Himalayan communities.

Climate change and the water crisis

In 2009, the RFSTE carried out a study on the impact of climate change in the Himalaya. In Uttarakhand, the participatory research analysis carried out in 165 villages revealed that about 35 per cent of perennial springs have died completely, and water discharge in the remaining springs has been reduced by an average of 67 per cent. In some of the villages water discharge was reduced by up to 90 per cent. Besides this, about 50 to 60 per cent villages depend on piped water supply, and in most cases reduction of this water has led to a decrease in the drinking water supply in connected villages. In more than 45 villages in Saterakhal-Chopata area of district Rudraprayag, drinking water is being supplied by water tankers. A similar situation is occurring in Agastyamuni, Gopeshwar, Purola and Nainbag townships.[1]

In Chakrata area there was an acute shortage of drinking water particularly in the villages located around Quansi town. Villagers, especially women, have to travel long distances to fetch drinking water both for themselves and their animals, and are sometimes forced to auction their animals because of water scarcity. Drinking water is being transported to villages by mules. Used bath water was being used for washing clothes and animals in Deoli village in district Uttarkashi, and about 70 per cent milch cattle have been auctioned to traders due to water and fodder crises. About two decades ago, the village had a big water spring that was used to cultivate irrigated paddy in a large chunk of land, but after construction of the Maneri-Bhali Phase II tunnel, this spring dried up completely. The crisis of drinking water has put an extra load on already overloaded women.

Ladakh was another region chosen for this community-based climate study. In Ladakh life depends on snow. It is a high altitude desert which receives an average of about 50 mm. of annual rainfall. Ladakh's water comes from the snowmelt – both the snow that falls on the land and provides the moisture for farming and pastures, as well as the snow of the glaciers that slowly melts and feeds the streams that are the lifeline of the settlements. Statistics compiled by the Indian Air Force show that the temperature of Ladakh has risen by 10°C over the last thirty-five years, which is alarming for the region. For centuries snow has supported human survival in Ladakh; now in village after village, farmers have either reduced their acreage or stopped farming completely, where snowmelt on the fields was the only source of moisture.

Reduced snowfall also means less snow in glaciers, and less stream-flow. The shorter period of snowfall prevents the snow from turning into hard ice crystals, therefore more of the glacier is liable to melt every summer. In recent years rainfall has been witnessed in place of snow even at higher altitudes. This has also accelerated the melting of glaciers. Meanwhile, heavy rainfall, which was unknown in the high altitude desert, has become more frequent, causing flash floods, washing away homes and fields, trees and livestock. Climate refugees are already being created in the Himalaya in villages such as Rongjuk. As one of the displaced women said, "We are afraid of black clouds now, when we see them in the sky we think they will wash away our new settlement."

Today, people are only concerned about procuring more and more water. The mainstay of Ladakh is subsistence agriculture – with such negligible rainfall, they have to depend on the glaciers that feed the groundwater. However, glaciers are now receding and people are digging borewells in order to cultivate the land.

Our survey results revealed that during the last decade an average of 25 per cent of perennial springs (60 out of 242) have either been converted into seasonal springs or abandoned completely. This percentage has gone up to 60 per cent in Rongjuk village in Nubra valley and to about 30 per cent in other villages around Leh, Nubra and the Zanskar valley.

A high percentage of these drying springs could be linked to recent erratic weather conditions, increasing frequency of tourism, road construction and other development activities in the region. Erratic and unprecedented rains are also a major problem for the 90 per cent traditional houses in this region which, being built with mud, get completely destroyed. It was also observed during the survey that about 20 per cent of irrigation channels were destroyed by flash floods in Nubra valley over the past ten years.

The traditional Ladakhi systems of water management and sanitation were in greater harmony with nature. Compost toilets were used in place of water, and soil and leaves of plants were used after defecation. Water from streams, fed by glaciers, was used for drinking purposes until recently; but now modern construction needs and an increased number of hotels and guesthouses in the region have resulted in an increase in flush toilets, needing more water. To overcome the water crisis, hoteliers have resorted to indiscriminate digging of bore-wells, leading to a rapid decline in the groundwater table. Unfortunately, there is no legislation or regulatory system in place to tackle this overuse. In addition, due to a lack of drainage systems, sewage water flows into the once-beautiful, pure streams, thereby polluting the source of drinking water for local inhabitants.

Getting real about climate change in the Himalaya

Navdanya's report on climate change at the Third Pole indicates that variations due to changing climate are clearly visible in effect: erratic rainfall, less snow in the higher reaches, rapid drying of the perennial streams or even conversion to seasonal streams over the last ten years; shift of plant species towards higher altitudes; and changes in growing as well as flowering and fruiting periods. The signals from the ground are very clear, and very disturbing. There has been a radical reduction in snowfall. Many villages that received snow a few decades back no longer get any, and where it still falls, it has decreased dramatically. This is leading to a thinning, and often a disappearance, of glaciers. The snowline is moving further upwards, reducing the snow cover of the Himalaya.[2]

From September 6-13, 2009, we undertook a climate yatra from Dehradun in Uttarakhand to Leh in Ladakh, covering three Himalayan states and creating awareness among different sections of society, from scientists to students, villagers to politicians.

In regions like Ladakh snowmelt from glaciers provides the only source of water; now it receives rains in July and flash floods, unknown in the desert, become a new climate-related disaster. In regions like Uttarakhand, the source of the mighty Ganga and Yamuna, while the monsoons provide rain in the peak season, it is the snowmelt and water conserved in forested catchments as perennial springs and streams, which provide water in the lean season when it is most needed.

Climate change and climate instability affect the Himalayan snows both through lower snow precipitation, which reduces the accumulation, and through higher temperatures which melt the snow and ice and further deplete the glaciers. According to climatologists, alpine glaciers, such as those in the Himalaya, are particularly sensitive indicators of climate change, and the particular vulnerability of Himalayan glaciers is due to the fact that they are "summer accumulation types," dependent on summer monsoonal precipitation and cool summer temperatures; consequently, the summer mass balance of these glaciers nearly equals the annual mass balance.

As global warming continues to increase the atmospheric temperature, it will lead to a continuous shift of the zero temperature line (snowline) towards higher altitudes. Thus glaciers will receive more liquid precipitation and less monsoonal snow precipitation. A shift in the snowline will result in lower input to the glacier mass balance during summer. Therefore, higher atmospheric temperatures and more liquid precipitation at higher altitudes in the Himalaya will lead to a rapid retreat of glaciers.

The impact of global warming is already being felt in the Himalaya, as the example of the 30.2 kms. long Gangotri glacier shows. The rate of retreat in the last three decades has been found to be more than three times the rate during the preceding two centuries. The average rate of recession has been computed by comparing the snout position on a 1985 toposheet map and 2001 panchromatic satellite imagery – the result shows that the average recession for this period was about 23 m/yr. This is attributed to the increased greenhouse gas emissions contributing to global warming. Climate change is not a one-dimensional linear phenomenon; it is complex, with many factors interacting to create an unstable climate. Changes in snowfall and rainfall patterns and in temperature are changing the very conditions which have maintained the fragile and young Himalaya as a stable and sustainable ecosystem on which 40 per cent of humanity depends, largely through its gift of water.

Meanwhile, a false debate about Himalayan glaciers has been created leading to complacency and inaction. Some scientists, without data and without monitoring, claimed that Himalayan glaciers would disappear by 2030 because of climate change. In response, glaciologists who have been studying glaciers diligently for decades, swung to the other extreme and said that there was nothing to worry about, that glaciers were not receding. They based their claim on three indicators: (*i*) that the rate of retreat of each glacier has varied over time; (*ii*) that the rate of retreat varies across glaciers; and (*iii*) that the snout of some glaciers has not retreated as significantly as the tributaries.

This variation is treated as proof of no climate change impact. Since climate change is not a linear and uniform phenomenon, there is no reason to expect uniform melting; and since most glaciologists are originally geologists, they think on a geological time-scale rather than a human time-scale, either of human impact on the climate, or the impact of climate change on human communities. It is true that the earth has had glacial ages and deglaciation in the past, independent of humans; but today's climate instability is human-induced and it will determine whether the human species survives or not.

We can afford neither hype nor denial, neithr panic nor complacency on the climate front. We need a new realism, and that realism will come from Himalayan ecosystems and communities who bear the brunt of climate instability. The Government of India has set up a National Climate Action Plan which has eight missions, one of which is for sustaining the Himalayan ecosystem. However, Himalayan communities are missing in the mission statement:

A mission for sustaining the Himalayan ecosystem will be launched to evolve management measures for sustaining and safeguarding the Himalayan glacier and mountain ecosystem. Himalayas, being the source of key perennial rivers, the Mission would, inter alia, seek to understand whether, and the extent to which, the Himalayan glaciers are in recession and how the problem could be addressed. This will require the joint efforts of climatologists, glaciologists and other experts.

People are only introduced to protect forests. "Community-based management of these ecosystems will be promoted with incentives to community organisations and panchayats for protection and enhancement of forested lands."

However, climate change is about more than forests. It is about flash floods and drought, it is about planning for a future which is not like today; for this, people need to be partners in monitoring and planning. No government machinery, no matter how sophisticated, can know every mountain, every glacier, every stream, and every field. People are experts on local ecosystems and the changes in their ecosystems due to a destabilised climate; it is this expertise which needs to be mobilised in order to evolve timely strategies for adaptation. People, their knowledge, their power, are central to the transition from climate war to climate peace.

References

[1] Vandana Shiva and Vinod Bhatt (eds.), *Climate Change at the Third Pole: Impact on Himalayan Ecosystems and Communities,* Delhi: Navdanya, 2009.
[2] Ibid.

5   Forest Wars and Forest Peace

ACCORDING TO RABINDRANATH Tagore the distinctiveness of Indian culture consists in its having defined life in the forest as the highest form of cultural evolution. Today we have a problem protecting our core life-support systems and our civilisational identity, because we have sacrificed the unifying principle of life in diversity and democratic pluralism for reductionist, mutually excluding categories which preclude coexistence. The tiger is pitted against the tribal, the tribal against trees. Mutuality is being replaced with antagonism, polarisation and exclusion which threaten everyone – tribal and tiger, and forest biodiversity.

Tribals, tigers and trees

This conflict between the protection of human and non-human species in our forests has been evident in two fierce debates that the nation has been preoccupied with – the debate around the disappearance of the tiger, and the debate around scheduled tribes (Recognition of Forest Rights Act, 2006). There used to be 40,000 tigers in our forests a century ago, today there are fewer than 3,000. In Sariska, in Rajasthan, the tiger has disappeared and tribals are being displaced from their homes to make way for dams, mines, highways. At a time when conservationists and tribal rights activists should be joining hands to protect our forests and diverse species to create a unified force against the predation by mining corporations, poachers, timber and land mafias, those who want to protect tigers, trees and tribals spend more time undermining each other than taking on their common adversary.

The protection of indigenous people in India has taken the form of an Act for the Recognition of Tribal Rights. I was on the technical support committee for the drafting of this Act, and as someone who cares deeply for tribals, tigers and trees in equal measure, my endeavour has been to protect the ecological space for all. There has, however, been an apprehension on the part of conservationists that the Act threatens forests, based largely on the misconception that it is granting *new* rights for the occupation of *new* forest lands. However, no new land is to be allotted, and conservation is intimately linked to the forest rights of tribals. The Act does not grant new rights to forest-dwelling tribes – it merely recognises their rights, correcting the historical injustice of ignoring the rights of original inhabitants. The Act was necessary because

> ...the forest rights on ancestral lands and their habitat were not adequately recognised in the consolidation of state forests during the colonial period, as well as in independent India, resulting in historical injustice to the forest-dwelling scheduled tribes who are integral to the very survival and sustainability of the forest ecosystems.

The Act is not just about tribal rights – it is also a forest conservation bill. The rights of indigenous people rest on their ecological responsibility.

> The recognised rights of the forest-dwelling scheduled tribes include the responsibilities and authority for sustainable use, conservation of biodiversity, and maintenance of ecological balance, thereby strengthening the conservation regime of the forests while ensuring livelihood and food security of the forest-dwelling scheduled tribes.

Another misconception is that recognising tribal forest rights will dismantle existing forest management and wildlife protection laws. This is a product of the either/or point of view, which leads to the polarised perception that either tribals can have rights, or state institutions can have powers; either we can have local governance or national regulation. In matters as vital as the survival of our forests and forest peoples we need both empowered communities and the empowered regulatory and protection systems of the state. Article 15 of the proposed law clearly states, "Save as otherwise provided in this Act, the provisions of this Act shall be in addition to and not in derogation of the provisions of any other law for the time being in force." We need strong national laws for conservation to deal with mining, timber and land mafias. Forest guardians joining forest guards is necessary for this strengthening.

Our colonial forest and wildlife conservation laws were based on the western bias that human and non-human species cannot coexist. Wilderness is people-less. Parks must be without people, and human settlements without biodiversity. This is the *terra nullius* assumption on the basis of which territories were colonised. If land and forests were conserved, they were not "developed" – hence in the Lockean paradigm of "property", they did not "belong" to the original inhabitants. As John Winthrop wrote in 1869,

> Natives in New England, they enclose no land, neither have they any settled habitation, nor any tame cattle to improve the land soe have no other but a Natural Right to those countries. Soe as if we leave them sufficient for their use, we may lawfully take the rest."

When colonising Australia, the British government used *terra nullius* to justify the dispossession of indigenous people who had lived there for at least 60,000 years. Aboriginal communities were defined into the native flora and fauna, denied their humanity and human rights. However, as the 1992 high court decision in the famous Mabo case ruled, non-recognition does not extinguish rights; the 1993 Native Title Act of Australia, like the proposed Tribal Act of India, is an act for recognition of *continuing* rights.

The tribal rights recognition law will in fact strengthen the protection of forests and wildlife by providing the real custodians and guardians of our forests the security of rights. Tribals, with forest and wildlife authorities, need to jointly protect forests from external encroachment. This is not an either / or issue, it needs both the people and the government to work in partnership.

Prof. B.D. Sharma who was commissioner, Scheduled Castes and Scheduled Tribes (1986-88) and is also a member of the technical support group for the tribal rights law, has clearly articulated an action plan for securing both tribal rights and forest ecosystems:

- Preparing a hamlet-wise list of land under the occupation of people in the hamlet, which may be authenticated by the occupants of the lands and also by officials of the forest and revenue departments in an open meeting convened for the purpose;
- Making an agreement between the village community and the concerned departments to the effect that (*a*) while the people on their part will undertake to prevent any further extension of cultivation in the forest and, in case they are not able to do so, to give information about the offenders to an official designated for that purpose; and (*b*) the government departments on their part may undertake (*i*) not to institute any cases in respect of land included in the list mentioned above; and (*ii*) withdraw old cases pending in the courts at different stages in respect of these lands;
- Working out a mutually agreed action plan with co-equal objectives of restoration of ecological balance and providing a viable economic base for the concerned people.

Conservation-based economic livelihoods have kept tribals and forests alive. If they are now poorer, it is not because biodiversity and forest-based livelihoods do not generate wealth, but because that wealth has been appropriated by outside commercial forces. Biodiverse agriculture and pastoral economies can be sustainable components of forest ecosystems. Non-sustainable commercial scale production with tractors, heavy machinery and toxic chemicals is not a forest activity, whether carried out by land-grab mafias or tribal communities. Sustenance of the forest is a real measure of indigenous lifestyles and cultures – the Maldharis in Gir in Gujarat cohabit with the Gir lion. Small-scale, biodiverse ecological farming that does not use chemicals and heavy machinery or ecological pastoralism can be as perennial as the forest and needs to be counted as forest activity. As Sir Albert Howard wrote in the *Agricultural Testament,*

> In the agriculture of Asia we find ourselves confronted with a system of peasant farming which, in essentials, soon became stabilised. What is happening today in the small fields of India and China took place many centuries ago. The agricultural practices of the Orient have passed the supreme test, they are almost as *permanent as those of the primeval forest,* of the prairie, or of the ocean.[1]

These principles of perennial production can be integrated into diversified, multifunctional forest management which conserves diverse species and protects both forests and the livelihoods of forest peoples. After all, this coexistence is not being invented now, it is as ancient as human evolution on this planet. We could, if we cared to, ensure that tigers, tribals and trees, and all other life forms, are protected and can continue their evolutionary journey in peace and harmony. If we fail, because our narrow aims blind us to our larger duties, we will destroy our very life-support systems, and destroy the lives and cultures of indigenous communities who know that humanity needs to make a transition to sustainable living on an extremely fragile planet in extremely fragile times.

Can commercialisation protect forests?

In the 1980s, forest activists joined hands in Penang in Malaysia to form the World Rainforest Movement as a response to the World Bank's push for commercial forestry under the garb of the Tropical Forest Action Plan and social forestry and watershed projects. The challenges we face today in Reducing Emissions from Deforestation and Degradation (REDD) and REDD+ are similar to those challenges faced thirty years ago; we can draw lessons from the struggle against the World Bank's Tropical Forest Action Plan to deal with the current threat by the commercialisation of forests and their ecological services.

The myth that 'experts' from Washington and global corporations and investors are needed for saving tropical forests is a renewal of an old myth – the British would 'conserve' India's forests when they had, in fact, depleted them at home and in the colonies.

As Stebbing reported in 1805, a dispatch was received from the Court of Directors of the East India Company enquiring to what extent the King's Navy might, in view of the growing deficiency of oak in England, depend on a permanent supply of teak timber from Malabar. Thus, the first real interest aroused in the forests of India originated from the colonial centre and the cause was the same as that which had kept forestry in the forefront in England through three centuries – the safety of the Empire, which depended upon its "wooden walls" – its supremacy at sea. When the British started exploiting Indian timber for military purposes, they did so rapaciously, because the great continent appeared to hold inexhaustible tracts convered with dense jungles.

The military requirement of Indian teak led to an immediate proclamation usurping the royalty right in teak trees from the royal courts in the South and vesting it in the East India Company. Under further pressure from the home government, it was decided to appoint a special officer to supervise forest exploitation. Captain Watson, a police officer, was appointed the first conservator of forests in India on November 10, 1806. Under the Proclamation of April 1807, he wielded great powers and interfered seriously in people's rights. The conservator soon established a timber monopoly throughout Malabar and Travancore for a plentiful supply of cheap timber, but the methods used were intolerable and gradually gave rise to such seething discontent that the conservatorship was abolished in 1823.

The introduction of colonial forestry was therefore not associated with superior forestry knowledge or scientific management, but with a dominant military need and the usurpation of rights. It was only after more than half a century of uncontrolled destruction by British commercial interests that an attempt was made to control the exploitation of forests. In 1865 the first Indian Forest Act (VII of 1865) was passed by the Supreme Legislative Council, which authorised the government to declare forests and wastelands (*benap* or unmeasured lands) as reserved forests. This was repealed later by the Forest Act of 1878. This legislation marked the beginning of what is called "scientific management", which became in effect, a policy for deforestation.

Under the theology of the market that the World Bank spread in the 1980s it is the commercialisation of forestry and land use that is the objective of maximising profitability. Forest ecosystems are therefore reduced to the timber mines of commercially valuable species. "Scientific forestry", in its present commercial form, is a reductionist system of knowledge which ignores the complex relationships within the forest community and between plant life and other resources, like soil and water. Its pattern of resource utilisation is based on increasing 'productivity' on these reductionist foundations. By ignoring the system's linkages within the forest ecosystem, this pattern of resource use generates instability and leads to a counterproductive use of natural resources in the ecosystem. Forest movements like Chipko are simultaneously a critique of reductionist forestry and an articulation of a framework for an alternative forestry science, in which forest resources are not viewed as isolated from other resources of the ecosystem; nor is the economic value of a forest reduced to the commercial value of timber. Two economic perspectives lead to two notions of 'productivity', 'yield' and economic 'value'. Thus, while for tribals and other forest communities a complex ecosystem is productive in terms of herbs, tubers, fibre and genepool, for the forester, these components are useless, unproductive and dispensable. Today we could add that land that is not 'improved' by mining, highways, factories and the commodification of ecological services, is waste. This is the recurrence of *terra nulllius* – land is empty if does not serve the aims of eco-imperialism.

As James A. Bethel, a forestry consultant, stated about the diversity of rainforests:

From the standpoint of industrial material supply, the important question is how much of the biomass represents trees and parts

of trees of preferred species that can be profitably marketed ...
By today's utilisation standards most of the trees in these humid
forests are, from an industrial materials standpoint, clearly weeds.[2]

The replacement of natural forests in India with eucalyptus plantations
has been justified on the grounds of improving productivity, because
pulpwood alone has been projected as a universally applicable measure
of productivity. The 'eucalyptus controversy' is in reality a conflict
between an ecological peoples' forestry and a reductionist partisan
forestry for commercial industrial requirements. But natural forests
and many indigenous tree species are more ecologically productive
than eucalyptus. The scientific conflict is in reality an economic conflict
over which needs, and whose needs, are more important.

Can commercialisation guarantee basic needs?

The World Bank social forestry projects in India were launched
primarily to correct the one-dimensional commercial forestry that
has made forest resources scarce for the poor; their aim was
supposedly to enhance the availability of organic fertiliser, food, fodder
and fuel for local populations. The result, however, is further erosion
of their rights and resources. More than 90 per cent of tree planting
under social forestry has been of eucalyptus, nearly all of it on fertile
agricultural land, and all of it has been marketed to urban industrial
centres, especially to the pulp industry. New enterprises have emerged
to produce 'green gold' on farmlands with the promise that "money
grows on trees". The result has been a serious reduction of food
availability, a decline in agricultural employment, and an accentuation
of the fuel, fodder and fertiliser scarcity in rural areas. It is critical to
keep in mind the distinction between two kinds of biodiversity
economies: (a) the survival or sustenance economy; and (b) the
commercial or market economy. In the first, production and
distribution are based on the organisation of rights and entitlements
that ensure that forest and tree produce reaches Gandhi's proverbial
"last man". In the second, they are based on the strength of purchasing
power, which the more than 50 per cent Indians living below the

poverty line do not have. Peasants and forest-dwellers depend on rights and entitlements, not on purchasing power, to satisfy their basic sustenance needs.

The flawed organisational assumption of different management structures is at the root of afforestation projects not reaching the poor. It is assumed that the outcome is the same, whether a resource is managed collectively by local tribals or privatised and managed by multinational corporations which serve the interests of the economically more powerful groups. However, as an ecological audit of different afforestation programmes has shown, the organisational structures effective in a market economy can actually be inconsistent with the needs of a survival economy. Large-scale, even aged, monocultures match the raw-material needs for pulpwood or the plantation industry; but for local needs, multipurpose tree planting is needed for food, fuel, fibre, fodder, fertiliser, oilseeds and medicines. Commercial tree planting success does not automatically translate into successful tree planting for a sustenance economy. Further, when plantations bring in a sixteen times higher return on investment than food production, tree planting for 'green gold' can disastrously aggravate the real energy crisis of food scarcity. Afforestation on farmlands is just one among the Bank's many other suggestions to the Government of India to move away from growing foodcrops altogether.

The Bank's model of forestry results in undermining food production not just at the site of the plantations, but throughout the country. Forestry investment involves borrowing, and debt repayment involves more and more production of primary commodities for export, so that land everywhere is diverted from food production for local consumption to cash crops for the global market. This exaggerated investment is based on not recognising that peasants everywhere have always planted and protected trees under economic and legal conditions that allow them to do so.

Can commercial tree planting ensure ecological recovery?

Recognising the ecological crisis generated by deforestation India has launched massive afforestation projects which, besides social forestry projects in each state, consist of World Bank-financed watershed projects in the Himalaya and a national wasteland development project.

The Nayar watershed project, with funding of $69.12 million, is intended to reverse ecological decline, but the project itself is largely a prescription for introducing commercial activities in the watershed area. The sophistication of agricultural practices in hill areas, including ancient techniques of soil conservation through terracing and mulching, have been ignored in the project, although they are recognised globally. It is an established fact that indigenous mixed and rotation cropping systems are the best mechanisms for soil and water conservation. While flood control and catchment stability is the main objective of watershed development, the success of watershed projects is generally measured only in terms of increased cash flow. The World Bank appraisal makes this shift in evaluation criteria explicit.

> The direct production effects generated by project actions provide sufficient economic justification for the project. The project is a pilot scheme leading to a long-term programme for control of erosion within upper watersheds of the Himalayas, aimed at reducing run-off and decreasing the silt load of the rivers. Little data is, however, at present available to evaluate the economic effects of controlling erosion and flooding.[3]

A project aimed primarily at conservation and rebuilding nature's economy in degraded catchments is not carried out in accordance with conservation criteria. On the contrary, land-use shifts are introduced which further threaten to destabilise soil and water systems. Such impacts, moreover, are neither anticipated nor monitored, leaving the further erosion of nature's economy as an invisible factor in catchment degradation.

The World Bank's Panar watershed project in Almora district similarly threatens to be an ecological and economic disaster. Eighty per cent of its outlay is for planting pine, converting the watershed into a mine of timber and resin, rather than a stable source of water.

The local population is seriously resisting the pine plantations, demanding instead mixed planting of indigenous species like oak, *bhimal, timil, buras,* which conserve the soil and water and provide rich fodder.

The World Bank also ignores ecological criteria for measuring success in the afforestation of upland watersheds. The district in Karnataka which tops the list in 'successful' social forestry also tops the list in drought – in water, food and fodder scarcity. The ecological ignorance and indifference of agencies like the World Bank become apparent in the investment profiles for the Tropical Forest Action Plan. First, India is shown as needing a total of $1,222 million for five years, which is far in excess of the investment for all of Africa, suggesting that it is not ecological survival, but market growth, that the Bank is interested in; while survival might be at stake in Africa, India's markets for wood products are far more promising. Second, the report has categorised forestry projects under three headings and earmarked funds for them as: "Fuelwood and Agro-forestry: ($500m), "Land-use on Upland Watersheds" ($500m), and "Forest Management for Industrial Uses" ($190 m). Only $32 million has been set aside for ecosystem conservation. The problem with this categorisation is that (*a*) it does not reveal that most "agro-forestry", "watershed development" or "social forestry" consists of commercial industrial plantations; and (*b*) that the World Bank sees agro-forestry and upland watershed management as not being part of ecosystem conservation.

It is therefore unsurprising that these projects fail to meet ecological criteria. All three categories of afforestation include large-scale, capital-intensive planting of commercial species like pine and eucalyptus which make no positive contribution to either the local ecology or its economy.

The Tropical Forestry Action Plan has recommended the expansion of these destructive activities; in India it recommended the expansion of its social forestry programme which has already desertified farmlands and displaced peasants at the rate of 200 mm-days per hectare, per year, at a cost of US $500 million. At the cost of another US $190 million the TFAP recommended exploiting 30 million hectares of natural forest to establish industrial plantations at the rate of 240,000 hectares per year. In Brazil, it recommended an investment of US $400 million to convert natural forests into plantations as a fuelwood and agro-forestry project; another US $325 million for managing five million hectares of Amazon forests for industrial wood production; and establishing 320,000 hectares of industrial plantations over a five-year period. If the Action Plan had been operationalised in India and Brazil alone, people would have had to bear the burden of US $1,415 million in loans to destroy millions of hectares of natural forests and prime farmland. This does not include the destruction of watersheds through commercial tree planting (US $500 million for India). This Plan should more appropriately be called the Action Plan for Tropical Forest Destruction.

The systemic inability of forestry projects to meet ecological and social needs arises, in our view, from false scientific and organisational assumptions. Scientifically, it is assumed that all trees and forest ecosystems are ecologically equivalent; this completely ignores the difference between the imperatives of temperate zone and tropical zone forest management, between commercial and conservation forestry, and differences in the ecology of different tree species. (The assumption that temperate zone practices are suitable for tropical eco-zones has been identified as a significant cause for the erosion of forest resources even when "scientifically" managed.) It also misses the physiological and architectural diversity in tree species which is matched to local eco-system diversity. Trees have their own water and nutrient relations and patterns of partitioning organic matter which are determined by their native habitat. The wrong species in the wrong place can undermine essential ecological processes and basic needs satisfaction. Different species and different silvi-cultural practices have a varied ecological and social impact. Some plantations cause major dislocations in nature's processes; to subsume all tree planting under a uniform category of "green cover" on the assumption of ecological equivalence is to ignore the diversity in nature and the diverse human needs that it supports. In Bihar and Madhya Pradesh, for example, teak and pine have become the embodiment of a political and technological structure which takes resources away from local populations, while sal allows their survival with local resources and under local control. The socio-ecological crisis arising from deforestation can be solved only if the processes from which it arises are reversed; for commercial forestry has caused the destabilisation of the water cycle and the nutrient cycle, the two cycles of life. Conservation presupposes the maintenance of diversity which can only be maintained locally. A people's action plan for saving tropical forests has to be based on respect for nature and for people's survival needs; on viewing trees as life-support systems which must be protected. In particular, it must build on the little traditions of little people which ensure the protection of nature and local communities.

Can commodification of ecological services protect the earth?

The Green Economy being created by the UN Programme on Reducing Emissions from Deforestation and Degradation uses market/financial incentives in order to reduce emissions from deforestation. REDD is presented as an "offset" scheme of carbon markets to produce carbon credits. Carbon offsets are "emissions–saving projects" which allow polluters to buy their way out through cheap projects in which local communities of the South bear the burden of their emissions. It commodifies the ecological functions of the forests and offers "deforestation" through the conversion of natural forests into biofuel plantations. The UN-REDD document states:

> Tropical forests are continuing to disappear at an alarming rate. Between 1990 and 2005, the rate of deforestation averaged about 13 million ha a year, occurring mostly in developing countries. These results are a result of land-use change, mainly the expansion of agricultural land, which in turn is closely connected to the conditions of rural livelihoods, the increasing demands for food, feed, fabric and the overall economic development.

However, the conversion of forests to agriculture is not driven by local communities, but by agribusiness, biofuels and land-grab; REDD fails to address these global forces which are contributing up to 18 per cent of greenhouse gas emission. Instead it maintains that:

> Reduced deforestation and forest degradation may play a significant role in climate change mitigation and adaptation, can yield significant sustainable development benefits, and may generate a new financing stream for sustainable forest management in developing countries. If cost-efficient carbon benefits can be achieved through REDD, increases in atmospheric CO_2 concentrations could be slowed, effectively buying much-needed time for countries to move to lower emissions technologies.

We do not need to wait for lower emission technologies, we already have them – biodiverse ecological farming can absorb 30 per cent of the CO_2 build-up in the atmosphere, if applied globally.

The UN admits that REDD programmes, if not carefully designed, "could marginalise the landless and those with informal land rights and communal use rights". It also recognises that governments and elites could "capture" the payments made for capturing atmospheric carbon. REDD proposes a partnership with World Bank's Forest Carbon Partnership.[4] The idea is to establish a "post-2012 REDD payment mechanism funded by multilaterals with an eye to preparing for integration with private carbon markets".[5] It is assumed that carbon markets will create more than $1 billion in trade; the World Bank estimates that carbon trade is already at $144 billion.[6]

Nature, the basis of life on earth, and all beings of the earth, have intrinsic value. These values are not reducible to market values. There are three important reasons why the reduction of nature's value to market values is misplaced. First, nature's economy exists prior to commerce. It is holistic, multi-dimensional and diverse. Our crude market calculus cannot capture the richness and diversity, complexity and multi-dimensionality, beauty and harmony of nature's web of life, nor be a management tool for the integrity of creation. At best, putting a market valuation on particular ecosystem services can act as a heuristic guide to avoid destruction. Knowing the contribution that bees and pollinators make to the food economy should act as an imperative to stop killing them with pesticides and pesticide-producing genetically engineered crops. Second, nature is the basis of the sustenance economy and the economy of the poor. Third, market instruments and valuations have proven to be unreliable even for managing the financial market, as the sub-prime housing crisis, the collapse of Wall Street in 2008, and the massive bail-out of banks has shown. To apply these failed and flawed tools to nature is foolhardy. Market fundamentalism leads to ecological and social disintegration; it cannot be the basis for repairing violated ecosystems and communities. Making peace with the forest involves recognising the integrity, diversity and unity of the forest – it cannot be reduced to the timber or pulp it provides, or to the carbon it absorbs.

References

[1] Sir Albert Howard, *Agricultural Testament*, Oxford: Oxford University Press, 1940.
[2] James A. Bethel "Sometimes the Word is Weed", in *Forest Management*, June 1984, pp. 17-22.
[3] World Bank, Mimeo, 1982 (?)
[4] http://www.un-redd.org/UN-REDD-pdf
[5] Paul Verghese, http://www.rightsresources.org documents/files doc-1220.pdf
[6] Earth Grab, *Geopiracy and the New Bio-masters*, Pazambuka Press, 2011.

PART II

Food Crises, Food Justice, Food Peace

6 Hunger by Design

WHY IS EVERY fourth Indian hungry? Why is every third woman in India anaemic and malnourished? Why is every second child underweight, stunted and wasted? Why has the hunger and malnutrition crisis deepened even as India has seen nine per cent growth? Why is "shining India" a starving India?

In my view, hunger is a structural part of the design of the green revolution, a design for scarcity. There is now much talk of a second "green revolution" in India and a "green revolution" in Africa. The second green revolution is based on genetic engineering which is being introduced into agriculture largely to allow corporations to claim intellectual property rights and patents on seeds. The floodgate of patenting seeds was opened through the Trade Related Intellectual Property Rights (TRIPS) agreement of WTO, written by corporations like Monsanto.

The Agreement on Agriculture (AoA) of the WTO was drafted by the MNC Cargill, and designed to allow it and other agribusiness corporations to have access to world markets by forcing countries to remove import restrictions (Quantitative Restrictions) and using $400 billion to subsidise and dump artificially cheap food commodities on countries of the South. The dumping of soya and the destruction of India's domestic edible oil production and distribution is an example of the global reach of MNCs; Indian farmers are losing $25 billion every year to falling prices but food prices continue to rise, creating a double burden of hunger for rural communities which is why half the hungry people in India and the world are farmers.

Globalised forced trade in food, falsely called free trade, has aggravated the hunger crisis by undermining food sovereignty and food democracy. With the deadlock in the Doha round of WTO, forced trade is being driven by bilateral agreements such as the US-India Knowledge Initiative in Agriculture, on whose board sit corporations like Monsanto, Cargill/ADM and Walmart. Sadly, India is trying to use the food crisis that trade liberalisation policies have created to hand over seed supply to Monsanto, food supply to Cargill and other corporations, and retail to Walmart, in line with the US-India Agreement on Agriculture signed with President Bush in 2005. Speaking at a conference on the crisis and food inflation on February 4, 2011, Prime Minister Manmohan Singh said India needs to "shore up farm supply chains by bringing in organised retail players" (read Walmart; *Business Line*, February 5, 2011). Recent research shows that globalised retail is destroying farmers' livelihoods, destroying livelihoods in small retail and leading to wastages of up to 50 per cent of food. This, too, is hunger by design.

Both the US and Indian governments are supporting US agribusiness corporations to expand markets and profits; the common citizen is politically orphaned in a world shaped by corporate rule – farmers' rights and people's right to food are extinguished. When the Supreme Court of India told the government to distribute the foodgrain that was rotting in its godowns, the prime minister said he could not do so because it would distort "the market". When the National Advisory Council (NAC) headed by Sonia Gandhi drafted a Food Security Act, the prime minister's appointed Rangarajan Committee said it would distort "the market". In other words, corporate rights to profit through the creation of hunger must be protected even as people die.

And even as corporate greed has led to the food crisis, the corporate takeover of seed, food and land is being offered up as a solution to it. The government has already allowed two million hectares of fertile farmland to go out of food production; new farmland is being given over to agribusinesses. Planning Commission vice-chairman, Montek Singh Ahluwalia, during a visit to Muscat, invited Gulf countries to farm in India and export food to their countries (*Outlook*, January 31, 2011). A Bahrain firm, the Nader and Ebrahim Group (NEG) recently tied up with Pune-based Sanghar group to grow bananas on 400 acres; so far 2.6 million kilos of bananas have been exported. Indian laws do not allow foreigners to buy land; the Planning Commission is encouraging foreign corporations to subvert India's land sovereignty by asking them to enter into partnerships with Indian companies, and by encouraging contract farming.

Diverting land from food for local communities to cash crops for the rich in US, Europe and the Gulf can only aggravate the food crisis. Biodiverse organic farming, if adopted nationally, can provide enough calories for 2.4 billion people, enough protein for 2.5 billion, enough carotene for 1.5 billion, and enough folic acid for 1.7 billion pregnant women. There is no place for hunger in a sustainable, just and democratic society. We must end it by building food democracy, by reclaiming our seed sovereignty, food sovereignty and land sovereignty.

India shining or India starving?

India became independent soon after the Great Bengal Famine of 1944 which took two million lives. *The Harijan,* a newspaper published by Mahatma Gandhi, was full of articles written by him during 1946-47 on how to deal with food scarcity, politically; and by Mira Behn, Kumarappa and Pyarelal on how to grow more food using internal resources. On June 10, 1947, referring to the food problem at a prayer meeting, Gandhi said:

> The first lesson we must learn is of self-help and self-reliance. If we assimilate this lesson, we shall at once free ourselves from disastrous dependence upon foreign countries and ultimate bankruptcy. This is not said in arrogance but as a matter of fact. We are not a small place, dependent for this food supply upon outside help. We are a subcontinent, a nation of nearly 400 million. We are a country of mighty rivers and a rich variety of agricultural land, with inexhaustible cattle-wealth. That our cattle give much less milk than we need is entirely our own fault. Our cattle-wealth

is any day capable of giving us all the milk we need. Our country, if it had not been neglected during the past few centuries, should today not only be providing herself with sufficient food, but also be playing a useful role in supplying the outside world with much-needed foodstuffs, of which the late war has unfortunately left practically the whole world in want. This does not exclude India.

Recognising that the crisis in agriculture was related to a breakdown of nature's processes, India's first agriculture minister, K.M. Munshi, worked out a detailed strategy on rebuilding and regenerating the ecological base of productivity in agriculture, based on a bottom-up, decentralised and participatory methodology. In a seminar on September 27, 1951, organised by the agriculture ministry, the programme of regeneration recognised the diversity of India's soils, crops and climates. Munshi told state directors of agricultural extension to consider every individual village, and sometimes every individual field, for the 'land transformation' programme:

> Study the life-cycle in the village under your charge in both its aspects – hydrological and nutritional. Find out where the cycle has been disturbed and estimate the steps necessary for restoring it. Work out the village in four of its aspects: (*i*) existing conditions; (*ii*) steps necessary for completing the hydrological cycle; (*iii*) steps necessary to complete the nutritional cycle, and a complete picture of the village when the cycle is restored; and (*iv*) have faith in yourself and the programme. Nothing is too mean and nothing too difficult for the man who believes that the restoration of the life-cycle is not only essential for the freedom and happiness of India but is essential for her very existence.

Ecological repair of the water and nutrient cycle, combined with land reform, investments in agriculture, fair prices for farmers and consumers through a universal public distribution system were holistic instruments for food security.

Per capita consumption today has dropped from 177 cal/day/capita to 150 cal/day/capita, as a result of the food chain being broken; tinkering with fragments of the broken chain will not fix it. The first link in the food chain begins with the natural capital of soil, water and seed; the second link is the labour of small, marginal farmers and landless peasants, most of whom are women; the final link is eating. The first link has been broken by ecological degradation – soil erosion, biodiversity erosion, water depletion, undernourished food production contribute to food insecurity. When peasants lose access to land, seed and water, they lose access to food; an increase in hunger is a direct consequence. The second link that has been broken is the capacity of the farmer to produce food. Rising costs of production and falling farm prices create debt and this creates food insecurity. The deliberate destruction of food procurement by dismantling the public distribution system, by using godowns to store liquor instead of food, by not guaranteeing a fair price to farmers, are signals that the government wants a food system without small farmers. Farmers are the backbone of India's food security and food sovereignty, and there can be no food security in a deepening agrarian crisis. The third link in the food chain is people's entitlement and right to food. Rising food prices and decreasing production of pulses and nutritious millets has reduced the access of the poor to adequate food and nutrition.

While millions of our fellow citizens starve, the government fiddles with figures and addresses a fragment of the consequences of the crisis. Poverty is a consequence, not a cause. Fiddling with poverty figures – 37 per cent in the Tendulkar Committee Report; 50 per cent in the Saxena Report; 77 per cent in the Unorganised Sector Report – is a deliberate attempt at not addressing the root causes of hunger and poverty. In this context, the proposed National Food Security Act (NFSA) is a mere fig-leaf. It is inadequate because it ignores the first two links in the food chain, and reduces the scope of existing schemes for the poor and vulnerable. The NFSA offers only 25 kgs. of grain instead of the 35 kgs. per family, per month, fixed by the Supreme Court. The Indian Council of Medical Research has fixed the caloric norms at 2400 Kcal in rural areas and 2100 Kcal in urban areas; the Tendulkar Committee (which is now the Planning Commission's official basis) fixes average calorie consumption at 1776

Kcal in urban areas and 1999 Kcal in rural areas. Through juggling figures the hungry become well-fed, the poor become non-poor.

Food security demands a universal PDS system which serves both poor farmers and poor consumers by *ensuring fair prices throughout the food chain.* Instead, the government is committed to ever narrowing "targets" because it is committed to handing over agriculture to global agribusiness, and handing over so-called "food security schemes" to companies like Walmart and Sodexo, Cargill, Unilever and Nestlé, through introducing cash transfers. This is undermining food security by abandoning the farmer and the public distribution system.

As small farmers are displaced by agribusinesses, the destruction of natural capital will increase, weakening the first link in the food chain, and the agrarian crisis facing two-thirds of rural India will deepen. Breaking the link between farmers and eaters, between production and consumption, through food stamps and food vouchers will completely break the food chain. The proposed solution is to reduce food subsidies; when PDS was replaced by targeted PDS under World Bank pressure, this was the argument used. However, the food subsidy bill increased from Rs. 2,500 crores to Rs. 50,000 crores; increased financially, but shrank socially from universal coverage to targeted PDS, thus effectively starving a quarter of our people. A further narrowing of the "target" will further increase the food subsidy because it will lead to an increase in the gap between the high cost of production and the cost of subsidised food, as well as a growing gap between rising market prices for food and financing subsidised food. Privatising our public food distribution system through cash transfers is a recipe for debt and hunger. Dismantling trade patterns that serve communities and replacing them with so-called "free-trade", which only increases market control and profits for agribusinesses, is akin to putting precious food in a global casino.

Why are one billion people starving?

The year 2008 witnessed a global food crisis, with food prices rising to unprecedented levels and food riots taking place in 40 countries;

in 2010, the food crisis re-surfaced. President Bush had an interesting analysis for the global rise in food prices in 2008. At an interactive session on the economy in Missouri, Bush argued that prosperity in countries like India had triggered an increased demand for better nutrition.

There are 350 million people in India who are classified as middle class. That's bigger than America. Their middle class is larger than our entire population. And when you start getting wealth, you start demanding better nutrition and better food, so demand is high and that causes prices to go up.

While this story might divert the US political debate from the role of US agribusiness in the current food crisis, both through speculation and through diversion of food to biofuels, and it might present economic globalisation as having benefited Indians, the reality is that Indians are nutritionally worse off today than they were before globalisation.

However, it was not just George Bush who blamed India for the price rise. Oxford economist, Paul Collier, in his book *The Plundered Planet* has stated, "The root cause of the sudden spike in prices was the spectacular economic growth of Asia. Asia is half the world. As Asian incomes rise, so too, does demand for food. Not only are Asians eating more, they are eating better."[1] It is being stated repeatedly that food prices rise due to "surging demand in emerging economies like China and India". This growth myth is false on many counts. First, while the Indian economy has indeed grown, the majority of Indians have grown poorer because they have lost their land and livelihoods. Most Indians are in fact eating less today than a decade ago; the per capita availability of food has declined from 177 kgs. per person, per year in 1991 to 152 kgs. per person, per year currently. The daily availability of food has declined from 485 to 419 gms. per day; daily calorie intake has dropped from 2220 cals/day to 2150 cals/day. One million children die every year for lack of food, and even as India's growth soars, it has emerged as the capital of hunger. India ranks 67 among 84 countries in the global hunger index, below China and

Pakistan, and is home to 42 per cent of the world's underweight children. The poor are worse off because their food and livelihoods have been destroyed. The middle classes are worse off because they are eating worse, not better, as junk food and processed food is forced on India through globalisation. India is passing through a dietary or nutritional transition, with malnutrition taking on a double face. On the one hand, malnutrition based on food deprivation, on the other, malnutrition linked to a junk-food diet and its equally debilitating health effects. The Indian middle class is eating less cereals today. In 1972-73, urban Indians spent 23 per cent on cereals; this is down to 10 per cent, because of US pressure through the US-India Agriculture Agreement to promote processed and packaged foods. Cereal consumption in the US has grown by 12 per cent compared to two per cent in India, largely as a result of diversion of food for biofuel. President Bush's biofuel policies which have diverted food to fuel, as well as the deregulation of the financial economy which has allowed speculation to enter the food economy, are the real reasons for food prices rising.

Cereal Consumption

Country	2006-07	2007-08	2008-09	2009-10	2010-11
China	382.2	389.1	397.04	411.50	420.90
US	277.6	310.4	325.20	330.40	340.60
India	193.1	197.3	203.00	207.00	212.00
World	2062.4	2105			

Source: FAO, *Food Outlook*, 2010.

According to the UN Special Rapporteur on the Right to Food, Olivier de Schutter, 10 per cent of the world's hungry are pastoralists, fisherfolk and forest dwellers; 20 per cent are the rural landless, such as farm labourers; and 50 per cent are, in fact, small-holding farmers. If 80 per cent of the world's hungry are producers of food, they are clearly not eating enough of what they produce. Hunger creation is built into the design of the unfree rules of "free trade", which turn farmers into seed slaves of the gene giants who patent and own seeds, and into indebted bonded labour of the grain giants who sell costly inputs and buy cheap commodities from farmers trapped in debt. Hunger creation is also built into the design of industrial processing, long-distance transport and large-volume retail. Even while countries like India are told that our short distribution chains waste food, the reality is that the industrial globalised food system *wastes 50 per cent of food produced.*

We have been told repeatedly that industrial agriculture is necessary to feed the world, that without the chemicals of the so-called green revolution and without genetically engineered organisms, the world will starve. We were told that free trade would make food cheap.

The food and hunger crisis is rooted in who owns natural capital – land, seeds and biodiversity, and water. It is determined by how we produce our food and how we distribute it. In the Indian context, agriculture, food and nutrition are addressed independently of each other, even though the food that is grown determines its nutritional value, its distribution patterns and entitlements. If we grow biodiversity, including millets and pulses, we will have more nutrition per capita; if we grow monocultures with chemicals, we will have less nutrition per acre and per capita. If we grow food ecologically with internal inputs, more food will stay with the farming household and there will be less malnutrition in rural children. If we have local community-controlled food systems, we can escape the volatility of the global market and the monopolies of global corporations. If we have globalised trade in agriculture and speculative trade in food commodities, we will have debt and farmers' suicides, price rise and a food crisis, hunger and famine. We can create either hunger or food sovereignty by design; the former is shaped by a food dictatorship, the latter by food democracy.

Food in the global casino

Growing food, processing, transforming and distributing it, involves

70 per cent of humanity, eating food involves all of us. Yet it is not culture or human rights that are shaping today's dominant food economy, it is speculation and profits. Putting food on the global financial casino is a design for hunger. After the US sub-prime crisis and the Wall Street crash, investors rushed to commodity markets, especially oil and agricultural commodities. While real production did not increase between 2005-07, commodity speculation in food increased 160 per cent. Speculation pushed up prices and pushed an additional 100 million people to hunger. A 2008 advertisement for Deutsche Bank stated:

> Do you enjoy rising prices? Everybody talks about commodities – with the Agriculture Euro Fund you can benefit from the increase in the value of the seven most important agricultural commodities. (Quoted in Peter Wahl, "Speculation Undermines the Right to Food", 2008.)[2]

The financial deregulation that destabilised the world's financial system is now destabilising the world's food system. Between 2003-2008, commodity index speculation increased by 1900 per cent, from $13 billion to $260 billion; 30 per cent of these index funds were invested in food commodities. As the Agribusiness Accountability Initiative states,

> We live in a brave new world of 24-hour electronic trading, triggered by algorithms of composite price indices, fits of investor 'lack of confidence' and of unregulated 'dark pools' of more than US $7 trillion in over-the-counter commodities derivatives trades.[3]

The world's commodity trading has no relationship to food, to its diversity, to its growers or eaters, to the seasons, to sowing or harvesting. Food diversity is reduced to eight commodities and bundled into "composite price indicas", seasons are replaced by 24-hour trading, food production driven by sunshine and photosynthesis is displaced by "dark pools of investment". The tragedy is that this unreal world is creating hunger for real people in the real world. In a cover story for *Harper's* magazine, Frederick Kaufman wrote about the food bubble, "How Wall Street starved millions and got away with it. The history of food took an ominous turn in 1991, at a time when no one was paying much attention. That was the year Goldman Sachs decided our daily bread might make an excellent investment." The entry of investors like Goldman Sachs, AIG Commodity Index, Bear Sterns, Oppenheimer Puneo, Barclays, allowed agribusiness to increase its profits. In the first quarter of 2008, Cargill attributed its 86 per cent jump in profits to commodity trading, and Conagra sold its trading arm to a hedge fund for $2.8 billion.

Gambling on the price of wheat for profits took food away from 250 million people. As Austin Damani told Fred Kaufman, "We're trading wheat, but it's wheat we're never going to see, it's a cerebral experience." Food is an ecological, sensory, biological experience; with speculation it has been removed from its own reality. Grain markets have been transformed, with futures trading by the grain giants in Chicago, Kansas City and Minneapolis, combined with speculation by investors. Kaufman says, "Imaginary wheat bought anywhere affects real wheat bought everywhere." And if we do not decommodify food, more and more people will be denied food, as more and more money is poured into the global casino for profits.[4]

The spike in world food prices began to reappear in 2011. According to the FAO, in January 2011, the food price index was up 3.4 per cent from December 2010; the cereal price index was three per cent above its December reading, and at the highest level since July 2008, though still 11 per cent below its peak in April 2008. The oils and fats index rose by 5.6 per cent, approximating the June 2008 record level. The dairy price index shot up 6.2 per cent and the sugar price index by 5.4 per cent. Wheat prices were up by 25 per cent compared to six months earlier. Prices of soyabean and palm-oil doubled over the second half of 2010.

In India, the price of onions jumped from Rs. 11/kg. in June 2010 to Rs. 75/kg. in January 2011. While the production of onions had gone up from 4.8 million tonnes in 2001-01 to 12 million tonnes in 2009-10, prices also went up, indicating that in a speculation-driven market there is no correlation between production and prices. The price difference between wholesale and retail prices was 135 per cent. Tomato prices shot up by more than 100 per cent between October and December 2010, from Rs. 15/kg. to Rs. 40-50/kg; prices of cabbage went up by 159 per cent; garlic, 140 per cent; potato 86 per cent; brinjal 72 per cent; and green peas, 66 per cent between March and December 2010. While traders gained, farmers were losing. Farmers got only Rs. 8/kg. for tomatoes selling at Rs. 50. The price of staples has also been going up systematically. Between December 2006 and December 2010, rice went from Rs. 14.50/kg. to Rs. 24/kg., sugar from Rs. 21/kg. to Rs. 34/kg., arhar dal from Rs. 32/kg. to Rs. 65/kg., moong dal from Rs. 46.50/kg. to Rs. 64/kg.[5]

Synthetic biology and biodiversity wars

Synthetic biology is the emerging technology for transforming biomass and biodiversity into commerce. Synthetic biology is an industry that creates "designer organisms to act as living factories". With synthetic biology, hopes are that by building biological systems from the ground up, they can create biological systems that will function like computers or factories. The goal is to make biology easier to engineer by using bio-bricks.

Agriculture and food production were transformed through two earlier "green revolutions", the first based on introducing chemistry to agriculture. For this, plants were made into dwarf varieties with the application of chemical fertilisers to prevent them from lodging. The second "green revolution" is based on the application of genetic engineering; and the emerging third "green revolution" introduces synthetic biology.

All three are based on an inappropriate and outmoded mechanistic paradigm. Living systems are based on self-organisation, diversity and complexity; green revolutions reduce life to raw material, complex systems to "machines", diversity to monocultures. The green revolution defined plants as factories, running on inputs from other factories producing synthetic fertilisers. Biotechnology, the second green revolution, is based on the obsolete paradigm of genetic reductionism, of genes as "atoms" of plants, at a time when we know genes do not act in isolation and a single gene does not carry one trait, but multiple traits like yield and resilience. Synthetic biology is even further removed from life.

To assess the promises and shortfalls of the emerging third "green revolution" we need to look at what the first and second green revolutions have delivered and the lessons that can be learnt from them. The first false claims of both earlier revolutions are that they declare themselves to be miracles. As Angus Wright has observed with respect to the green revolution,

> One way in which agricultural research went wrong was in saying, and allowing it to be said, that some miracle was being produced.... Historically, science and technology made their first advances by rejecting the idea of miracles in the natural world. Perhaps it would be best to return to that position.[6]

The second false claim is that of exaggerated benefits. Both earlier green revolutions have been declared miracle solutions to hunger. In the case of the first, it is said that HYVS (High-Yielding Varieties) saved millions from famine.

This is not true. First, as Dr. Palmer concluded in the United Nations Research Institute for Social Development's 15-nation study of the impact of new seeds, the term "high yielding varieties" is a misnomer because it implies that the new seeds are high yielding in and of themselves. The distinguishing feature of the new seeds, however, is that they are highly responsive to certain key inputs such as fertilisers and irrigation. Palmer therefore suggested the term "high responsive varieties" (HRV) be used instead.

Further, by transforming biodiverse systems into monocultures, and by replacing tall straw, high biomass production varieties to dwarf varieties, the output of food, nutrition and biomass actually went down. Biodiverse ecological systems produce more food and nutrition per unit acre, as Navdanya's study, "Health Per Acre" has shown.

For example, in just one biodiverse system the following was observed:

	Biodiverse	Monoculture
Protein	33 × 8.3 kgs.	90 kgs.
Carbohydrate	680 kgs.	920 kgs.
Fat	107.8 kgs.	12 kgs.
Carotene	2540 mgs.	24 mgs.
Folic acid	554 mgs.	0
Vitamin C	400 mgs.	0
Ca	3420 mgs.	120 mgs.
Fe	100.8 g	38.4 g
P	6013 g	2280 g
Kg	2389 g	1884 g
Na	79 g	0
K	4272 g	0

Overall, in energy terms, industrial agriculture is a negative energy system, using ten units of input to produce one unit of output. Industrial agriculture in the US uses 380 times more energy per ha. to produce rice than a traditional farm in the Philippines; and energy use per kilo of rice is 80 times higher in the US than in the Philippines. Energy use for maize production in the US is 176 times more per ha. than a traditional farm in Mexico, and 33 times more per kilogram.

The first green revolution spread monocultures of rice, wheat and corn. The second green revolution has spread monocultures of corn, soya, canola and cotton. The third green revolution will spread monocultures for biofuels. Biomass advocates refer to "marginal", "unproductive", "idle", "degraded" and "abandoned lands and wastelands" as the target for biomass extraction. European researchers have said "a prerequisite for the bio-energy potential in all regions is that the present inefficient and low-intensive agricultural management systems are replaced by 2050 by the best practice agricultural management systems and technologies".

The industrialisation of life is being sold as the new "bio economy" "clean tech", the "green economy". While biodiversity economies are genuine bio economies, they are being eclipsed with the rise of bio economy as an industrial order based on biological materials and industrial processes. International organisations are already referring to it as follows: the OECD calls it bio-based economy; the European Union refers to it as knowledge-based bio economy; the World Economic Forum calls it a bio-refinery industry; the Biotechnology Industry Organisation calls it biotechnology; while UNEP calls it the green economy, and the US government's Biomass Research and Development Board calls it the bioeconomic revolution.

The ETC Report, *Biomasters,* quotes Craig Venter, the founder of synthetic genomics as saying,

> Whoever produces abundant biofuels could end up making more than just big bucks – they will make history. The companies, the countries, that succeed in this will be the economic winners of the next age to the same extent that the oil-rich nations are today.[7]

The new bio-economy imagined by Craig Venter is an extension of the oil economy. Instead of oil being mined from fossilised biological matter, it will now be squeezed out from living biological matter or biomass. Major players of the oil age are now engaged in a scramble for the biodiversity that performs ecological services in nature's economy, and provides basic needs of food, fodder, fuel, fertiliser in people's sustenance economy. As the ETC Report says, "With 24 per cent of the world's annual terrestrial biomass so far appropriated for human use, today's compounding crises are an opportunity to commodify and monopolise the remaining 76 per cent that Wall Street hasn't yet reached."

Industrial sectors with an interest in the biodiversity and biomass of the planet include the energy, chemical, plastics, food, textiles, pharmaceuticals, paper products, and building supplies industries. Along with carbon, this is a market of $17 trillion. Global corporations are joining in this earth-grab, and include oil companies such as British Petroleum, Shell, Exxon Mobil; chemical and biotechnology companies like BASF and Dupont, Monsanto, Amyris, Synthetic Genomics, Syngenta; forestry and agribusiness companies like Cargill, Archer Daniel Midlands, Weyerhauser; food companies such as Procter & Gamble, Unilever, Coca-Cola; and financial giants, Goldman Sachs, J.P. Morgan, Microsoft. As Craig Venter has said, "We have modest goals of replacing the whole petrochemical industry and becoming a major source of energy."

The 76 per cent non-commercialised, non-commoditised biomass is the basis of biodiversity-based local economies. Biomass encompasses over 230 billion tonnes of "living stuff" that supports local living economies today, and could support them in the future.

> This annual bounty, known as earth's 'primary production' is most abundant in the global South – in tropical oceans, forests, and fast-growing grasslands – sustaining the livelihoods, cultures and basic needs of most of the world's inhabitants. What is being sold as a benign and beneficial switch from black carbon to green carbon is, in fact, a red-hot resource-grab (from South to North) to capture a new source of wealth. If the grab succeeds, then plundering the biomasters of the South to cheaply run the industrial economies of the North will be an act of 21st century imperialism that deepens injustice and worsens poverty and hunger. Moreover, pillaging fragile ecosystems for their carbon and sugar stocks is a murderous move on an already overstressed planet.[8]

The biodiversity-based knowledge possessed by peasant communities to control pests and increase fertility, is centuries old. The insecticidal use of nicotine, the alkaloid present in tobacco, dates back to the seventeenth century, long before it was isolated. The range of insects subject to control by nicotine is very wide, and the alkaloid has been used successfully by farmers against aphids, leaf rotters, moths, fruit tree borers, termites, cabbage butterfly larvae, etc.

The neem (*azadirachta indica juss*), a large evergreen tree, is a native of India. The use of neem to ward off damage by pests has been known since antiquity, and farmers have always mixed neem leaves with grain for storage. Neem contains several aromatic principles that repel insects; for example, demonstration of the anti-feedant properties of the neem kernel against the desert locust has generated tremendous interest in the insect-controlling properties of the plant. Spray applications of neem oil to rice plants was reported to inhibit the feeding responses of brown plant hopper and leaf folder, both rice pests. The application of neem oil to cow pea has demonstrated its effect in protecting the pulse from the infestation of bruchids. Farmers' experiments have indicated it as promising material for increasing biological nitrogen fixation in wetland paddy fields.

There are many other plants which our farmers use as insecticides and pesticides, building on their knowledge that has evolved over centuries. Chrysanthemum is a cosmopolitan genus comprising 300 species of herbs and undershrubs, of which only a few have the insecticidal property. Pyrethrum, the relevant substance present in the flower, is one of the safest insecticides known; it has low mammalian toxicity and an instantaneous knock-down effect. Its repellent action towards insects even in very low concentrations makes it useful for the preservation of food grains and preparation of insect-resistant packaging. Indian farmers plant it around their fields to provide protection to other plants. The oil-cake left after extraction of oil from seeds of *pangamia glabra* trees also serves as a very potent pest control agent when added to the soil. The tree kasorka (*strychnos muxuomica*) found in Malnad forests grows up to 60-90 ft.in height. The pesticidal properties present in its seeds and leaves have been known to our farmers who have been using its leaves, barks and twigs for pesticidal purposes since time immemorial.

Indian farmers depend on biodiversity for green and organic manure for their fields as well as fodder for their livestock. Soil is often described as consisting of solid particles, water, gaseous elements, humus and raw organic matter. Organic matter serves as a nutrient store from which the nutrients are slowly released into the soil and made available to plants. Trees, shrubs, cover crops, grain, legumes, grasses, weeds, ferns and algae all provide green manure; green manure crops contribute 30 to 60 kgs. of nitrogen per hectare annually. The cumulative effects of the continued use of green manure are important not only in terms of nitrogen supply, but also with regard to soil organic matter and micro-elements.

Deep-rooted green manure crops in rotation can help recover nutrients leached to the subsoil. Similarly, there is a balance maintained between the animal population and fodder availability in the ecosystem. Trees, including fodder trees, are grown in combination with agricultural crops useful for producing fodder for livestock.

Long before the introduction of chemical fertilisers in Indian agriculture, oil-seed cakes, particularly those of peanut *(arachis hypogaea)*, castor *(ricinus coimmunis)*, and mohua *(bassia latifolia)* were used as a source of plant nutrients. Scientists have reported on the value of the seed, bark and leaf of karanji *(pongamia glabtra)* as manure in the Deccan region. Other plants which contribute to green manure are thangadi *(Cassia anriculosts),* yekka *(calitropics gigantea)*, neem *(azadirachta indica)*, the creeper uganishambu *(pettsonia spp)*, and wild indigo *(tephrosia purpurea)*. Other kinds of green manure collected from the jungle are: Portia *(thespesia populnuraa)*, four o' clock plant *(mirabiulis jalepe)* and all pilli persara *(phaseolus aconitifilius)*. Crops that contribute to green manure are pulses, for example, green gram, horse gram, black gram, cow peas and other legumes.

As for fodder for the animals, the tree *prosopis cineraria* is a most useful plant in dry parts of the country. There is a popular saying among farmers that death will not visit a man even during a famine if he has a *prosopis cineraria*, a goat and a camel, because the three together will sustain him even under the most trying conditions. In wetland cultivation, it has been observed that green manure directly enhances soil conditions, whereas in dryland areas, fodder from animal dung is a rich source of manure. Local tall varieties of rice and millet are also an important source of fodder, which in turn returns to the soil as farmyard manure.

Thus, farmers' traditional knowledge of biodiversity use helps in increasing yields and protecting the environment by providing internal inputs as substitutes to economically expensive and environmentally destructive agro-chemicals.

The conflict and contest between the two systems – one based on eco-imperalism, bio-imperialism and eco-apartheid, the other based on earth democracy and bio-democracy, will intensify over the next decade. People will have to strengthen their defences to protect their local, living economies through local, living democracy.

References

1 Paul Collier, *The Plundered Planet,* Oxford: Oxford University Press, 2010.
2 Personal communication from the author.
3 Agribusiness Accountability Initiative, "Time to Act on Food Price Speculation", April 20, 2008. http:www.agribusinessaccountability.org
4 Frederick Kaufman, "The Food Bubble", *Harper's* Magazine, July 2010.
5 Data from Navdanya/RFSTE field study, "Skyrocketing Prices", January 2011.
6 Angus Wright, *The Death of Ramon Gonzalez: The Modern Agricultural Dilemma*, Austin: University of Texas Press, 1990.
7 The New Biomasters Report, www.etcgroup.org
8 Earth Grab, op.cit., p. 1.

7 Seed Wars as Wars against the Earth

FERTILISERS COME FROM explosives factories. In recent years, in Oklahoma and Afghanistan, in Mumbai and Oslo, explosives factories were retooled to make fertiliser bombs. Fertilisers are implicated in the violence against the atmosphere – N_2O is three hundred times more deadly as a climate changing gas than CO_2. Today, Punjab is the toxic capital of India. The monocultures of rice and wheat are a perfect breeding ground for pests. While pests are not a problem in ecologically balanced agriculture, in an unstable agricultural system they pose a series of challenges to agronomy.

Genetic engineering was supposed to provide an alternative to toxic chemicals, instead it has led to an increase in the use of pesticides and herbicides. It has failed as a tool to control and has instead created super pests and super weeds, because it is based on a violence that ruptures the resilience and metabolism of the plant and introduces genes for producing or tolerating higher doses of toxins. There are so far only two tools used to transfer genes from one organism to another – one is the use of a gene gun, the other is the use of a cancer infection. This is biological warfare at the genetic level.

On September 8, 2006, nine farmers' unions of Punjab organised a public hearing on farmers' suicides, and I was invited to be a member of the citizens' jury. The Diwan Hall of Gurdwara Haaji Rattan in Bhatinda was overflowing with a sea of women – all widows of suicide victims. The farmers' organisations had collected information on 2,860 suicides and mobilised family members to give evidence at the public hearing. (This was building on an earlier public hearing organised by Navdanya on April 1 and 2, 2006.)

Forty-two year old Sukhbir Singh of Chak Sadoke, block Jalalabad, district Ferozepur, ended his life on October 26, 2003, by jumping into a river, because he was unable to repay a debt of Rs. 1.9 million in spite of selling off seven acres of his land. He left behind a widow with two children; 21 year-old Harjinder Singh of Ratla Thark who lost seven acres to moneylenders ended his life by consuming pesticides; 60 year-old Jeet Singh of the same village burnt himself to death; 28 year-old Hardev Singh of Urmmat Puria in Hoga drank pesticide on July, 12, 2002 when he could not repay his loan of Rs. 0.7 million even after selling eight acres; 26 year-old Avatar Singh of Machika village died on March 28, 2006, after consuming pesticide; 48 year-old Jagtar Singh of Doda in Muktsar left behind a widow and daughter after drinking pesticide. He had sold two acres to partially repay a debt of Rs. 150,000. Twenty-eight year-old Raghubir Singh mortgaged four acres, could not clear his loan, and ended his life on April 28, 2004 by consuming pesticide. His mother, widow and two children are left to struggle on.

One by one the women came forward to share their pain, their loss, their tragedy. The names were different, the faces were different, but the tragedy was the same, the avoidable tragedy of poisoning farmers' fields and farmers' lives for profit. Thirty other women gave testimonies about their husbands' and sons' suicides by drinking the lethal and debt-creating pesticide ... and there were thousands more. The pesticides which had created debt also became the source for ending indebted lives. Those who survive suicide in Punjab are dying of cancer. There is a "cancer" train that leaves Punjab for the treatment of villagers at a charitable hospital in Bikaner. This toxic economy is the "gift" of the green revolution; and this toxic gift was also behind the tragedy of Bhopal. Pesticides are designed to kill – and from Punjab to Bhopal, they have killed thousands. Our breadbasket in Punjab does not have to be the epicentre of toxicity; the people of Bhopal did not need to die. There are alternatives to Bt-cotton and toxic pesticides. Through Navdanya we have promoted organic farming and seeds of hope to help farmers move away from Monsanto's seeds of suicide. Organic farmers in Vidharbha in

Maharashtra are earning Rs. 6,287 per acre on average, compared to Bt-cotton farmers who are earning Rs.714 per acre on average. Many Bt-cotton farmers have a negative income, hence the suicides.) Technologies are tools. When the tool fails it needs to be replaced. Bt-cotton technology has failed to control pests or secure farmers' lives and livelihoods; it is time to replace GM technology with ecological farming, time to stop farmers' suicides.

On April 17, 2011, World Peasant Day, I joined the victims of Kasargod in Kerala for a conference. Shahina, who has lost her brother and is herself severly crippled, opened the meeting with the following words:

> India is my country, I am proud to be an Indian. But the stand of India to oppose the global proposal for the ban of the dreadful poison, Endosulfan, is heavily painful to me. Pure air, pure water, pure food are the rights of any citizen. Hence ban of this poison is the basic duty of the government. I feel ashamed of the fact that my country is supporting this, in spite of 81 countries opposing it. I demand my government to implement the ban on Endosulfan on a national level in the forthcoming COP at Geneva. I demand India shall cast the first vote for the ban of Endosulfan.

Endosulfan is a broad-spectrum organochlorine insecticide which is acutely toxic and an endocrine disruptor. It also has the potential to bio-accumulate. It was developed in the 1980s by Hoechst (now Bayer) and its worldwide production was about 9,000 metric tonnes. By the 1990s, its use had increased to 12,800 tonnes per year. In 2000, its use for homes and gardens was banned in the US; and in 2002, the US restricted its use in agriculture. In 2007, Bayer withdrew Endosulfan from the US. In 2009, the Stockholm Convention's Persistent Organic Pollutants Review Committee agreed that Endosulfan is a persistent organic pollutant; in 2010, Endosulfan was added to the list of chemicals to be banned.

The government of Kerala has already imposed a ban on Endosulfan following a survey by the Kerala state health department which identified 4,000 victims. One hundred and seventy-five specialists from 11 departments of medical colleges screened patients in 17 camps. In spite of these surveys and the scientific knowledge that Endosulfan is a neuro-toxin, a carcinogen and an endocrine disruptor which leads to reproductive disorders and congenital malformation, the pesticide lobby continues to talk of it as "harmless". Their influence on the Indian government led the agriculture minister, Sharad Pawar, to block the national and international ban on Endosulfan. Mr. Pawar misled Parliament, falsely stating that there was opposition from some states to a national ban. However, right to information activists have found that no state government has written to the centre opposing a ban. In May 2011, the Supreme Court ordered an interim ban on Endosulfan.

Soil and climate resilience

Industrial agriculture contributes to climate change through the direct use of fossil fuels and the emission of CO_2, as well as through the use of fossil fuel-based nitrogen fertilisers which emit nitrogen oxide, which is 300 times more damaging to the climate than CO_2. Organic farming and organic soils contribute to mitigation of climate change by (*a*) getting rid of agri-chemicals like synthetic fertilisers; (*b*) sequestering carbon in the soil.

For every 100 kgs. of N-input, 3-5 kgs. of N_2O emissions go into the atmosphere.[1] In addition, fossil fuels are used for making chemical fertilisers; the energy used for nitrogen fertilisers is:

69.5 MJ / kgs. for production
2.6 MJ / kgs. for packaging
4.5 MJ / kgs. for transportation
1.6 MJ / kgs. for application
a total of 78.2 MJ / kgs. or 2.03 litres diesel equivalent / kgs.[2]

The energy used for synthetic nitrogen fertilisers, which are totally excluded in organic systems, represents upto $0.34 - 0.6$ G + CO_2 emission.[3]

In the UK 26 per cent of the energy burden in wheat is accounted for by chemical fertilisers and 11 per cent by pesticides. In the US 30-40 per cent of the energy used in corn is for fertilisers and 9-11 per cent for pesticides.[4] By avoiding these emissions, organic farming mitigates climate change. Sustainable soil fertility comes from organic manuring, and soil rich in organic matter is a major carbon sink. Since the beginning of industrial agriculture, soils have lost one to two per cent organic matter in the top 30 cms. of soil; this is equivalent to 150,000-250,000 million tonnes of lost organic matter. If we were able to put this organic matter back into the soil, we would remove 220,000-330,000 million tonnes of CO_2 from the air. This amounts to 30 per cent of excess CO_2 in the atmosphere.

Capturing Carbon Dioxide by Building Soil Organic Matter (SOM)

CO_2 in the atmosphere	2,867,500 m tonnes
Excess CO_2 in the atmosphere	717,8001 m tonnes
World's agricultural land	5,000 m ha
World's cultivated land	1,800 m ha
Typical reported SOM loss in cultivated land	2 percentage points
Typical reported SOM loss in prairies and non-cultivated land	1 percentage point
Amount of organic matter lost from the soil	150,000-205,000 m tonnes
Amount of CO_2 that would be sequestered if losses were recuperated	220,000-300,000 m tonnes

Source: *Grain, Seedling,* October 2009, p. 13.

In a study of nine farming systems, it was found that soil carbon concentrates in organically farmed soils are 14 per cent higher than conventional soils, and liable soil organic matter was 30 to 40 per cent higher.[5]

The carbon sequestration efficiency (tonnes CO_2-C per ha) of organic systems in temperate climates is almost double that of conventional ones, when the total above-and-below-ground biomass of cash crops and weeds is calculated. Organic fields sequester three to eight tonnes of carbon per hectare.[6] In a two-year study carried out by Navdanya across different agro-ecosystems in India, we found that carbon return to soil can increase by upto 200 per cent with organic practices compared to chemical farming – the result showed an additional increase of 62.5 to 83 mg g^{-1} soil carbon in organic agriculture, irrespective of the crop growth. In general, the carbon build-up was higher under humid agro-ecosystems.

Ecozones	*Additional increase ($\mu g\,g^{-1}$)*	
	Range	*Mean*
Arid	49 - 83	62.5
Semi-arid	57 - 98	71.9
Sub-humid	61 - 101	75.5
Humid	68 - 102	83.0

This would definitely help in microbial growth, nutrient recycling and moisture retention of the soil; it also helps in reduction of soil erosion, especially in arid and semi-arid areas.

Soil and water

Industrial agriculture is a thirsty agriculture; 70 per cent of water on the planet is being used to irrigate chemical farms that use ten times more water to produce the same amount of food as ecological farms. Intensification of drought, floods and cyclones is one of the predictable outcomes of climate change and climate instability. The failure of the monsoon in India in 2009 and the consequent drought impacted two-thirds of the country, especially the breadbasket of its fertile Gangetic plains. Bihar had a 43 per cent rainfall deficit; Jharkhand, 47 per cent; Uttar Pradesh, 64 per cent; Haryana, 61 per cent; Punjab, 26 per cent; Himachal Pradesh, 63 per cent; and Uttarakhand, 42 per cent. In the final analysis, India's food security rests on the monsoons which recharge the groundwater and surface water systems. In 2009, because of drought, there was reduced recharge; since 1966, as a consequence of the green revolution model of water-intensive chemical farming, India has over-exploited her groundwater, creating a water famine. In the 1970s the World Bank gave massive loans to India to promote groundwater mining; it forced states like Maharashtra to stop growing water-prudent millets like jowar which needs just 300 mm. of water, and shift to water-guzzling crops like sugarcane which needs 2,500 mm. of water. In a region with 600 mm. rainfall and 10 per cent groundwater recharge, this is a recipe for water famine.[7]

A new study by Matthew Rodell of Nasa's Goddard Space Flight Center in Maryland, published in *Nature*, has shown that water levels in north India have fallen by 1.6 inches (4 cms. per year) and more than 26 cubic miles of groundwater have disappeared from aquifers between August 2002 and August 2008. Most of this groundwater has been extracted for chemical farming.

The solutions for the climate crisis, the food crisis, or the water crisis are the same: biodiversity-based organic farming systems. Biodiverse organic systems also address the water crisis. First, production is based on water-prudent crops; second, they use one-tenth the water that chemical systems do; third, the increase in organic matter content transforms the soil into a water reservoir, which reduces irrigation demand and helps conserve water in agriculture. Maximising biodiversity and organic matter production thus simultaneously increases climate resilience, food security and water security. In a recent article, "Fight Drought with Science", Henry Miller, author of *The Frankenfood Myth*, has said that, "The first drought-resistant crop, maize, is expected to be commercialised by 2010. If field testing goes well, India could be a potential market for this variety."[8] What Miller fails to mention is that India has hundreds of thousands of drought-resistant crops, some of which are conserved in, and distributed from, Navdanya's community seed banks which farmers used in the drought year of 2009. While cultivation of rice has gone down from 25.673 million ha. to 19.13 million ha., the area under water-prudent, drought-resistant nutritious crops – unfortunately called "coarse grains" – has gone up from 15.325 ha. to 15.956 million ha. The biotechnology industry is clearly a laggard in breeding for drought resistance compared to centuries of breeding by India's farmers. Miller also fails to mention that the genetically engineered drought-resistant maize seed performs badly in normal years. This is not science. Another example of corporate opportunism in this period of drought was the pushing of Round-Up, a broad-spectrum herbicide, under the Zero Tillage and Conservation Tillage programmes, that kills everything green.

The 1965-66 drought was used to push the green revolution which has increased vulnerability to drought; the 2009 drought was similarly being used to push the second green revolution with GMO seeds and patents on seeds. It is vital that the government does not use climate emergency and act as a marketer of GM seeds and Round-Up. The alternative is clear. It involves: (*i*) conservation and large-scale distribution of open-pollinated varieties and open-source seeds of water-prudent crops; (*ii*) promotion of organic agriculture to increase climate resilience and food and water security; (*iii*) incentives to farmers for a shift from water-guzzling green revolution agriculture to water-conserving biodiverse organic farming.

Punjab's green revolution agriculture requires 4.37 million metres of water, of which surface canals from the Bhakra dam provide 1.45 million ha-metres and groundwater supplies 2.9 million ha-metres. As a result groundwater is declining by 30 cms. every year. Of the 138 blocks, 73 have over-exploited their water by 100 per cent, 11 have exploited it by 85-100 per cent, 16 have over-exploited it by 65-85 per cent.[9] Water contamination is so high that it is causing DNA mutations, according to a study commissioned by the Punjab Water Pollution Control Board and conducted by senior doctors of the Post-Graduate Institute of Medical Education in Chandigarh.

Pesticides were found in all samples; 65 per cent blood samples showed DNA mutation and 57.7 per cent had arsenic.[10]

India has become the world's largest groundwater user, using 230 cubic kilometres per year, which is 25 per cent of the world's total. In five states – Gujarat, Haryana, Maharashtra, Rajasthan and Tamil Nadu – groundwater mining has already led to a severe water crisis.

In organic systems, water retention and drainage capacity of the ecosystem are enhanced and the risk of floods or droughts, reduced. Molecules of soil organic matter can absorb upto 100 times as much water as those of dust, and they can retain and later release to plants a similar proportion of nutrients, protecting the soil from erosion. Organic soil is a major water reservoir because it can absorb rain and slowly release it to lakes, rivers and plants. Soil management techniques become water management techniques; organic soils contribute to groundwater recharge, an environmental service that protects the whole ecosystem.

Navdanya's study based on ten farms in four agro-ecosystems shows increased water-holding capacity in organic soils.

Ecozones	% Increase over Chemical Farming	
	Range	Mean
Arid	2 - 9	5.3
Semi-arid	3 - 16	7.2
Sub-humid	4 - 15	6.9
Humid	3 - 17	6.8

The results clearly showed between five and seven per cent increase in the water-holding capacity in each agro-ecosystem due to organic agriculture. As this is the key for improvement in soil health, microbial growth, nutrient recycling, better maintenance of soil temperature and ultimate crop production, organic agriculture definitely improves the soil environment.

A study comparing soils farmed organically and conventionally in the state of Washington (USA) found organic fields had topsoils

16 cms. deeper and a higher organic matter content, with soils being less prone to erosion.[11] A long-term Swiss study found the aggregate and percolation stability of both bio-dynamic and organic plots were significantly higher (10-60 per cent) than conventionally farmed plots.[12] The long-term Rodale farm studies showed that organic systems had an impressive increase of 574 kgs. per ha. in the legume-based, and 981 kgs. per ha. in the manure-based systems.[13]

Land hunger

The World Bank estimates that by 2030 land conversion from food to industrial agriculture, especially biofuels, will be in the range of 18 to 44 million ha.[14] Global biofuel consumption is estimated to jump from about 70 billion litres in 2008 to 280 billion litres in 2020. For the EU, the jump will be from 13 billion litres to 55 billion litres. The demand for land in the South to grow industrial biofuels could reach 17.5 million ha.; in just five countries – Ethiopia, Ghana, Madagascar, Mali and Sudan – 2.5 million ha. have been grabbed by investors, with 1.1 million for biofuels. The land-grab in Africa is driven by the convergence of the fuel crisis, the food crisis and the financial crisis. In India, laws for common lands were changed in Rajasthan to allow industry to plant jatropha for biofuels.

The world food crisis and the demand for biofuels has made land a strategic asset. Morgan Stanley purchased 40,000 ha. of farmland in Ukraine, and Goldman Sachs took over the Chinese poultry and meat industry in September 2008. Blackrock has set up a $200 million agricultural hedge fund, of which $30 million will acquire farmland. Swedish investment groups, Black Earth Farming and Alpiot-Agro, have joined the British investment group, Landkom, to acquire 600,000 ha. in Russia and Ukraine. An Abu Dhabi-based investment company, Al Qudia, has bought large tracts of farmland in Morocco and Algeria and is scouting for land in Pakistan, Syria, Vietnam, Thailand, Sudan and India.[15] The United Arab Emirates has acquired 900,000 ha. in land-scarce Pakistan and 378,000 in Sudan.[16]

While 5.6 million refugees are being fed by the World Food

Programme in Sudan, US investor Phillipe Heilberg (formerly with AIG and now CEO of Jarch Capital), leased 4,000 sq. kms. of land in Sudan, and in mid-April 2009, added another 3,000 square miles (800,000 ha.) to create a gigantic agricultural plantation.[17] Heilberg is betting on the disintegration of the African state.[18] Investors are the new buccaneers and merchant adventurers; what we are witnessing is a recolonisation of Africa. Instead of erstwhile kings and queens of Europe, it is the kings of the financial world who are grabbing land in this new colonisation; contemporary land-grab is based on financial conquest, not armed conquest. First food was transformed into a globally-traded commodity, now land is being similarly transformed. Private equity funds, hedge funds and other actors in the financial world are snapping up land worldwide in what is being called the "treasure hunt" for fertile farmland.

A report by FAO/IFAD titled, "Land-Grab or Development Opportunity" has assessed that two million ha. have been signed over to foreign investors in Africa, including a 10,000 ha. project in Mali and a 450,000 ha. plantation for agro-fuels in Madagascar. In July 2009, the government of Ethiopia allowed investors to take 1.6 million ha. of land, extendable to 2.7 million ha., to develop commercial farms. When I asked an Ethiopian taxi driver about the land-grab in his country, he said it was "wasteland", that Ethiopians were "primitive" and did not know how to practice "civilized agriculture", by which he meant industrial agriculture. Land was declared "empty", it had to be "improved"; since rights then and now were framed as "property rights", grabbing the land and violating the ancestral claims of indigenous local communities was acceptable, as land was not "property" for them. John Locke argued for property as an extension of man's self, but this implied that those for whom land was *identity*, not *property*, could be alienated from it by those with power and capital who could make it their property. The relationship of natural resources, including land, with capital has over-ruled their relationship with communities. In a system dominated by capital and investments, the land rights of communities can be systematically violated. This is why land-grab was easy in colonial times and is easy today.

Countries like China, which are destroying their farmland at home for rapid industrialisation and urbanisation, are also grabbing land. As GRAIN reports in *Seized*:

> Beijing has been gradually outsourcing part of its food production since well before the global food crisis broke out in 2007. Through China's new geopolitical diplomacy and the government's aggressive 'go abroad' outward investment strategy, some thirty agricultural cooperation deals have been sealed in recent years to give Chinese firms access to 'friendly country' farmland.[19]

Most of China's offshore farming is dedicated to the cultivation of rice, soya beans and maize, alongwith biofuel crops like sugarcane, cassava or sorghum. The farming is industrial, the farmers and experts are Chinese. There is no place for the indigenous and local, either in terms of farmers or farming systems. With US $1.8 trillion in foreign exchange reserves, China is a major global investor and there is nothing better than land to invest in.

The oil rich gulf states – Bahrain, Kuwait, Oman, Qatar, Saudi Arabia and the United Arab Emirates – are also on a land hunt. They are collectively outsourcing their food production and are looking for land in Myanmar, Cambodia, Indonesia, Laos, Phillipines, Thailand, Vietnam, Turkey, Kazakhistan, Ukraine, Georgia, Uganda, Brazil … Cambodia has leased large tracts of paddy land for $600 million to Qatar and Kuwait. At the same time, the World Food Programme has had to start shipping US $35 million in food aid to Cambodia for hungry Cambodians.[20] In 2009, Saudi Arabia received its first shipment of rice produced on land it had acquired in Ethiopia, even as the World Food Programme was feeding five million Ethiopians. In the Democratic Republic of Congo, China acquired seven million ha. of land for palm-oil, while millions of the country's citizens live on food aid.[21] While 'food security' is the justification for land-grab, intensifying food insecurity is its inevitable consequence.

Foreign direct investment in land was US $1 billion during 1989-91, $3 billion during 2005-2007. As GRAIN reports –

> Not all investment is development. "Investment in Agriculture"

has become the rallying cry of virtually all authorities and experts charged with solving the global food crisis, into which perhaps the uninvited land-grab boom fits well. It should be abundantly clear that behind the rhetoric of win-win deals, the real aim of these contracts is not agricultural development, much less rural development, but simply agribusiness development.[22]

The Oakland Institute report on "The Great Land-Grab" warns that "There is a dangerous disconnect between increasing investment in agriculture through rich countries taking over land in poor countries, and the goal of securing food supplies for poor and vulnerable populations." [23]

The UN Special Rapporteur on Food cautioned in an open letter that large-scale investments could negatively affect the right to food, as well as other human rights, through the forcible eviction of land-users with no formal security of tenure over the land they have been cultivating for decades; the loss of access to land for indigenous peoples and pastoral populations, competition for water resources and decreased food security if local populations are deprived of access to productive resources; or if, as a result of this development, a country further increases its dependency on food aid or imports for its national food security.

Obama and the US corporate take-over of agriculture in India and Africa

The main focus of US President Barack Obama's three-day visit to India in 2011 was to firm up business deals for US corporations that would create jobs in the US. Trade deals worth over $10 billion were finalised, with a focus on defence, energy and agriculture. In fact, Mr Obama's speech at St Xavier's College, Mumbai, focused almost entirely on how India owed it to the US to open its markets to US companies and agribusinesses. What he failed to mention, however, is that India has already been forced to give market access to the US in the areas of oilseeds, pulses and genetically-modified organisms at the cost of Indian farmers, and India's biodiversity and environment.

India's imports of edible oils from the US are growing disproportionately and, since 2008, have jumped 2,666 per cent – they were expected to reach 9.3 million tonnes in 2010-11, while returns to Indian farmers are declining. The flooding of domestic markets with artificially cheap imports is challenging the livelihoods of local farmers and food processors by destroying the rich diversity of indigenous oilseeds, including mustard, sesame, linseed, groundnut, coconut, etc. The reliance on imported oilseeds can easily trigger violence and instability, as Indonesia's food riots illustrate. The destruction of India's pulse diversity through the green revolution has led to pulses, the only proteins in a vegetarian diet, becoming completely unaffordable in most Indian households, with the US now dumping subsidised "yellow pea dal", which is no substitute for our indigenous flavourful pulses.

US-based Monsanto's monopoly in the Indian seed market has allowed the US corporation to harvest huge royalties through Intellectual Property Rights while Indian farmers are pushed into debt and suicide. Two hundred thousand farmers, mostly in the cotton belt, have committed suicide in India since 1997, the leading cause being debt, linked to crop failure of the Monsanto Bt-cotton, the spread of monocultures and of highly expensive, capital-intensive inputs that made cultivation economically unviable.

President Obama is also trying to pursue George W. Bush's agenda of unleashing Walmart on India's retail economy – the argument used is reduction of waste and creation of jobs. However, Jonathan Bloom's recently published book, *American Wasteland: How America Throws Away Nearly Half of Its Food*, places the blame for the destruction of food squarely on the Walmart model. India cannot afford such an expensive mistake. Further, retail generates 400 million jobs through self-employment; instead of exporting unemployment to India from the US, Mr Obama should be importing innovative ideas of employment generation by learning from India's small-scale entrepreneurs.

Mr Obama is also continuing Mr Bush's legacy with the Agriculture Knowledge Initiative (AKI) of 2008. At a time when the world recognises the productivity and ecological sustainability of small farmers, the US-India AKI is pushing India to adopt hazardous technologies. It is no coincidence that at the time of signing the AKI, US multinationals on the negotiating table – Monsanto, Walmart, Syngenta – lobbied for a change in India's IPR laws so as to claim exclusive ownership of, and extract royalties on, agricultural inputs, leading to the creation of a stronger technological monopoly.

A recent newspaper report stated that "India and the US may team up to tap farm opportunities in Africa. The proposal is a spin-off from the India-US agriculture dialogue." Ben Rhodes, the US's deputy national adviser for strategic communication, said,

> "The US has been part of food security initiatives in Africa, where we are trying to apply technology, innovation and capacity-building to help African farmers lift their countries and their standard of living. We see great potential for the US and India to cooperate, not just within India but in African countries as well."[24]

But African movements have staunchly rejected the green revolution model for Africa: what stakeholders want is a sustainable, inclusive and indigenous solution that increases food sovereignty – not dependency on markets, expensive chemical inputs and GMOs.

The UN's International Assessment of Agricultural Knowledge, Science and Technology for Development, which engaged 400 scientists for four years to assess the performance of different models of agriculture, has concluded that neither the green revolution nor genetic engineering can offer food security; only ecological agriculture has the potential for increasing food production.

Energy hunger

Biomass has always been used as energy by the poor who did not participate in the fossil fuel economy. With rising prices of oil and growing concern about the contribution of the use of fossil fuels to climate change, there is a scramble for transforming biomass into liquid fuel for the vehicles of the rich.

US and EU subsidies and energy policies have encouraged the diversion of food to fuel, thus contributing to hunger. The first generation of biofuels use soya and palm-oil for bio-diesel, and corn and sugarcane for ethanol. While these are offered as a renewable energy solution which can address both climate change and peak oil, more fossil fuels are used to produce industrial biofuel than are substituted. Biofuel production is a net negative energy system.

In Europe, the biofuel industry was supported by financial incentives of Euros 4.4 billion. If the target of 10 per cent blending of petrol and diesel with ethanol and bio-diesel has to be met by 2020, the industry would need to be subsidised with Euros 13.7 billion per year. This subsidy pulls food away from the hungry. At least 30 per cent of the global food price rise in 2008 was due to biofuels; by 2020 food prices could rise by an additional 76 per cent because of diversion.[25] According to FAO in 2008-09, 125 million tonnes of cereals were diverted to produce biofuels. Around 40 per cent of the maize in the US is being converted into ethanol.[26]

The former president of the World Bank, Paul Wolfowitz, said,

"Biofuels are an opportunity to add to the world supply of energy to meet the enormous growing demand, and hopefully to mitigate some of the price effect. It's an opportunity to do so in an environmentally friendly way and in a way that is carbon neutral."

In 2008, Robert Zoellick, current president of the World Bank stated,

"While many worry about filling their gas tanks, many others around the world are struggling to fill their stomachs. And it's getting more and more difficult every day."

Even when non-food crops such as jatropha are used, food-growing land is diverted to biofuel production. Our study, "Food *vs* Fuel", shows how pastures and common lands in Rajasthan, and rice-growing land in the tribal areas of Chhattisgarh were appropriated for jatropha cultivation for bio-diesel.[27]

There are new discussions about second generation biofuels which will use cellulosic biomass rather than food and forest produce, and agricultural bio-products such as wheat and maize straw. These are not expected to reach the market before 2018. The challenge is to separate the cellulose from the legnin and reduce it to simpler sugars by applying intense heat or strong chemicals. But if plantations are grown for biofuel, they will also divert land from agriculture which could have produced food for local communities. If agricultural by-products like straw are diverted to biofuels, no organic matter will be returned to the soil, thus having a negative impact on soil fertility and food security.

Biofuel markets accounted for $76 billion dollars in sales in 2010 and are expected to rise to $247 billion by 2020, and $280 billion by 2022.[28] The diversion of food to biofuel is built into the reduction of food to a commodity which flows to wherever more profits can be made. That is why the commodification of food has gone hand-in-hand with its diversion to feed and fuel.

World Cereal Production and "End Use"

	2007-08 million tonnes	2008-09 million tonnes	% Change	Change 2007/08 – 2008/09
Total production	2132	2287	+1.3%	155 m tonnes
Total utilisation	2120	2202		
Food	1013	1029	+1.5%	+16 m tonnes
Annual feed	748	773	+3.3%	+25 m tonnes
Other uses (including biofuel)	359	401	+11.7%	+42 m tonnes

Source: FAO

In 2008-09, cereals produced were used more for cattle-feed and biofuels (1,107 million tonnes) than for feeding people (1013 million tonnes).[29] Thus, in spite of an increase in food production, there have been food riots in 40 countries. It is estimated that over the period 2008-18, biofuels will account for 52 per cent of the increased demand for maize and wheat, and 32 per cent of that for oilseeds.[30]

Gene giants and seed monopolies

There are two ways in which corporate control is being introduced into Indian agriculture; the first is through the structural adjustment programmes of the World Bank; the second through WTO rules and dispute rulings.

Monopolies over seed are being established through mergers and cross-licencing arrangements. Monsanto now controls the world's biggest seed company, Seminis, which has bought up Peto Seed, Bruinismo, Genecorp, Barhan, Horticere, Agroceres, Royal Suis, Choon Ang, Hungnong. Other seed acquisitions and joint ventures of Monsanto are: Asgrow, De Rinter, Monsoy, FT Sementes, Carma, Advanta Canola, China Seed, CNDK, ISG, Wertern, Protec, Calgene, Deltapine Land, Syngenta Global Cotton Division, Agracetus, Marneot, EID Parry Rallis, CDM Mandiyu, Ciagro, Renessan, Cargill, Terrazawa, Cargill International Seed Division, Hybritech, Jacob Hartz 1995, Agriprowheat, Cotton States, Linagrain Canada, Alypanticipacoes, First Line, Mahyco, Corn States International, Corn States Hybrid, Agroeste, Seusako, Emergent Genetics, Mahendra, Indusem, Darhnfeldt, Paras, Unilever, Dekelb, Lustum, Farm Seed, Deklbayala, Ayala, Polon, Ecogen, PBIC.

In addition, Monsanto has cross-licencing arrangements with BASF, Bayer, DuPont, Sygenta and Dow. They have agreements to share patented genetically engineered seed traits with each other; giant seed corporations are not competing with each other, they are competing with peasants and farmers over the control of seed supply.

In 2004, two laws were proposed – a Seed Act and a Patent Ordinance which could forever destroy the biodiversity of our seeds and crops, and rob farmers of all freedom by establishing a seed dictatorship. Eighty per cent of all seed in India is still saved by farmers whose indigenous varieties are the basis of our ecological and food security. Coastal farmers have evolved salt-resistant varieties; Bihar and

World's Top Ten Seed Companies

Company	2007 seed sales (US $ million)	% of global propriety seed market
Monsanto (US)	$ 4694	23%
DuPont (US)	$ 3300	15%
Syngenta (Switzerland)	$ 2018	9%
Groupe Linagrain (France)	$ 1226	6%
Land O'Lakes (US)	$ 917	4%
KWS AG (Germany)	$ 702	3%
Bayer Corp (Germany)	$ 524	2%
Sahata (Japan)	$ 396	< 2%
DLF Trifolum (Denmark)	$ 391	< 2%
Takii (Japan)	$ 347	< 2%
Total	$ 14785	67%

ETC: "Who Owns Nature?" http://www.etcgroup.org/upload/publication

Bengal farmers have evolved flood-resistant varieties; farmers of Rajasthan and the semi-arid Deccan have evolved drought-resistant varieties; Himalayan farmers have evolved frost-resistant varieties. Pulses, millets, oilseeds, rice, wheat, vegetables, provide the diverse basis of our health and nutrition security. This is the sector being targeted by the Seed Act: the indigenous farmers' varieties of diverse crops – thousands of rice, hundreds of wheat, oilseeds such as linseed, sesame, groundnut, coconut, pulses including gahat, narrangi, rajma, urad, moong, masur, tur, vegetables and fruits. The Seed Act is designed to "enclose" the free economy of farmers' seed varieties and destroy it through compulsory registration, by making it illegal to plant unlicensed varieties, thereby making farmers dependent on a corporate monopoly of patented seed. The Seed Act is therefore the handmaiden of the Patent Amendment Acts which have introduced patents on seed.

New IPR laws are creating monopolies over seeds and plant genetic resources, and redefining seed saving and seed exchange that are the basic freedoms of farmers. There are many examples of how seed acts and the introduction of IPRs in various countries prevent farmers from engaging in their own seed production. Josef Albrecht, an organic farmer in Germany, was not satisfied with commercially available seed; he developed his own ecological varieties of wheat; ten other organic farmers from neighbouring villages took his wheat seeds. Albrecht was fined by his government because he traded in uncertified seed. He has challenged the penalty because he feels restricted in freely exercising his occupation as an organic farmer.

In Scotland, a large number of farmers grew seed potato and sold it to other farmers. They could, until the early 1990s, freely sell this to other seed potato growers, merchants, or farmers. In the 1990s, holders of plant breeders' rights issued notices to potato growers through the British Society of Plant Breeders and made the selling of seed potato by farmers illegal. They had to grow varieties under contract to the seed industry, which specified the price at which the contracting company would take back the crop and barred growers from selling it to anyone else. Soon, the companies started to reduce the acreage and prices; in 1994, seed potato bought from Scottish farmers for £140 was sold for more than double that price to English farmers, whilst the two sets of farmers were prevented from dealing directly with each other. Seed potato growers signed a petition complaining about the stranglehold of a few companies acting as a cartel. They also started selling non-certified seed directly to English farmers; the seed industry claimed they were losing £4 million in seed sales through these direct sales. In February 1995, the British Society of Plant Breeders proceeded with a high profile court case against a farmer from Aberdeenshire, who was forced to pay £30,000 as compensation to cover lost royalties by direct farmer-to-farmer exchange. Existing United Kingdom and European Union laws thus prevent farmers from exchanging uncertified seed as well as protected varieties.

In the US, as well, farmer-to-farmer exchange has been made illegal. Dennis and Becky Winterboer owned a 500-acre farm in Iowa; since 1987, they had derived a sizeable portion of their income from 'brown-bagging' sales of their crops, i.e., selling the harvest as seed to other farmers. Asgrow (now owned by Monsanto which has plant variety protection for its soybean seeds) filed a suit against them for violation of its property rights. The Winterboers argued that they had acted within the law since the Plant Variety Act allowed farmers to sell seed provided both the farmer and seller were farmers. Subsequently, in 1994, the Plant Variety Act was amended and the farmers' privilege to save and exchange seed suspended, establishing an absolute monopoly of the seed industry by making farmer-to-farmer exchange and sales illegal.

In India, the entire country is being taken for a ride with the introduction of a similar law, the Seed Act, 2004, on the grounds of guaranteeing seed quality. However, the Seed Act, 1966, already performs the function of seed testing and certification, for which twenty laboratories have been identified in different states; nine seed corporations have been identified as certification agencies. Under pressure from the World Bank the seed policy of 1988 started to dismantle our robust public sector seed supply system, which accounted for 20 per cent of the seeds that farmers grow. Eighty per cent of the seed prior to globalisation was the farmers' own varieties which have been saved, exchanged and reproduced freely and have guaranteed our food security.

GMOs: a false solution to hunger

Genetically Modified Organisms continue to be promoted as the only solution to hunger and food security. However, the tools of genetic engineering merely transfer genes across species boundaries; they are not tools of breeding, which is still done through conventional methods that also determine the yield of a crop. Yield is a multigenetic trait, and genetic engineering cannot deal with complex traits. The report, "Failure to Yield", of the Union of Concerned Scientists shows that in no crop has genetic engineering contributed to yield increase. The yield trait comes from the variety into which a GM trait is introduced.[31]

Over twenty years of the commercialisation of GMOs, two traits account for most genetic modification.These are crops into which a gene has been added to resist herbicides or to resist pests (Bt. crops); the former are supposed to control weeds, the latter to control pests. However, these crops have led to the evolution of super weeds and the creation of super pests. Monsanto, which controls 95 per cent of all GM seeds sold, introduced Round-up Ready Crops for herbicide resistance. When super weeds started to overtake the crops, Monsanto introduced Round-Up Ready II. In 2010, it introduced Smart Stax with eight toxic genes – six for insecticides and two for herbicide resistance. Its strategy was to "create a captive customer base", but it was a failure. Monsanto lost 47 per cent of its shares, and is paying US farmers $12/acre to deal with the problems created by its GM seeds. The solution is the use of lethal herbicides like 2,4-D, an ingredient of Agent Orange which was used in the Vietnam war. If one toxic gene does not control pests, stacking six insecticidal genes will only accelerate the emergence of resistance. Monsanto, and others who promote GMOs, forget Einstein's observation that insanity means doing the same thing over and over again and expecting a different result.

Another serious result of GMOs is the destruction of biodiversity and the creation of monocultures and monopolies. India had 1,500 varieties of cotton; today 95 per cent of the cotton grown is Bt. cotton, most of it owned and controlled by Monsanto through licencing arrangements. Monsanto charges Rs. 50 lakhs as an initial licence fee, and then royalty. When Bt. cotton was introduced, prices of cotton seed jumped from Rs. 5/kg. to Rs. 1,600/450 gms. of which the royalty was Rs. 725. If this extraction of super profits had continued, it translated into an annual transfer of Rs. 1,000 crores or Rs. 10 billion from poor Indian farmers to Monsanto. For the farmer this means debt, and debt has pushed 250,000 farmers to suicide over the past fifteen years. Most of these suicides are concentrated in the cotton belt, and most of the cotton grown is now GMO cotton. An anti-trust case against Monsanto filed by the government of Andhra Pradesh has forced the company to reduce the price of Bt. cotton, but the introduction of Bollgard II has pushed the prices up again.

Another serious issue is conflict of interest. In India, the same scientists who promote GMOs sit on regulatory bodies. When the environment minister asked the six national academies of science to provide their scientific inputs for the Bt. brinjal moratorium in 2010, what they submitted was propaganda material lifted verbatim from industry literature. Even in Europe, the revolving door exists between industry and regulatory bodies. Suzy Renkins, who worked for the European Food Safety Authority, was also associated with Syngenta; Dr. Harry Kruper, the chair of an EFSA panel, was also involved in a research programme involving Bayer, Monsanto and Syngenta. The situation is worse in the US where the biotechnology industry literally runs all government agencies – that is why the US government tried to sue Europe in the WTO for the GMO bans in some countries. We had to organise a massive global campaign beginning in 2003, and submitted 60 million signatures to WTO at the Hong Kong ministerial conference to prevent the removal of the bans. News released through WikiLeaks reveals that the US Ambassador, Craig Stapleton, urged then President George Bush to start a military style trade war against GM-sceptics in Europe. "Country team Paris recommends that we calibrate a target retaliation list that causes some pain across the EU since this is a collective responsibility, but that also focuses in part on the worst culprits," he wrote. Nina Fedroff, technology advisor to the US government, State Department, was sent to India in February 2010 to try and prevent the moratorium on Bt. brinjal. At a biotechnology industry conference, a US State Department official said, "We will aggressively confront the naysayers around the world."

India is planning to replace the rules under the Environment Protection Act with a Biotechnology Regulatory Authority of India (BRAI) Act, which would give fast-track approvals to GMOs and throw critics into jail. The recently-appointed minister for science and technology, Ashwini Kumar, has announced that the government is planning to introduce four bills in Parliament, namely Biotechnology Regulatory Authority of India Bill; DNA Profiling Bill; Regional Centre for Biotechnology Bill; and Public Funded R&D (Protection and Utilisation of Public Funded Intellectual Property) Bill. The Prime Minister's Office has written to the states to establish partnerships with corporations in the seed sector; Monsanto has signed MoUs with six states.

A failed and hazardous technology such as genetic engineering can only be pushed through by dictatorial means; GMOs and democracy cannot co-exist. GMO-free food and agriculture are necessary for creating food security and defending food democracy.

Failed technology, false promises

Navdanya's research in India has shown that contrary to Monsanto's claim of Bt. cotton yield of 1,500 kgs. per acre, the reality is that the yield averages 400-500 kgs. per acre. Although Monsanto's Indian advertising campaign reports a 50 per cent increase in yields for its Bollgard cotton, a survey conducted by the Research Foundation for Science, Technology and Ecology found that the yields in all trial plots were lower than that promised by the company. Bollgard's failure to deliver higher yields has been reported all over the world. The Mississippi Seed Arbitration Council ruled that, in 1997, Monsanto's Round-up Ready cotton failed to perform as advertised, recommending payments of nearly $2 million to three cotton farmers who suffered severe crop losses. Australian research shows that conventional crops outperform GM crops.

Yield Comparison of GM Canola Trials in Australia

	2001	
Conventional	1144	
Round-Up Ready GM	1055	(two applications of Round-Up)
	977	(one application of Round-Up)

Source: http://www.non-gm-farmers.com/documents/gmcanola

New South Wales

	2001
In Vigor (GM)	109
Hyola (Conventional)	120

Source: Bayer Crop Science Website

Despite Monsanto adding the Round-Up Ready gene to 'elite varieties', the best Australian trials of Round-Up Ready Canola yielded only 1.055 t/ha, at least 16 per cent below the national average of 1.23 t/ha.[32]

As Marc Lappe and Britt Bailey report in their book, *Against the Grain*, herbicide-resistant soybeans yielded 36 to 38 bushels per acre, while hand-tilled soybeans yielded 38.2 bushels per acre, which raises the possibility that the gene inserted into these engineered plants may selectively disadvantage their growth when herbicides are not applied. "If true, data such as these cast doubt on Monsanto's principal point that their genetic engineering is both botanically and environmentally neutral."[33]

While increased food productivity is the argument used to promote genetic engineering, when the issue of potential adverse impacts on farmers is brought up, the biotechnology industry itself argues that genetic engineering does not lead to increased productivity. Thus Robert Shapiro, CEO of Monsanto, while referring to Posilac (Monsanto's bovine growth hormone) in *Business Ethics,* said on the one hand that, "There is need for agricultural productivity, including dairy productivity, to double if we want to feed all the people who will be joining us, so I think this is unequivocally a good product." On the other hand, when asked about the product's economic impact on farmers, he said that it would "play a relatively small role in the process of increasing dairy productivity".[34]

Bt. crops: a recipe for super pests

Bt. (*Bacillus thuringiensis*) is a naturally occurring organism which produces a toxin; corporations are now adding genes for Bt. toxins to a wide array of crops to enable the plants to produce their own insecticide. Monsanto sells its Bt. potato as Nature Mark in Canada, and describes it as a plant using "sunshine, air and soil nutrients to make a biodegradable protein that affects just one specific insect pest, and only those individual insects that actually take a bite of the plants". The camouflaged description of a transgenic crop hides many of the ecological impacts of genetically engineered crops. The illusion of sustainability is manufactured through the following distortions.

1. The Bt. plant does not merely use "sunshine, air and soil nutrients"; it is transgenic and has a gene from the Bt. bacteria which produces the Bt. toxin. In addition, it has antibiotic resistance marker genes and genes from viruses as promoters.
2. The so-called "biodegradable protein" is actually a toxin which the gene continuously produces in the plant. It has been found in the blood of pregnant women and their foetuses.
3. Insect pests, like the cotton bollworm which destroys cotton, can actually develop resistance because of continuous release of the toxin and hence become 'super pests'. Monsanto has admitted this has happened in India and has now introduced Bollgard II.
4. The Bt. crop does not affect "just one specific pest" but also beneficial insects like bees and ladybirds. A Cornell University study showed that Bt. toxin affected the Monarch butterfly; Navdanya's studies have shown that soil micro-organisms are negatively affected.

Bt. cotton is among the 'miracles' being pushed by corporations like Monsanto as a solution to the pesticide crisis. One of its brochures had a picture of a few worms and stated, "You will see these in your cotton and that's ok. Don't spray." However, in Texas, Monsanto faced a law suit filed by 25 farmers who suffered cotton bollworm damage on 18,000 acres, and had to use pesticides in spite of the corporate propaganda that genetic engineering meant an end to the pesticide era.

The widespread use of Bt-containing crops could accelerate the development of insect-pest resistance to Bt. which is used for organic pest control. Already eight species of insects have developed resistance to Bt. toxins, either in the field or laboratory, including diamond-back moth, Indian meal moth, tobacco budworm, Colorado potato beetle and two species of mosquitoes. Bt. crops continuously express the Bt. toxin throughout the growing season, and long-term exposure develops resistance in insect populations which could lead to resistance in all stages of the insect pest, on all parts of the plant, for the entire season.

Due to this risk of pest resistance, the US Environment Protection Agency offers only conditional and temporary registration of varieties producing Bt., and requires four per cent 'refugia' with Bt. cotton, i.e., four per cent of conventional planted cotton which does not express the Bt. toxin. It therefore acts as a refuge for insects to survive and breed, and hence keeps the overall level of resistance in the population low. Even at a four per cent refugia level, insect resistance will evolve in as little as three to four years.

Herbicide-resistant crops: a recipe for super weeds

In 1994, research scientists in Denmark reported strong evidence that an oilseed rape plant, genetically engineered to be herbicide-tolerant, transmitted its transgene to a weedy natural relative, *Brassica campestris ssp. Campestris*. This transfer can take place over just two generations of the plant. In Denmark, *B.campestris* is a common weed in cultivated oilseed rape fields, where selective elimination by herbicides is now impossible. Its wild relative is spread over large parts of the world. One way to assess the risk of releasing transgenic oilseed rape is to measure the rate of natural hybridisation with *B.campestris*, because certain transgenes could make its wild relative a more aggressive weed, even harder to control.

But natural inter-specific crosses with oilseed rape was generally thought to be rare. Artificial crosses by hand pollination carried out in a risk assessment project in the UK were reportedly unsuccessful.

However, a few studies have reported spontaneous hybridisation between oilseed rape and the parental species, *B.campestris*, in field experiments and, as early as 1962, hybridisation rates of 0-8.8 per cent were measured. The results of the Danish team showed that high levels of hybridisation can occur in the field; their tests revealed that between 9 to 93 per cent of hybrid seeds were produced under different conditions.[35]

Scientists also warn that as the gene for herbicide resistance is likely to be transferred to the weed, this strategy will be useless after a few years. Like many other weeds, *B.campestris* is characterised by seed dormancy and longevity; therefore, *B.campestris* with transgenes from oilseed rape may be preserved for many years in spite of efforts to exterminate it. They conclude that weedy *B.campestris* with this herbicide-tolerant transgene may present economic risks to farmers and the biotechnology industry. Finally, natural ecosystems may also be affected. Other concerned scientists add that the potential spread of the transgene will indeed be wide because oilseed rape is insect-pollinated and bees are known to fly long distances; its existence in large parts of the world poses serious hazards once the transgenic oilseed rape is marketed commercially. In response to the Danish findings, the governments of Denmark and Norway have acted against the commercial planting of the engineered plant, but the UK government has approved its marketing.

Wild beets have become a major problem in European sugar beet production since the 1970s. These weedy populations arise from seeds originating from the accidental pollination of cultivated beets by adventitious beets. The existence of gene exchange via seed and pollen between weed beets and cultivated beets shows genetically engineered sugar beets to be herbicide resistant; this would broaden the niche for weeds and create super weeds resistant to herbicides. The efficacy of herbicide-resistant crops would therefore be totally undermined.[36]

Current surveys indicate that almost 20 per cent of US producers have found glyphosate-resistant weeds on their farms.[37] Referring to Round-Up resistant weeds, Andrew Wargo III, president of the

Arkansas Association of Conservation Districts said, "It is the single largest threat to production agriculture that we have ever seen."[38] There are now ten resistant species in at least twenty-two states, infesting millions of acres, predominantly soyabean, cotton and corn; weeds include pigweed, ragweed and horseweed. Today Round-Up Ready crops account for 90 per cent soyabean and 70 per cent corn and cotton grown.

The problem of super weeds is so severe that US Congress was forced to organise a hearing on it titled, "Are Super Weeds an Outgrowth of USDA Biotech Policy?"[39] Roy Troush, an Indiana farmer, stated in his testimony,

> In 2005 we first began to encounter problems with glyphosate resistance in the plants, marestant and lambs quarters, in both our soybean and corn crops. Despite well-documented proof that glyphosate-tolerant weeds were becoming a significant problem, the Monsanto scientist instructed me to increase my application rates. The increase in application proved ineffectual. In 2008, we were forced to include the use of 2,4-D and an AIS residual in our program. Like most farmers, we are very sensitive to environmental issues, and we were very reluctant to return to using tillage and more toxic herbicides for weed control. However, no other solutions were then or now readily available to eradicate the weed problems caused by development of glyphosate resistance.[40]

When introduced to countries such as China, Taiwan, Japan, Korea and the former USSR, where wild relatives of soya are found, Monsanto's Round-Up Ready soya bean could transfer the herbicide-resistant genes to wild relatives leading to new weed problems. The native biodiversity richness of the South thus increases the environmental risks of genetically modified species.

Reduced use of chemicals

Despite claims that GMOs will lower the levels of chemicals (pesticides and herbicides) used, this has not been the case. A survey was conducted by Navdanya of Bt. cotton-growing areas in Vidharbha. Twenty-five fields were selected where Bt. cotton had been grown for three years, and compared with the adjoining fields which grew either other varieties of cotton or other crops. The survey covered areas between Nagpur, Amravati, Wardha and adjoining areas. The result showed significant reduction in acid phosphatase (26.6 per cent), nitrogenase (22.6 per cent) and dehydrogenase (10.3 per cent) activities under Bt. cotton-growing fields. A slight reduction in esterase (7.6 per cent) and alkaline phosphatase (0.7 per cent) activity was observed, but the results are not statistically significant. The results clearly demonstrated that Bt. cotton cultivation definitely affects soil biological health, especially beneficial micro-organisms (actinomycetes, bacteria) and enzymes (acid phosphatase, nitrogenase and dehydrogenase).[41]

In India

- A study recently published in the *Review of Agrarian Studies* also showed a higher expenditure on chemical pesticides for Bt. cotton than for other varieties for small farmers.[42]
- Non-target pest populations in Bt. cotton fields have exploded, which will likely counteract any decrease in pesticide use.[43]

In China

- Populations of mirid bugs, pests that previously posed only a minor problem, have increased twelve-fold since 1997. A 2008 study in the *International Journal of Biotechnology* found that any financial benefits of planting Bt. cotton had been eroded by the increased use of pesticides needed to combat non-target pests.[44]

In the US

- Herbicide use increased 15 per cent (318 million additional pounds) from 1994 to 2005 – an average increase of 0.25 pound per each acre planted with GM seeds – according to a 2009 report published by the Organic Center.[45]
- The same report found that in 2008, GM crops required

26 per cent more pounds of pesticides per acre than acres planted with conventional varieties, and projects that this trend will continue due to the spread of glysophate-resistant weeds.[46] This made it necessary to combat these weeds by employing other, often more toxic, herbicides. This trend is confirmed by 2010 USDA pesticide data which show skyrocketing glysophate use accompanied by constant or increasing rates of use for other, more toxic, herbicides.[47]

- Moreover, the introduction of Bt. corn in the US has had no impact on insecticide use, and while Bt. cotton is associated with a decrease in insecticide use in some areas, insecticide applications in Alabama, where Bt. cotton is planted widely, doubled between 1997 and 2000.[48]

In Argentina
- Overall glysophate use more than tripled by 2005-06. A 2001 report found that Round-up Ready soya growers in Argentina used more than twice as much herbicide as conventional soya growers.[49]
- In 2007, a glysophate-resistant version of Johnsongrass (considered one of the worst and most difficult weeds in the world) was reported on over 120,000 hectares of prime agricultural land – a consequence of the increase in glysophate use. As a result, it was recommended that farmers use a mix of herbicides other than glysophate to combat the resistant weeds, and it is estimated that an additional 25 litres of herbicides will be needed each year to control them.

In Brazil
- GM crops became legally available in 2005, and now make up 45 per cent of all row crops planted in Brazil – a percentage that is only expected to increase.[50]
- Of 18 herbicide-resistant weed species reported, five are glysophate resistant.[51]
- In 2009, total herbicide active ingredient use was 18.7 per cent higher for GM crops than conventional.[52]

Climate resilience

Monsanto has been claiming that through genetic engineering it can breed crops for drought tolerance and other climate-resilient traits. This is a false promise. As the US Department of Agriculture (USDA) has said in its draft environmental assessment of the new drought-resistant GE corn, "Equally comparable varieties produced through conventional breeding techniques are readily available in irrigated corn production reviews."[53] Helen Wallace of GeneWatch, UK cautions: "The GE industry must now stop its cynical attempts to manipulate the public into believing that GE crops are needed to feed the world."[54]

Other biotech industries also falsely claim that they are inventing climate-resilient traits. Ram Kaundiya, CEO of Advanta, India, and chairman of Biotech Led Enterprises – Agriculture Group writes,

> Very exciting input traits are in the pipeline. For example, water-use efficiency trait, which will reduce the water requirements of the crops considerably and can help vast numbers of farmers who cultivate rainfed crops in the country in more than 100 million ha. Similarly, the nitrogen-use efficiency trait, which will reduce the use of nitrogenous fertiliser on the crops by an estimated 30 per cent. Another trait that is waiting in the wings is salt tolerance trait, which can help farmers grow crops in saline soils of more than 20 million ha. in India.[55]

All these traits have already been evolved by Indian farmers. Navdanya's seed collections have drought-tolerant varieties like nalibakuri, kalakaya, atia, inkiri, etc.; flood-tolerant varieties like nalidhulia, ravana, seulapuni, dhosarakhuda, etc; and salt-tolerant varieties like bhundi, kalambank, lunabakada, sankarchin, etc. Pulses and beans are nitrogen fixing crops. None of these traits is "invented" by genetic engineering, they are pirated from nature and farmers. There are 1,600 patents on climate-resilient crops.[56]

Safety

Among the false claims made by Monsanto and the biotechnology industry is that GM foods are safe. There are enough independent studies to show that GE foods can cause serious health damage. The Committee of Independent Research and Information on Genetic Engineering (CRIGEN) and universities at Caen and Rouen were able to get raw data on Monsanto's 2002 feeding trials on rats, ordered by the European Council, and made it public in 2005. The researchers found that rats fed with three approved GE corn varieties – Mon 863, Mon 810, and Round-up Ready herbicide–absorbing HK 603 – were linked to organ damage. The data "clearly underlines adverse impacts on kidneys and liver, the dietary detoxifying organs, as well as different levels of damage to the heart, adrenal glands, spleen and haematopoetic systems," according to Dr. Gilles Eric Seralina, a molecular biologist at the University of Caen.[57]

A Canadian study has shown that traces of Bt. toxin from Monsanto Bt. corn were found in the blood of 93 per cent women and in 80 per cent of their umbilical cord and foetal blood.[58] Monsanto's false argument for safety was that Bt. toxin in Bt. crops poses no danger to human health because the protein breaks down in the human gut. However, the study shows that the Bt. toxin survives in the blood of pregnant women and is also detected in foetal blood.

Evidence was found of liver and kidney toxicity when rats were fed an approved GM maize variety (Mon 863).[59] Similar effects were observed when Monsanto fed its GT-73 Round-up Ready canola variety to rats – they showed a 12-16 per cent increase in liver weight.[60]

In 2005, the Council for Scientific and Industrial Research in India abandoned a decade-long project to develop GM peas after tests showed they caused allergic lung damage in mice.[61]

In general, the main health concerns for humans are toxicity and allergenicity; even the WHO cautions that,

> Different GM organisms include different genes inserted in different ways. This means that individual GM foods and their safety should be assessed on a case-by-case basis, and that it is

not possible to make general statements on the safety of all GM foods."[62]

The myth of substantial equivalence

The safety debate has been repeatedly suppressed by bad science parading as 'sound science'. One of the unscientific strategies used to extinguish the safety discussion is to tautologically define a novel organism or novel food created through genetic engineering as 'substantially equivalent' to conventional organisms and foods. However, a GE crop or food is different because it has genes from unrelated organisms. In fact, the biotechnology industry itself gives up the claim of substantial equivalence when it claims patents on GMOs on grounds of novelty. While governments and government agencies refer to 'sound science' as the basis for their decisions, they are manipulating scientific data and research to promote genetic engineering and the interests of the biotechnology industry, at the risk of citizen health and the environment. The report of the scientists of EPA titled, *Genetic Gene: the premature commercial release of genetically engineered bacteria* and the report by Andrew Christiansen, *Recombinant Bovine Growth Hormone: alarming tests, unfounded approval: the story behind the rush to bring RBGH to the market* show, in detail, how regulatory agencies have been manipulated on issues of safety.[63]

The scientific corruption by the biotech industry and the sacrifice of knowledge sovereignty began in 1992 with the concoction of the false principle of substantial equivalence; this was introduced by President Bush in US policy immediately after the Earth Summit in Rio, to blunt the call for biosafety regulation and undo the articles in the Convention on Biological Diversity. It was later formalised and introduced in 1993 by the UN Organisation for Economic Cooperation and Development, and subsequently endorsed by the FAO and WHO. The OECD document states:

> For foods and food components from organisms developed by the application of modern biotechnology, the most practical approach to the determination is to consider whether they are

substantially equivalent to analogous food products, if such exist. The concept of substantial equivalence embodies the idea that existing organisms used as foods, or as a source of food, can be used as the basis for comparison when assessing the safety of human consumption of food or food component that has been modified or is new.

Apart from being vague, this definition is unsound. Foods with Bt. toxin genes are not the same as foods without; herbicide-resistant crops are different from existing varieties because they have introduced new genes. To treat these differences as insignificant when it is a question of safety, and as significant when it is a question of patentability, is totally unscientific. As Millstone, Brunner and Mayer have stated in "Beyond Susbtantial Equivalence",

> Substantial equivalence is a pseudo-scientific concept because it is a commercial and political judgment masquerading as if it were scientific. It is, moreover, inherently anti-scientific because it was created primarily to provide an excuse for not requiring biochemical or toxicological tests. It therefore serves to discourage and inhibit scientific research.
>
> –*Nature*, October 7, 1999

Scientific agencies have been split and polarised into two communities – a corporate science community and a public science community. The former participates in distorting and manipulating science, such as the assumption of substantial equivalence which is falsified both by the research done by the public science community as well as by the intellectual property rights claims of the biotechnology industry itself.

When industry wants to avoid risk assessment and issues of liability, the argument used is that the genetically engineered organism is substantially equivalent to the non-engineered parent. However, when industry wants property rights, the same GMO becomes 'novel' or substantially unequivalent to the parent organism. When these discourses of the genetic engineering industry are examined, what emerges is an unscientific, incoherent, undemocratic structure for total control through which absolute rights are claimed and all responsibility is denied and disclaimed. This ontological schizophrenia is based on and leads to incoherence, which is a characteristic of bad science. Good science is based on coherence. The consistency and incoherence between the discourse on property rights and on issues of safety contribute to an undemocratic structure in which there are no mechanisms to protect citizens from corporate irresponsibility.

A second unscientific concept used to ignore biosafety considerations is 'significance'. Thus the EPA has argued that because we are surrounded by bacteria, the risk of introducing pathogenic bacteria through gene transfer is not significant, and that as the problem of antibiotic resistance already exists, any new risk is insignificant. Yet another strategy used to suppress good science is in the design of trials, and the extrapolation of data from artificially constructed contexts to real ecosystems. The final strategy is direct arm-twisting. This was used repeatedly by the US administration to kill the Biosafety Protocol in the Convention on Biological Diversity (CBD), even though the US is not a party to the Convention. Despite this, the countries of the world adopted the Cartagena Protocol on Biosafety in 2000; the world also agreed to GMO labelling in the Codex Alimentarius. It is often claimed that there have been no adverse consequences from over 500 field releases in the US. However, the term 'releases' is completely misleading. The tests undertaken were largely unscientific, not of realistic ecological concerns, yet this sort of non-data on non-releases has been cited in policy circles, as though 500 true releases have now informed scientists that there are no legitimate scientific concerns.

Recently, for the first time, the data from the US Department of Agriculture field trials were evaluated by the Union of Concerned Scientists (UCS) to see whether they support the safety claims. They found that these data on small-scale tests have little value for commercial risk assessment. Many reports fail to even mention – much less measure – environmental risks, and of those that do, most have only visually scanned field plots looking for stray plants or isolated test crops from relatives. The UCS concluded that the observations that nothing happened in those hundreds of tests do not say much. In many cases, adverse impacts are subtle and would never be registered by scanning a field; in other cases, failure to observe evidence of the risk is due to the contained conditions of the tests. Many test crops are routinely isolated from wild relatives, a situation that guarantees no out-crossing. The UCS cautioned that "…care should be taken in citing the field test record as strong evidence for the safety of genetically engineered crops".[64]

Genetic contamination is inevitable, co-existence impossible

At a recent conference in Washington DC on the future of farming, US secretary of agriculture, Tom Vilsack, referring to organic farming and GMOs said, "I have two sons, I love them both and I want them to coexist." Filmmaker Debra Grazia responded from the floor, "But one of your sons is a bully."

GMOs contaminate non-GM crops. Contamination is inevitable, since cross-pollination is inevitable within the same species or with close relatives. The most dramatic case of contamination and genetic pollution is that of Percy Schmeiser, a Canadian canola seed grower, whose crop was contaminated by Monsanto's Round-Up Ready canola. Instead of paying Percy for the damage of contamination in accordance with the "polluter pays" principle, Monsanto sued Percy for "intellectual property theft". The contamination of canola in Canada is so severe that 90 per cent of certified non-GM canola seed samples contain GM material.[65] As Arnold Taylor, chair of the Organic Agriculture Protection Fund said, "There is no organic canola in Canada any more, virtually none, because the seed stock is basically contaminated … we've lost that crop."[66] Canadian researchers tested 33 samples of certified non-GM canola seed and found 32 samples contaminated with GM varieties – with three samples having contamination levels of more than two per cent.[67]

Another study in the US found that virtually all samples of non-GM corn, soya beans and canola seed were contaminated by GM varieties.[68]

A study in the UK found that GM canola cross-pollinated with non-GM canola more than 26 kms. away.[69]

An Australian study found that gene-carrying pollen from GM canola can travel up to 3 kms. on wind or insects. The present isolation distance in Canada between GM and non-GM canola is a mere 100 metres. In a 2007 report by the Network of Concerned Farmers on the economies of genetically modified canola, it was assessed that if GM canola was introduced in Australia and 20 per cent farmers adopted it, non-GM farmers would suffer losses of $65.52 million due to contamination.[70] In December 2010 organic farmer, Steve Marsh, in Australia lost his organic status because his harvest was found contaminated with the genetically modified Round-Up Ready canola of Monsanto.[71]

In June 2006, trace amounts of Bayer's experimental genetically engineered liberty link rice was found to have contaminated 30 per cent of the rice-land in Texas, Louisiana, Missouri, Arkansas and Mississippi. Trials for the GM rice were being undertaken by Bayer and Louisiana State University at Crowley (La.) Within four days, the news of contamination led to a decline in futures prices by 14 per cent, costing growers $150 million. Exports fell as the European Union, Japan and Russia stopped importing long-grain rice grown in the US; 11,000 US rice farmers sued Bayer for contaminating their rice and ruining their exports. On July 1, Bayer agreed to pay the farmers $750 million to settle.[72]

The contamination has spread to Japanese ecosystems. A report of the Japanese Institute for Environmental Studies (JIES) confirmed that herbicide-resistant genetically engineered canola plants had escaped into Japanese ecosystems at major shipping ports along the Japanese coast.[73]

As early as 1997, GM maize was found growing in Mexico (where it is not approved.) This is doubly worrisome because Mexico is the centre of origin for corn. Contamination was ultimately found in nine states, with levels as high as 33 per cent.[74] In 2001, D. Quist and I. Chapela of the University of Mexico published a study in *Nature*, "Transgenic DNA Introgressed into Traditional Maize Land in Oaxaca,

Mexico." Their study showed that native maize had been contaminated by GM corn.[75] (Mexico is where corn was domesticated and where the highest diversity of corn exists. According to the government, the contamination took place when farmers planted corn imported from the US, not knowing it was genetically modified.) In April 2002, the Mexican government confirmed the contamination of native corn by GM corn. Jorge Sobiron, secretary of Mexico's Biodiversity Commission stated, "This is the world's worst case of contamination by genetically modified material because it happened in the place of origin of a major crop. It is confirmed. There is no doubt about it."[76]

In 2003, native corn in Mexico was found contaminated by genetically manipulated varieties in cornfields in the states of Chihuaha, Morelos, Durango, Mexico State, Puebla, Oaxaca, San Luis Potosi, Tlaxcale and Veracruz. The analysis was carried out by a coalition of farmers' organisations, and contamination was as high as 33 per cent in some samples.

In 2000, Starlink Corn, a GM crop patented by Aventis (newly acquired by Bayer) which had not been approved for human consumption, was found in supermarket products in the US, when a coalition of environmental groups commissioned a testing of corn products. This Bt. corn has toxic genes to produce an insecticide protein (Cry 9c 2000.) More than 70 types of corn chips and 80 types of taco shells had to be recalled, leading to major disruptions in US and international markets.

The peaceful coexistence of GMOs and conventional crops is a myth: environmental contamination via cross-pollination, which poses a serious threat to biodiversity, is unavoidable. GM pollen can potentially cross-pollinate with both non-GM crops and weeds, creating pest-resistant super weeds. Insects and wind can carry pollen over kilometres, and the seeds can lie in the soil for years before germinating. Moreover, there is no sure way to prevent human error or illegal planting of GM seeds.[77] Separating fields of GM and non-GM seeds is not a sufficient precaution: low levels of pollution can be found as far as several hundred metres away, and it's difficult to draw the line at which contamination can be prevented.

- In Canada, there have been numerous reports of GM canola sprouting up where it wasn't planted, and tests found GM genes in over 50 per cent of canola plants. Similar reports exist from Japan, the US and Australia.[78]
- In the US, an estimated 50 per cent of maize seeds, 50 per cent of cotton seeds, and 80 per cent of canola seeds now contain GM DNA, according to a study by the Union of Concerned Scientists.
- In Hawaii, 30-50 per cent of papaya was found to be ontaminated with GM genes.[79]
- In 2004, GM papaya field trials in Thailand were found to be the source of widespread genetic contamination; more was found in 2005 after the Department of Agriculture claimed it had all been eradicated.[80]
- In 2005, 13,500 tonnes of maize in New Zealand were found to be contaminated by GM material during routine testing – the sixth such incident in three years.[81]
- In Japan in 2005, GM crops (corn, soya) were found growing all over ports as a result of seeds being spilled during unloading and transporation.[82]
- A 2004 report found widespread contamination of soya in Brazil.[83]

Right to know, right to choose

In June 1997, the US Trade Representative, Charlene Barshefshy, warned the European Union Agriculture Commissioner, Franz Fischler, not to go through with proposals requiring the labelling of GMOs or their segregation from regular products. She told the Senate Agriculture Committee that the US could not tolerate a step that would cause a major disruption in US exports to the EU. The EU Commissioner was under pressure from European consumers to label GMO foods as their democratic right to information and choice. However, consumer rights were defined by the US Trade Representative as "arbitrary, politicised and scientifically unjustified" rules. The insistence of consumers to pursue "non-science based restrictions" would lead to a "trade war of major dimensions". In a letter to the US Secreary of Agriculture on June 12, 1997, US agribusiness corporations stated that segregation of crops for labelling was both scientifically unjustified and commercially unfeasible.

According to US industry, the labelling of foods violates the WTO agreement on free trade; the sanitary and phyto-sanitary measures in WTO are thus viewed by industry as protecting their interests. The denial of labelling is one dimension of totalitarian structures associated with the introduction of genetical engineering in food and agriculture.

We filed a case in India in 2006 to demand labelling of GM foods. A law was drafted by the health ministry and labelling was made mandatory in June 2012.

On July 5, 2011, Codex Alimentarius, the international food safety body, recognised the right of countries to label GMO foods. This ended twenty years of struggle by citizens to the right to labelling of GM foods at the international level. As *Consumer International* states,

> The new Codex agreement means that any country wishing to adopt GM food labelling will no longer face the threat of a legal challenge from the World Trade Organization. This is because national measures based on Codex guidance or standards cannot be challenged as a barrier to trade.[84]

We now need to build on this Right to Know and ensure GMO labelling in all our countries.

GMOs and food democracy

Food democracy is everyone's right and responsibility, and we can only have it when we are able to exercise our choice to have GMO-free seed and food. This choice is being systematically undermined as seed is genetically engineered and patented, food systems are increasingly controlled by giant corporations, and chemical and genetic pollution spreads uncontrolled, making our food unsafe. Each of us must defend our food freedom and urge our governments to protect the rights of their citizens.

In February, 2010, then minister for environment, Jairam Ramesh, placed a moratorium on Bt. brinjal. In 2011 he was pushing trials of GM rubber onto Kerala, which is a GMO-free state. Kerala chief minister, V.S. Achuthanandan, and agriculture minister, Mullakkara Ratnakaran, have both reiterated their commitment to keep Kerala GMO-free. Jairam Ramesh stated that GM rubber is not transgenic, i.e., it does not have genes from unrelated species. This is totally false. The gene MnSOD, which comes from the rubber, is transgenic. It contains CaMV35s, a virus used as a promoter, an antibiotic resistance marker npt II (Kanamycin) and a CUS reporter gene from bacteria (E.coli.). Introducing viruses and bacteria into a plant is a transgenic transformation.

GM rubber is being developed to spread rubber cultivation to regions beyond Kerala by making it drought resistant. However, engineering drought resistance is linked to a "pleiotropic effect", which is the ability of a single genetic change to cause unintended physiological effects throughout a plant. Researchers pursuing genetically engineered drought tolerance are finding that these genes can have unpredictable and unwanted effects on other traits, including yield and quality. Like a sluggish computer that's overloaded with bloated software, the genes associated with drought tolerance slow down the plant's development, resulting in smaller plants and delayed flowering. According to a report by Australia's Grain Research & Development Corporation, "The flaw is a profound one. It amounts to shifting the yield losses experienced in dry seasons onto the good years."[85]

Researchers at the International Crops Research Institute for the Semi-Arid Tropics (ICRISAT) in India also report drawbacks to working with stress-responsive genes in transgenic crops. In a 2007 article they write:

> Evaluation of the transgenic plants under stress conditions and understanding the physiological effect of the inserted genes at the whole plant level, remain as major challenges to overcome. The genetic engineering is thus not a reliable technology for drought tolerance.[86]

Besides the ecological risks of adding viruses and bacteria into plants, GM rubber will promote monocultures and displace diversity. By replacing food crops in other regions it will aggravate the hunger crisis in India, which has deprived half the children and one-third of adults their share of adequate, safe and nutritious food.

The blind acceptance of GMOs as a solution to hunger is the real superstition because genetic engineering does not increase the yield of crops. It is a crude tool, based on reductionist science, which ignores the latest developments in the fields of gene ecology, epigenetics and agro-economy. The International Assessment of Agricultural Knowledge, Science and Technology for Development (IAASTD), carried out by four hundred scientists over four years for the UN, has categorically stated that the future of food security does not lie in genetic engineering; this is the largest and latest assessment of genetic engineering available from the scientific community. Genetic engineering is a sloppy technology based on bad science which fails to take into account the complexity and self-organisation of living systems.

As the Knowledge Manifesto of the International Commission on the Future of Food and Agriculture states, the following principles are now generally accepted by the scientific community: (a) living and non-living systems are all dynamically interconnected, with the consequence that any change in one element will necessarily lead to not fully predictable changes in other parts of the network; (b) variability is the basis of change and adaptation while its absence leads inevitably to death; (c) living systems actively change the environment and are changed by it in a reciprocal way. It is time to remove reductionist blinkers that allow genetic engineering to be seen as a sustainable and safe solution to hunger. We need real science and real sustainability, not the pseudo science and pseudo sustainability being offered by corporations and their scientists. The alternative to GM monocultures spreading across the country is promoting biodiverse ecological production, towards food security through increased nutrition per acre, as well as climate resilience.

The tools of corporate agribusiness are tools for profit, not science. Adopting the paradigms of corporate science is to fall prey to corporate superstitions.

References

1. P. J. Critzen, et al, "N_2O Release from Agro-biofuel Production Negates Global Warming Reduction by Replacing Fossil Fuels," *Atmospheric Chemistry and Physics Discussions*, 7: 11191-11205, 2007.

2. Caroline Lucas, et al, "Fuelling a Food Crisis," December 2006, and personal communication.

3. A.G. Williams, et al, "Determining the Environmental Burdens and Resource Use in the Production of Agricultural and Horticultural Commodities," Main Report, DEFRA Research Product ISO 205, Cranfield University and DEFRA.

4. D. Pimental, "Impact of Organic Farming on the Efficiency of Energy Use in Agriculture," Cornell University: The Organic Center, 2006.

5. E. E. Marriott and M. M. Wander, "Total and Liable Soil Organic Matter in Organic and Conventional Farming Systems," *Social Science Society Journal*, 70-950-59.

6. Johannes Kotschi and Karl Müller-Samann, "The Role of Organic Agriculture in Mitigating Climate Change: A Scoping Study," Bonn: IFOAM, p. 64, 2004.

7. Navdanya's "Financing the Water Crisis: World Bank, International Aid Agencies and Water Privatisation," Dehradun: RFSTE, 2005.

8. Henry Miller, *The Frankenfood Myth*, New York: Praeger, 2004.

9. www.dswcpunjab.gov.in

10. "Contaminated Ground Water in Punjab Causing DNA Mutations in People", November 30, 2007, http://www.theindianews.com.

11. J. P. Reganold, et al, "Long-term Effects of Organic and Conventional Farming on Soil Erosion", *Nature*, 330, 370-72, 1987.

12. P. Mader, et.al, "Soil Fertility and Biodiversity in Organic Agriculture", *Science*, 296, 1694–97.

13. Paul Hepperly, et.al, "The Rodale Farming System Trial, 1981-2005", in *International Society of Organic Agriculture Research* (ISOFAR), Bonn, 2008.

14. World Bank, "Rising Global Interest in Farmland", 2011.

15. M. Montenegro "Hungry for Land," *Seedling*, April 27, 2009.

16. Julian Cribb, *The Coming Famine*, Berkeley: University of California

Press, 2010, p. 51.

[17] J. Blas and W. Wallis, "US Investor Buys Sudanese Warlord's Land," *The Financial Times*, January 9, 2009.

[18] J. Godoy, "The Second Scramble for Africa Starts," Inter Press Service, April 20, 2009.

[19] GRAIN, "Seized: The 2008 Land-Grab for Food and Financial Security". www.grain.org/article/entries/93-seized-the-2008 landgrab-for-food-and-financial-security

[20] Ibid.

[21] Madeline Bunting, "How Land Grabs in Africa Could Herald a New Dystopian Age of Hunger" *The Guardian*, 2000.

[22] GRAIN, "Seized", op.cit.

[23] GRAIN, "Seized", op.cit.

[24] *Livemint*, November 1, 2010. www.livemint.com/2010/10/usindia-may-tie-up-to-tap-fa.html

[25] Action Aid, "Meals per Gallon," www.actionaid.org.uk/doc-lib meals-per-gallon-final.pdf

[26] http://triplecrisis.com/frenzy-in-food-markets/

[27] Vandana Shiva, *Soil Not Oil: Climate Change, Peak Oil and Food Insecurity*, Delhi: Women Unlimited, 2009.

[28] Alex Salkever, "Global Biofuels Market to Hit $247 Billion by 2020," *Daily Finance*, July 24, 2009.

[29] FAO 2009b, "Crop Prospects and Food Situation." http://www.fao.org/docrep/011/ai481a/ai481e04.htm and FAO 2009c; "Food Outlook," http://www.fao.org/docrep/011/ai 482e/ai 48202.htm; and Action Aid "Meals per Gallon."

[30] Organisation for Economic Cooperation and Development and FAO 2010, "Agricultural Outlook," Paris and Rome; "Rising Global Interest in Farmland," World Bank, 2011.

[31] www.ucsusn.org/assets/documents/food-and-failure-to-yield.pdf

[32] http://www.non-gm-farmers.com/document/gmcanola

[33] Marc Lappe and Britt Bailey, *Against the Grain: Biotechnology and the Corporate Takeover of Your Food*, Maine: Common Courage Press, 1998.

[34] Robert Shapiro interviewed by Mary Scott in *Business Ethics*, January-February, 1996.

[35] R.B. Jorgensen and B. Anderson, "Spontaneous Hybridization Between Oilseed Rape (*Brassica Napus*) and Weedy B. (*Campestris Brassicaceae*): A Risk of Growing Genetically Modified Oilseed Rape," *American Journal of Botany*, 1994.

[36] P. Bondry, et al, "The Origin and Evolution of Weed Beets: Consequences for the Breeding and Release of Herbicide-Resistant

Transgenic Sugar Beets": *Theor-Appl Genet* (1993), 87:471-78.

37 http://farmindustrynews.coms/crop-protection/diversification prevents-weed-resistance-glyphosate

38 William Neuman and Andrew Pollack, "Farmers Cope with Round-Up Resistance Weeds", *New York Times*, May 4, 2010.

39 http://westernfarmpress.com/management/superweeds-put usda-hotseat

40 http://westernpress.com/management/superweeds-put-usda-hotseat

41 Navdanya, "Effect on Soil Biological Activities due to Cultivation of Bt. Cotton", Delhi, 2008.

42 Madhura Swaminathan and Vikas Rawal "Are there Benefits from the Cultivation of Bt. Cotton?" *Review of Agrarian Studies* Vol 1(1) January-June 2011.

43 Glenn Davis Stone, "Field versus Farm in Warangal: Bt. Cotton, Higher Yields and Larger Questions." *World Development*, 2011; 39 (3): 387.

44 "Benefits of Bt. Cotton Elude Farmers in China." http: www.gmwatch.org/latest-listing/1-news-items/13089

45 http://www.organic-center.org/ science. pest.php?action=view&report_id=159

46 http://www.organic-center.org/ science.pest.php?action=view&report_id=159

47 GM Watch, "Despite Industry Claims, Herbicide Use Fails to Decline with GM Crops." . http://www.gmwatch.org/latest-listing/1-news items/13089

48 Charles Benbrook. "Do GM Crops Mean Less Pesticide Use?" *Pesticide Outlook*, October 2001. http://www.biotech-info.net/ brook_outlook.pdf

49 Friends of the Earth International, "Who Benefits from GM Crops? Feed the Biotech Giants, Not the World's Poor." February 2009. http:/ /www.foei.org/en/resources/publications/pdfs/2009 gmcrops2009exec.pdf

50 *Soybean and Corn Advisor*, "Brazilian Farmers are Rapidly Adopting Genetically Modified Crops." March 10, 2010. http: www.soybeansandcorn.com/news/Mar10_10-Brazilian-Farmers Are-Rapidly-Adopting-Genetically-Modified-Crops

51 GM Watch, "Use of Pesticides in Brazil Continues to Grow." April 18, 2011. http://www.gmwatch.org/latest-listing/1-news-items/ 13072-use-of-pesticides-in-brazil-continues-to-grow

52 Graham Brookes and Peter Barfoot, "GM Crops: Global Socio-economic and Environmental Impacts 1996-2009." P G Economics

Ltd. UK, 2011. http://www.pgeconomics.co.uk/../2010-global-gm-crop-impact-study-final

53 "USDA Looks to Approve Monsanto's Drought-Tolerant Corn," *New York Times*, May 11, 2011.

54 GeneWatch UK press release, "Drought-Tolerant GM Corn Will Not Feed the World," May 13, 2011.

55 Ram Kaundiya, "Bt.Brinjal and Biryani." www.thehindubusinessline.com/opinion, July 23, 2011.

56 Navdanya/RFSTE, "Biopiracy of Climate Resilient Crops: Gene Giants Steal Farmers' Innovation in Drought-Resistant, Flood-Resistant and Soil-Resistant Varieties," June 2009 & www.etcgroup.org

57 Joel Spiroux de Veu de Mois, et al, "A Comparison of the Effects of Three GM Corn Varieties on Mammalian Health," *International Journal of Biological Sciences*, 2009, 5: 706-726.

58 A. Aris and S. Leblanc, "Maternal and Fetal Exposure to Pesticides Associated to Genetically Modified Foods in Eastern Township of Quebec", *Reproductive Toxicology*, May 31, 2011 (4) 526-33, Epub 2011 Feb/8.

59 G.E. Seralin, et al, "New Analysis of Rat-Feeding Study with a GM Maize," Archives of Environmental Contamination and Toxicology, 10,1007, S 00244-006-01495, 2007.

60 Greenpeace Critique of Monsanto's Round-up Ready Oilseed Rape, GT-73, http://www.saveourseeds.org/downloads/9p-GT731-comments, 2004.

61 E. Young, "GM Pea Causes Allergic Damage in Mice," *New Scientist*, http://www.newscientist.com/article.ns

62 World Health Organization, "20 Questions on Genetically Modified Foods." http://www.who.int/foodsafety/publications/biotech/20questions/en/

63 Quoted in Navdanya, "The Biopiracy of Climate Resilient Crops", op.cit., p. 31.

64 Jane Rissler & Margaret Mellon, *The Ecological Risks of Engineered Crops*, Cambridge: MIT Press, 1996.

65 www.lynnmaclaren.org.au/media-release-major-grain-traders-reject-gm-canola

66 "GM Canola 'Contaminated' Canadian Farms," The Age.com.au, July 5, 2011.

67 L. Freisa, et al, "Evidence of Contamination of Pedigreed Canola Seed Lots in Western Canada with Genetically Engineered Herbicide Resistance Traits." *Agronomy Journal*, 95, 2003, pp. 1342-1347.

68 M. Mellon and J. Rissler, "Gone to Seed: Transgenic Contaminates in

the Traditional Seed Supply", Union of Concerned Scientists, 2004.

69 G. Ramsay, et al, "Quantifying Landscape-Scale Gene Flow in Oilseed Rape", Scottish Crop Research Institute and UK Department of Environment, Food and Rural Affairs (DEFRA), October 2004, p.4.www.defra.gov.uk/environment/gm/research/pdf/epg-rg0216.pdf

70 www.lynnmaclaren.org.au/media-release-major-grain-traders-reject-gm-canola

71 http://www.perthnow.com/au/news/special-features/gm-contamination-of-organic-crop-confirmed

72 "Bayer Settles with Farmers Over Modified Rice Seeds," *New York Times*, July 2, 2011. http://www.nytimes.com/2011/07/02/business/02rice.html, 2011.

73 http://www.greenpeace.org/international/en/publications/reports/canola-report

74 Silvia Rebeiro, "The Day the Sun Dies: Contamination and Resistance in Mexico". GRAIN.org. July 2004. http://www.grain.org/seedling/?id=292#_3

75 *Nature*, 414, 6863, November 29, 2001, pp. 541-543.

76 C. Clover, "Worst-ever GM Crop Invasion," *Daily Telegraph*, April 19, 2002; P. Brown, "Mexico's Vital Gene Reservoir Polluted by Modified Maize", *The Guardian*, April 19, 2002.

77 Friends of the Earth, "GM Contaminations Briefing." January, 2006. http://www.foe.co.uk/resource/briefing_notes/gene_escape.pdf

78 Special Report: "Genetically Modified Canola Contamination in Japan." Nishoren.org. October 29, 2010. http://www.nishoren.org en/?p=888

79 Hawaii SEED, "Hawaiian Papaya: GMO Contaminated," 2006. http://www.grain.org/research_files/Contamination_Papaya.pdf

80 http://www.greenpeace.org/international/en/news/features/ge papaya-010606

81 http://www.grain.org/research/contamination.cfm?id=337

82 http://www.grain.org/research/contamination.cfm?id=265

83 http://www.grain.org/research/contamination.cfm?id=164

84 http://foodfreedom.wordpress.com/2011/07/05/codex alimentarius-adopts-labeling-of-genetically-modified-foods/

85 Gio Braidotti, "Scientists Share Keys of Drought Tolerance", Grain Research and Development Corporation, Issue 72, January-February 2008.

86 Pooja Bhatnagar, et al, "Transgenic Approaches for Abiotic Stress Tolerance in Plants", *Plant Cell Reports*, 27 (3), 2008, p. 411.

8 Hunger via Corporate-Controlled Trade

THE URUGUAY ROUND agreement on agriculture should be called the Cargill agreement, as it was former Cargill vice-president, Dan Amstutz, who drafted the original text. Its primary aim was opening up southern markets and converting peasant agriculture into corporate agriculture; WTO rules are not just about trade, they determine how food is produced and who controls its production. For Cargill, capturing Asian markets is the key, as it happens to be the largest agricultural economy in the world, with the majority involved in agriculture. Converting self-sufficient food economies into food-dependent economies is the Cargill vision and the WTO strategy.

Because the WTO Agriculture Agreement is an *agribusiness* treaty it distorts production and trade from the perspective of nature, small farmers and all consumers, especially the poor, and is a recipe for ecological destruction, devastation of family farms and ruination of citizens' health. Behind the apparent neutrality of rules for "domestic support", "market access" and "export competition" lie distorted assumptions and myths about food production and distribution.

The first myth is that America is the best region for growing the best food; the reality is that America is a model of how *not* to grow and produce food. The second myth is that free trade allows food to be delivered "efficiently"; the reality is that without massive subsidies and dumping, US corporations could not capture markets in the South, and "free trade" is based on a "food swap", with countries importing and exporting the same commodity, and pushed into trade in a handful of commodities controlled by the agribusiness giants – not on exporting what a country can uniquely produce and importing what it cannot. The related myth is that dumping "frees" up incomes of farmers who can then buy "motorbikes, cellular phones and computers"; the reality is that dumping destroys domestic markets, livelihoods and incomes, and the collapse of rural incomes erodes purchasing power and entitlements. Impoverished farmers join the ranks of the hungry, indebted farmers commit suicide. Starvation deaths and farm suicides are the tragic outcome of the trade liberalisation of food systems.

As a result of globalisation, India's imports jumped from Rs. 12 billion in 1990-91 to Rs. 220 billion in 2005-06. Edible oil accounted for two-thirds of total agricultural imports and in 2009-10, were expected to jump by 46 per cent.[1] In any case, price collapse is not a linear mechanical phenomenon dependent on percentage of imports; it is more appropriately described in terms of non-linear perturbation in a complex equation which can slide the system into chaos and disintegration. Therefore, even in the case of products where imports are low, removal of import restrictions has sent domestic prices into a downward spin, leaving producers in crisis and the agricultural economy in a shambles.

Humanity has consumed more than 80,000 edible plants throughout its evolution; more than 3,000 have been used consistently. However, we now rely on *just eight crops* to provide 75 per cent of the world's food, and with genetic engineering, production has narrowed down to three crops – corn, soya, canola. Monocultures are destroying biodiversity, our health, and the quality and diversity of food. They have been promoted as an essential component of industrial and globalised agriculture; they create pseudo surpluses and real scarcity by destroying biodiversity, local food systems and food cultures.

In 1998, India's indigenous edible oils made from mustard, coconut, sesame, linseed and groundnut processed in artisanal cold press mills were banned, using "food safety" as an excuse. Restrictions on the import of soya oil were simultaneously removed and ten million farmers' livelihoods were threatened. One million oil mills in villages were closed, more than twenty farmers were killed while protesting against the dumping of soya on the Indian market, which was leading to a fall in prices of domestic oil seed crops. And millions of tons of artificially cheap GM soya oil continue to be dumped on India.

Women from the slums of Delhi came out in a movement to dump GM soya and bring back mustard oil. "Sarson Bachao, Soyabean Bhagao" (save the mustard, drive out the soyabean) was their slogan, and we succeeded in bringing back mustard through our Sarson Satyagraha (non-cooperation with the ban on mustard oil).

I was in the Amazon in 2006, where the same companies that dumped soya on India – Cargill and ADM – are destroying millions of acres in the Amazon rainforest – the lung and heart of the global climate system – to grow soya for export. Cargill has built an illegal port at Santaren in Para and is driving this expansion of soya. Armed gangs take over the forest and use slaves to cultivate it. When people like Sister Dorothy Stang oppose the destruction of the forests and the violence against people, they are assassinated. In the US and Europe, 80 per cent of soya is used as cattle-feed to provide cheap meat. Feeding factory-farmed animals is destroying both the Amazon rainforest as well as people's health in rich countries.

Soya, which is now found in 60 per cent of all processed food, was not eaten by any culture 50 years ago. It has high levels of isoflavones and phyto-oestrogens which produce hormone imbalances in humans. (Traditional fermentation, as in the food cultures of China and Japan, reduces the levels of isoflavones in it.) The promotion of soya in food is a huge experiment promoted with US $13 billion in subsidies from the government between 1998 and 2004. According to the *Farmers' Weekly*, 70 per cent of the soya value came from government subsidies which led to a 25 per cent increase in soya planting in the US since 1998.[2] The US has enlarged agriculture subsidies through the Farm Security and Rural Investment Act of 2002 and the Food Conservation and Energy Act of 2008, as well as by US $80 million a year from the American soya industry.[3]

Corporate control thrives on monocultures. Bringing back biodiversity to our farms goes hand-in-hand with bringing back small farmers on the land. Citizens' food freedom depends on biodiversity. Human freedom and the freedom of other species are mutually reinforcing, not mutually exclusive.

Industrialised globalised production creates pseudo surpluses because most of the food produced is not accessible to the hungry. In India, the rotting grain in godowns is a pseudo surplus and has accumulated because, under World Bank and corporate pressure, the government has dismantled the public distribution system. On July 5, 2010, the country was at a standstill because of a Bharat Bandh (national lock-down) called by opposition parties to force the government to address the crisis of rising prices of essential commodities, including food. Basic items of consumption such as wheat, rice and milk that form the minimum survival basket for the common man and woman, were out of reach even for better-off consumers with rice, for example, witnessing a 50 per cent increase in price over 2009-2011. The poor spend most of their meagre income on food, and high inflation automatically translates into an increase in hunger and malnutrition.

India has become food-insecure since the 1990s and the liberalisation of agriculture. The opening up of this employment-intensive sector to foreign players has led to a total monopoly over Indian food production systems in the hands of a few powerful corporations. The government engages in regulatory schizophrenia, deregulating corporations and regulating our farmers more and more. Worse still, it is consistently devolving social responsibility to corporations with murky past records of unethical and unfair business practices.

While the nation protests, the government is doing everything to deepen the crisis. The Food Security Act was offered as a solution to the hunger and malnutrition crisis; yet it does not address the real causes of hunger, nor does it tackle malnutrition. In fact it proposes to dismantle the public distribution system by encouraging cash transfers instead of food distribution. This means the government will not procure food from farmers, thus abandoning them and deepening the agrarian and food crises.

The proposed Food Security Bill, as it stood drafted by the empowered group of ministers, sees a *decrease* in the quantities allotted to poor households from 35 kgs. to 25 kgs. at Rs. 3; it also takes an extremely reductive figure for Below Poverty Line households, and plans to do away with the public distribution system core strength of distributing foodgrains, to be replaced with coupons or so-called "smart cards" provided by private companies. Recent developments in the debate over the Food Security Act have seen a push from the National Advisory Council, headed by Sonia Gandhi, who, realising the incongruence between promises and practice with regard to tackling hunger, called for changes in the Bill. Addressing food insecurity requires changing the policies that create hunger, pushing towards fixing the amount of subsidised grains at 35 kgs., while enlarging the basket of subsidised items to the poor to include edible oil and pulses. Pricing food items at a maximum retail price for *all households*, following a universal principle, is also being considered along with special provisions for the most vulnerable.

The "smart cards" idea came under criticism from NAC members as the system is prone to corruption and wouldn't serve the interests of the poor, being based on the false assumption that poor people have the money to buy food first, and then be reimbursed. The PDS has been one of the most crucial determinants of food policy and food security in the country. It started as a rationing system in the backdrop of the Bengal Famine of 1943-44, as well as a wartime measure during World War II. Over the years the system expanded enormously, emerging as a poverty alleviation measure to become a permanent feature in the country's food economy. In the context of new economic and liberalisation policies, it is regarded as a safety net for the poor, who number more than 330 million and are nutritionally at risk.

With a network of about 451,000 Fair Price Shops (FPS) for the distribution of commodities worth over Rs. 150 billion to about 180 million households throughout the country, the PDS in India is perhaps the largest distribution network of its type in the world. The rationing mechanism entitles households to essential commodities such as rice, wheat, sugar, kerosene and edible oils at subsidised rates. The responsibility of operation is shared by central and state governments; the central government procures stocks, supplies the grain and absorbs the cost of these operations, while state governments 'lift' the grains and distribute them to retail PDS outlets.

The Public Distribution System was designed with three objectives: (*i*) to protect the interests of farmers and producers by providing them remunerative prices; (*ii*) to provide foodgrains, especially to vulnerable sections of society, at reasonable prices; and (*iii*) to provide food security by maintaining buffer stocks of foodgrains to meet the exigencies arising out of natural calamities like droughts, floods and cyclones.

The World Bank used structural adjustment conditionalities to dismantle India's universal public distribution system and reduce it to a targeted PDS (TPDS), because a universal system that subsidised food for those who could afford it was a "waste" of public funds. Paradoxically, the public expenditure on food subsidies has actually increased from Rs. 2,450 crores in 1990-91 to Rs. 32,667 crores in 2008-09, a 1600 per cent increase.

Central Subsidy on Food
1976-77 to 2008-09

Year	Food subsidy (in crores)
1976-77	477
1977-78	480
1978-79	569
1979-80	600
1980-81	650
1981-82	700
1982-83	711
1983-84	835
1984-85	1,101
1985-86	1,650
1986-87	2,000
1987-88	2,000

1988-89	2,200
1989-90	2,476
1990-91	2,450
1991-92	2,850
1992-93	2,800
1993-94	5,537
1994-95	5,100
1995-96	5,377
1996-97	6,066
1997-98	7,900
1998-99	9,100
1999-2000	9,434
2000-01	12,060
2001-02	17,499
2002-03	24,176
2003-04	25,181
2004-05	25,798
2005-06	23,077
2006-07	24,204
2007-08	25,696
2008-09	32,667

The government of India finalised a National Food Security Act in 2012, guaranteeing food for all vulnerable sections of society through legislation, unlike the existing allocation-based schemes. However, there are still intense debates on the issue of providing food to the hungry; the impact of globalisation on the creation of hunger has become evident in India in less than two decades.

Dismantling our mandis

In spite of the deep crisis, corporations are pushing for foreign direct investment in multibrand retail. The spin given to the corporate hijack of retail is that it will control inflation. To allow corporations like Walmart and Cargill to take over distribution, there is an imperative to dismantle India's distribution system based on mandis (local markets) and small retailers.

Agricultural markets in most parts of the country are established and regulated under the State Agricultural Produce Marketing Committee (APMC) Act. The entire geographical area in a state is divided, and if a particular area is declared a market area it falls under the jurisdiction of the market committee – no person or agency is allowed to freely carry on wholesale marketing activities. Under the pressures of trade liberalisation, the title of the Act has now been changed to The State Agricultural Produce Marketing (Development and Regulation Act,) 2003, and a new chapter on "Contract Farming" has been added; this provides for compulsory registration and recording of all contract farming argreements, sponsors, resolution of disputes, if any, arising out of such agreements, exemption from levy of market fee on produce covered by contract farming, and an indemnity to producers' title/possession over land from any claim arising out of the agreement.

The union ministry of agriculture appointed an expert committee and a task force which, in their reports of June 2001 and 2002, respectively, suggested various reforms relating to agricultural marketing in the country. Their recommendations were discussed at the National Conference of State Ministers organised by the union ministry of agriculture on September 27, 2002, in New Delhi, and later by the standing committee of state ministers under the chairmanship of Hukumdev Narayan Yadav, the union minister of state for agriculture on January 29, 2003. The ministry of agriculture accordingly set up a committee under the chairmanship of additional secretary, department of agriculture, to formulate a model law for agricultural marketing. The draft model legislation was fully discussed and finalised by the committee in September 2003. Titled the State Agricultural Produce Marketing (Development and Regulation) Act, 2003, it provides, apart from other objectives, for the establishment of private markets/yards; direct purchase centres; promotion of public-private partnerships; contract farming; E-trading; and forward/ futures trading. The model legislation also intends to facilitate the emergence of competitive agricultural markets in private and cooperative sectors; create an environment conducive to massive investment in marketing-related infrastructure, leading to modernising and strengthening exporting markets.

The union agriculture minister has asked all states to amend their APMC Acts to bring in private investment and develop alternative competitive marketing structures, bypassing licenced traders. State governments would have to allocate land to agencies to set up alternative markets and exempt them from the purview of the APMC Act.[4]

The government of India has approved Rs. 190 crores for setting up new markets and strengthening and modernising existing ones, but only those states that have made certain policy changes in the APMC Act can qualify for this scheme. By linking it to reform, the government is offering incentives to states reluctant to amend the Act for fear of losing revenue from state-owned mandis. Karnataka, Madhya Pradesh and Andhra Pradesh have already amended their Acts.[5] The Gujarat government has told the Centre that it is not interested in amending its legal provisions in order to allow free play to the corporate sector in agriculture, but the ministry of agriculture is insisting that the WTO provisions on deregularisation of the rural agricultural marketing sector be respected by amending legal provisions.[6]

Multinational corporations are now making direct assaults on domestic markets by manipulating central and state governments. Agriculture, under the Indian Constitution is a state subject, but the Centre is pressurising states through financial incentives. As the report in *Indian Express* states:

> These changes, driven by trade liberalisation, benefit MNCs but remove protections from exploitation for farmers. The changes are a combination of more freedom for MNCs' operations and more centralised control over indigenous, domestic trade and marketing, by state bureaucracies. The changes replace democratic structures with state structures, which then create rules that favour

MNCs and displace local traders while also leaving MNCs free to exploit small farmers.[7]

The old Agricultural Produce Marketing Acts were designed by states, and their main objective was to ensure that farmers received a fair price, that traders and brokers were not free to exploit them by buying their produce at lower prices. The mandis governed by the Acts also offered farmers transportation, storage, grading, besides guaranteeing a just procurement price. The markets and mandis were governed and managed by elected market committees, with a predominance of agriculturists who were defined as those "whose livelihood depends solely on farming". The "model" act that the Centre is attempting to impose on states replaces the elected committees with a chief executive officer and other members appointed by the government. The definition of agriculturists has also been changed from those who depend on farming as a livelihood, to a person resident in the notified area of the market, who is engaged in the production of agricultural produce by himself or by hired labour or otherwise.

The most significant change in the marketing law is the removal of any regulations for MNCs regarding location of purchase, price and volume. Old APMC Acts prohibited the purchase of produce by traders outside the mandi or market yard; the sale of agricultural produce was carried out by open auction from which commission agents were barred. By having many traders and a ceiling on volumes traded, monopolies could not emerge in mandis. Payments had to be made the same day, or a penalty interest of one per cent per day for five days was imposed. Licences were cancelled if payments were not made. The mandis also had storage facilities in case of no-sale. The marketing laws were thus intended primarily to prevent the exploitation of farmers by traders. That exploitation takes place in spite of the law is part of the corruption that seeps through in our society and it needs to be addressed. Amendments in the marketing acts, however, are designed to remove legal instruments preventing farmers' exploitation altogether. Giant corporations can now set up private markets that are not regulated by any market committee.

This is how the India Tobacco Company (ITC) has set up its E-chaupals in Madhya Pradesh, against which there were protests and statewide strikes. Nothing in the law exists to prevent ITC from buying cheap from farmers, after one or two years of getting them hooked into a dependency on seeds and chemicals from the ITC chaupal. Since input costs have outstripped the prices of produce, agribusiness corporations, without market regulation, will make profits selling costly seeds, buying cheap farm produce, and locking farmers into debt. This has been the process by which the small family farmer has disappeared in the US, Argentina and Europe.

The Act regulates trading through mandis but allows corporations to determine the terms of trade. Section 40(1) has an exemption for agribusiness which states, "Provided, further, that it will not be necessary to bring agricultural produce covered under contract farming to the market/yard sub-market/yard/private yard and it may be directly sold to contract farming sponsor from farmers' fields." While local traders will have to buy through open auction in mandis, the MNCs have the freedom to fix prices. Local traders cannot engage in wholesale transactions but agribusiness can buy any amount from farmers anywhere [41(3)].

Local traders have to pay upto Rs.2 for every Rs.100 of the price as market fees; but there is no market fee for agribusinesses buying in private yards. This unequal taxation was granted to the East India Company through the Farukhsheer Firman of 1716, called the Free Trade Treaty of that period, which destroyed local trade and local manufacture. Today the 'reform' of the agricultural marketing laws have built-in inequality – freedom from regulation and taxes for MNCs.[8]

India produces thousands of crops on millions of farms, agribusinesses trade in a handful of commodities. The new Act has contract farming built into its structure; the Model Contract Farming Agreement refers to corporations as "contract farming sponsors". Contracts oblige farmers to produce, but do not oblige corporations to buy; in case of disputes, farmers cannot seek justice from courts. Section 9 on "Dispute Resolution Mechanism" states:

> In majority of cases, it is highly unlikely that a sponsor will take legal action against a small holder for breach of contract. The costs involved are inclined to be far in excess of the claims amount and legal action threatens the relationship between the sponsor and all farmers, not just those against whom action is being taken. Action by a farmer against a sponsor is similarly impossible. As neither side is likely to seek a legal remedy through the courts, it is important that quick and easy ways of resolving disputes are identified in the agreement.

The Model Act puts a bar on civil suits. (Act 105) Article 89 states,

> No court shall take cognisance of any offence punishable under this Act or any rule or any bye-laws made thereunder, except on the complaint made by the collector or chairman, vice chairman, chief executive officer of the market committee or of any person duly authorised by the market committee in this behalf.

In other words, farmers are disenfranchised from all legal and civil rights. This is corporate dictatorship, implemented by a corporate state.

The E-chaupal redefines the chaupal, the village square, where elders meet to discuss matters of importance. "E" stands for an Internet connection for farmers to gather and interact, not just among themselves but with people anywhere in the country and even beyond. The ITC E-chaupal initiative has already reached three million Indian farmers and by 2012, it hopes to reach 10 million. Within two years ITC's Aashirwad brand of atta (wheat) has captured 15 per cent of the market share.[9]

ITC and other corporations are not interested in the empowerment of small farmers, their main aim is the expansion of their business empire in rural areas. ITC launched Aashirwad in Uttar Pradesh because it wanted an entry into the state to buy wheat. Similarly, as the company owns Wills Sports and other garment brands, it plans to enter cotton procurement, which will help it forge linkages between fibre and fashion. Within a few years, the company will supply branded seeds to farmers, even though these seeds may be ten times more expensive. There is endless scope for making money from E-chaupals.

Traders in Madhya Pradesh, especially those who operate in the Krishi Upaj Mandis (agriculture produce markets) went on strike on December 13, 2004, to protest against the government ending their monopoly in the sale and purchase of agricultural produce. All traders in the 330 mandis of the state stopped work. The decision to grant licences to multinationals and Indian corporates to trade in agricultural produce had been taken one year earlier, but the real impact of the decision was being felt now.[10]

The ITC is one of the mass operators in the area with 1,750 E-chaupals all over the state. Now many mandis wear a deserted look and grain traders are almost jobless. The non-arrival of soyabean and other produce has also hit the hammals (loaders) who depend solely on the business in mandis for their livelihood. ITC acquired around Rs 1,500 crores worth of agricultural commodities in 2005, some 40 per cent of which would be marketed directly by the company. It is also retailing third party products, teaming up with other companies who want to sell to farmers.[11] According to Gopal Agarwal, spokesman of the traders, the new system besides hitting traders, has also affected the income of the government, which used to net huge sums in the form of mandi tax; used to be so rich in the past that governments even borrowed from tax income to overcome financial crises.[12]

An efficient marketing system for farm produce ensures an increase in farm production, and translates into an increase in the level of income, thereby stimulating the emergence of additional income. Consumers benefit because goods are available at the lowest possible cost. The ideal marketing system should aim at giving remunerative prices of produce to producers. All these emphasise the fact that agricultural marketing plays an important role in the economic development of the nation.

To explore the likely implications of an amended APMC Act and the arrival of wheat, a study was conducted by Navdanya in 2005 in the following mandis of Madhya Pradesh, which was the first state to implement the Act: Ganj Basoda, Beena, Khurai, Bhopal, Sihor, Sanyogata Gunj, Laxmibai Nagar, Khandwa, Ashla, Sonkuteh, Dewas, Sanawad, Badgaon and Sagar. The study found that the entire economy of small towns like Ganj Basoda and Khurai revolved around mandis. While the traders, hammals, women workers, cart-pullers and others depend directly on mandis for their livelihood, others like hotels, restaurants, shopkeepers and vendors depend on them indirectly. Allowing E-chaupals and big companies in is likely to affect the livelihood of millions of people in the state. According to Anil Yadav, a local veteran and journalist with the Hindi daily, *Nai Duniya*,

> In Ganj Basoda, apart from more than 390 traders, there are more than 3,000 labourers, which includes 700 hammals (who load and unload the sacks), 80 tulia (who weigh the grain), about 2,000-2,500 women (for cleaning the grain), and 125 cart-pullers.

In the town, the mandi supports the livelihood of another 30,000-35,000 persons. Traders blame the government for discriminating against them and giving large concessions that are not available even to government or semi-government agencies to E-chaupals. While traders are permitted to buy only within the mandi, a chaupal can buy outside it; if a trader wants to buy outside the mandi, he will have to buy at least 20,000 quintals. "When traders applied for the licence to do so, their applications were rejected," says Virendra Shah, president of Grain and Tilhan Traders in Ganj Basoda. He adds,

> Not only this, E-chaupal is allowed to pay after cleaning the dirt, waste and broken grains. This concession is not extended to traders, which means E-chaupal pays at least Rs. 20-25 less per quintal than traders. Even government agencies like NAFED are not permitted this concession.

Traders also claim that ITC does not pay a fair price; if it offers Rs. 1,250 for one quintal of soyabean, it cuts Rs. 30 to 40 for moisture, damage, etc., and pays only Rs. 1,220, whereas a mandi trader pays the rate fixed in an auction for Fair Average Quality (FAQ). If the quality of the consignment is not upto FAQ level, ITC does not pay the price which farmers get in the mandi.

At a conference on food sovereignty organised by Navdanya and the Council for Social Development on July 29, 2011, Dr. Jaya Mehta, an eminent economist, pointed out that in 1950 India had 256 mandis, today it has 7,700. The argument used for the corporate takeover of food distribution is that it will get rid of middlemen; what it hides is that it gets rid of small producers and small traders. Instead of farmers selling to one thousand buyers in a mandi, they sell to one corporation.

Retail democracy *vs* retail dictatorship

India is a land of retail democracy – hundreds of thousands of weekly haats and bazaars take place across the length and breadth of the country through people's own organisational capacities. Our streets are bazaars – lively, vibrant, safe, and the source of livelihoods for millions. India has the highest shop density in the world, with eleven outlets per 1,000 people; this does not include village haats. Our retail democracy is characterised by high levels of livelihood in retail with nearly 40 million employed, which accounts for eight per cent of employment and four per cent of the entire population; high levels of self-organisation; low capital input; and a high degree of decentralisation.

However, our diversified and decentralised retail economy is under severe assault from giant corporations like Reliance and Walmart who are trying to establish a retail dictatorship, whereby they will control the entire supply chain, from production to retail. This assault has both cultural and economic components. A well-crafted cultural assault, in which language and semantics play an important role, is being mounted to project India's retail democracy as inferior, and Walmart or Reliance monopolies as culturally superior. Thus the self-organised sector of retail democracy is now defined as "unorganised", and the corporate monopoly sector is defined as "organised". The subtle implication is to project the transition from retail democracy to retail dictatorship as a transition from an unorganised to an organised state.

Similarly, indigenous trading arrangements and the destruction of the livelihoods of 40 million people are projected as the removal of "middlemen". The imposition of giant middlemen like Reliance and Walmart goes unquestioned. The logic of corporate trade monopolies is to "buy cheap, sell dear"; in the short run, in order to capture markets through predatory pricing, they will of course "buy dear and sell cheap"; once alternative markets for the producer and the consumer are eradicated, they will drive down the price of produce, and thus drive down farmers' incomes.

Dr. Tim Lang reported in *Food Wars* that Walmart drove down prices by 13 per cent within ten years of entering the food trade. By 2010, seven major US retailers were forecast to control close to 10 per cent of the food-retailing environment, with Walmart increasing its food retail share to 22 per cent. In Europe the share of the top ten grocery retailers is expected to increase from 37 per cent to 60 per cent in just one decade.[13] The UK government's 2000 Competition Commission inquiry listed twenty-seven practices by supermarkets that went against the public interest. The Commission also uncovered regular selling, by all five main retailers – Tesco, Sainsbury, ASDA/ Walmart, Safeway and Sourcefield – of some frequently purchased products, below cost. Supermarkets and their suppliers have a one-sided business relationship; suppliers have very low margins of four to two per cent, with some even having a negative margin.

The entry of giant corporate retail in India's food market will have a direct impact on India's 650 million farmers and the 40 million employed in small retail. More than 6,600 mega stores are planned with a Rs. 40,000 crores ($2.5 billion) investment. Reliance plans to invest $5 billion over the next four years to open thousands of stores. Walmart's partner, Bharti, plans to invest upto $2.5 billion in new stores in the next eight years. Since 2005, Walmart has tried every trick in the trade to enter India and hijack the Indian retail sector. It tried to enter directly by pressurising the government to allow FDI in retail, but protests in Parliament and among people forced the government to restrict FDI to single brands. This did not stop Walmart; it joined hands with Bharti, which owns Airtel, India's largest mobile service provider. When Sunil Mittal of Bharti was asked about Walmart squeezing margins, his reply was, "I went to different Walmart stores, I didn't see any angry or grumpy faces. Yes, they employ Hispanics at $8 an hour – but they are smiling." (*Indian Express*, April 8, 2007.)

Walmart Stores is the largest retailer in the world, and was formerly the largest corporation in the world, based on revenues for 2004. It operates retail department stores selling a wide range of products, and its main focus is on "supercenters" which sell everything from grocery items to clothing and electronic goods. It also operates Sam's Club, a "warehouse club" that sells merchandise, often in large quantities, to customers who pay an annual fee for shopping there. There has been much criticism of Walmart. Specific areas of controversy include the company's foreign product sourcing; treatment of employees and product supplies; environmental carelessness; extraction of public subsidies (corporate welfare); availability of prescription contraceptives at its pharmacy counters; and store impacts on local communities and businesses. Walmart owns:

- 100 per cent of England's ASDA Group
- 100 per cent of Brazilian Bompreco
- 100 per cent of USA's McLane Co. Inc.
- 53.56 per cent of Japanese Seiyo
- 53 per cent of Mexico's Cifra Group

In September 2005, Walmart acquired 33.3 per cent of Central American Retail Holding Company, and in March 2006 increased its holding to 51 per cent.

Walmart became an international company in 1991, with the opening of Sam's Club near Mexico City. It now has more than 2,660 units in 14 countries (excluding the US). It is present in Argentina, Brazil, Canada, China, Costa Rica, El Salvador, Germany, Guatemala, Honduras, Japan, Mexico, Nicaragua, Puerto Rico and United

Kingdom. India now joins this list. In 1990, Walmart had only nine supercentres; by the end of 2000, it had 888 in the US and had become the number one retailer in the country. Today it is the biggest grocery seller in the world. In the US it controls 16 per cent of the grocery market, and in some cities its share is 30 per cent. Walmart now has 3,811 stores in the US. It has become the largest retailer in Mexico and Canada, the second largest grocery seller in UK – all in a few years. A typical Walmart store sells 60,000 different items, and a supercentre sells 120,000, 80 per cent of which are sourced from China. Walmart is one of the most successful beneficiaries of corporate-led globalisation, and has made communities dependent on supplies from thousands of miles away for everyday items – including the food we eat and the clothes we wear.

The three arguments used to justify the Walmart model of retail are employment generation, efficiency and low cost. Each claim is false. Its long distance supply chain is considered the most "efficient" model of distribution. As Thomas Friedman says admiringly in *The World is Flat*,

> I had never seen what a supply chain looked like in action until I visited Walmart headquarters in Bentonville, Arkansas. My Walmart hosts took me over to the 1.2 million sq. ft. distribution center, where we climbed up to a viewing perch and watched the show. On one side of the building, scores of white Walmart trailer trucks were dropping off boxes of merchandise from thousands of different suppliers. Boxes large and small were fed up a conveyor belt at each loading dock. These little conveyor belts fed into a bigger belt, like streams feeding into a powerful river. Twenty-four hours a day, seven days a week, the suppliers' trucks feed the twelve miles of conveyor streams, and the conveyor streams feed into a huge Walmart river that flows along, an electric eye reads the bar codes on each box on its way to the other side of the building. There, the river parts again into a hundred streams. Electric arms from each stream reach out and guide the boxes – ordered by particular Walmart stores – off

the main river and down its stream, where another conveyor belt sweeps them into a waiting Walmart truck, which will rush these particular products onto the shelves of a particular Walmart store somewhere in the country. There, a consumer will lift one of these products off the shelf and the cashier will scan it in, and the moment that happens, a signal will be generated. That signal will go out across the Walmart network to the supplier of that product – whether that supplier's factory is in coastal China or coastal Maine. That signal will pop up on the supplier's computer screen and prompt him to make another of that item and ship it via the Walmart supply chain, and the whole cycle will start anew. So no sooner does your arm lift a product off the local Walmart's shelf and onto the checkout counter than another mechanical arm starts making another one somewhere in the world. Call it "the Walmart Symphony" in multiple movements – with no finale. It just plays over and over 24/7/365: delivery, sorting, packing, distributing, buying, manufacturing, reordering, delivery, sorting, packing....[14]

This model appears efficient if one ignores ecological limits and human needs and human rights, including the need for livelihoods and the right to work. India's retail is based on local supply from small producers to small retailers. Vegetables grown in small holdings around cities are carried in headloads and then distributed by hawkers and vendors in every village, town and street. On the one hand, this involves millions of humans in creating economic activity, on the other, it avoids carbon dioxide emissions which are leading to global warming and climate catastrophe. Walmart's entry into India threatens this ecologically sustainable and socially just model of retail. Food miles will increase, and with it CO_2 emissions, further destabilising the climate. Ecologically and socially, the Walmart model of retail is highly inefficient.

In the US, Walmart has been prosecuted several times for predatory pricing behaviour, which is defined as the practice of temporarily lowering prices in order to drive competitors out of business so that prices may be raised afterwards in a competition-free environment (monopoly). Kenneth E. Stone of Iowa State University has published several studies on Walmart. In 1997, he found that small towns "lost up to 47 per cent of their retail trade after ten years of Walmart stores nearby". An earlier study carried out by him, in 1995, on the impact of Walmart's growth found that, over ten years, 7,326 Iowa businesses closed, including: 555 grocery stores; 298 hardware stores; 293 building suppliers; 161 variety shops; 158 women's stores; and 116 pharmacies.[15]

Walmart can displace low-cost options available through corner shops, street vendors and hawkers only through a cultural and legal assault. The pull towards Walmart's mega stores will come by promoting shopping in super stores as fashionable among the middle classes. The push towards Walmart and giant retail chains will be made by legally banning street vendors and local retail, as is being done in city after city in India in the name of "cleaning it up". (Many observers interpret the force behind successive "sealing" drives in Delhi, through which commercial establishments and retail are being shut down under new zoning criteria, as being the result of giant retail chains and supermarkets coming up on the outskirts of cities. Why would people drive 20 kms. out if vegetables and groceries are available at their doorsteps? And what happens to 96 per cent of India which does not own a car?)

Low prices at Walmart will also be achieved by creating monopoly markets; the volumes that Walmart buys makes suppliers dependent on selling to it – and lowering prices is always possible when there is a monopoly buyer. Giant retail is driving down prices of agricultural produce, increasing the agrarian crisis. What we have seen of farmers' suicides in the cotton growing regions of India could well spread to regions where Walmart will procure its vegetables and groceries.

In a report, "Oligopoly Inc. 2005", the ETC group has shown that consolidation, cut-throat competition and aggressive global expansion are the driving forces in the food retail sector. In 2004, the top ten global food retailers accounted for combined sales of $840 billion, 24 per cent of the estimated \$3.5 trillion global market, up from \$513.7 billion in 2001.[16]

Official estimates put the figures of small retail at 40 million, but I do not think this takes into account the farmer who sells directly at the village haat, or the millions of hawkers and vendors who do not have a "shop". My estimate is that retail in India provides livelihoods to 100 million people, and supports at least 300 million through incomes that retail brings in. Today both agriculture and small retail are under attack from agribusiness and giant corporate retail. The attack is multifaceted, and cultural.

We need to defend our retail democracy which offers a different model from Walmart's retail dictatorship. We cannot allow our livelihoods, ecological sustainability and the cultural vitality of our streets and localities to be destroyed. Retail democracy in India is a survival imperative for millions of Indians, it is also a survival imperative for the planet.

Revenue of Top Ten Global Food Retailers

Company	2004 revenue US $ millions	Global market share % grocery retail
1. Walmart (US)	$287,989	8%
2. Carrefour (France)	$99,119	3%
3. Metro AG (Germany)	$76,942	2%
4. Ahold (Netherlands)	$70,439	2%
5. Tesco (UK)	$65,175	2%
6. Kroger (US)	$56,434	2%
7. Costco (US)	$52,935	2%
8. ITM Enterprises (France)	$51,800	1%
9. Albertson's (for sale) (US)	$39,897	1%
10. Edeka Zentrale (Germany)	$39,100	1%

Source: ETC. Group

Explosive growth for these giant food retailers is predicted in Asia and Latin America – with Asia forecast to account for 41 per cent share of the global retail market in 2020. People in India and Vietnam spend more than half their income on food, while the Chinese spend more than a third. A global open food system would be one where the regions that grow food best are linked through with regions that need their food most. According to IGD, a UK-based market research firm, India will become the fourth largest grocery retail market by 2020. Multinational food retailers like Walmart wield extraordinary economic and trade power. According to ETC,

> These companies decide where and by whom a staggering share of the world's food is produced, processed and procured. Thus Walmart sources most of its products from factories in China, where 80 per cent of the 6,000 factories that supply Walmart are located. The FAO has warned that the dominance of global supermarkets "has led to consolidated supply chains in which buyers for a handful of giant food processors and retailers wield increasing power to set standards, prices and delivery schedules".

Hypermarkets displace diversity, quality and taste and replace it with uniformity, quantity and appearance. As Tobias Reichart says,

> To ensure timely delivery to numerous retail outlets, companies like Walmart prefer to buy large amounts of products, meeting uniform standards, from a limited number of suppliers. The contracts are often designed in a way that allows retailers to place orders on very short notice, refuse products for quality reasons and pay only several months after delivery, thereby capturing value while passing business risks to suppliers and farms.[17]

In Kenya, as retail chains started to influence food production and food distribution, the share of small farmers in horticultural exports decreased from 70 per cent to only 18 per cent in the 1990s, while large commercial farms and export companies with their own production made up more than 80 per cent.

The Walmart model of long distance supply chains is energy-intensive and hence greenhouse gas-intensive. As the huge retail chains claim they provide every vegetable and fruit from any part of the country at any time, the average distance travelled by food will increase. Traffic congestion is already a real problem for many towns and cities, so stores generating thousands of new car journeys will significantly add to local problems. Recent work for DEFRA (the UK environmental and food agency) suggests that car use for food shopping results in costs to society of more than £3.5 billion per year, from traffic emissions, noise, accidents and congestion. Traffic congestion occurs on a larger scale, too – the distribution systems used by supermarkets generate huge volumes of traffic, both in this country and overseas. This will lead to high levels of carbon dioxide emission and global warming as a long-term result.

- When shopping gets so centralised, one might have to drive for every article of shopping that could be provided by local markets.
- For refrigerating vegetables and fruits for the whole year, at least 6,000 megawatts of electricity is needed.
- For air-conditioning four million sq. ft. of built-up area, one will need at least 150 megawatts of electricity (only for Reliance stores).

Supermarket lorries travel 408 million miles a year only for the major UK supermarket chains. This is equivalent to going to the moon and back 854 times – more than two return trips per day. This results in 600,000 tonnes of carbon dioxide emissions per year.

Area of UK: 244,820 sq kms.
Area of India: 3,287,590 sq. kms. (more than 13 times the area of UK)
UK's population: 60,609,153
India's population: more than 1.2 billion (more than 18 times the population of UK)

Thus, even if we go by conservative estimates, supermarket trucks in India will generate more than seven million tonnes of carbon dioxide per year, adding more problems to the already fragile environment of the country and further contributing to climate chaos. And for producing this huge amount of carbon dioxide in the air, corporate retail trucks will consume one billion litres of diesel/ petrol.

In an article on Walmart's vision for India published in the *Financial Express*, June 1, 2007, Raj Jain, president, Emerging Markets, stated: "One key reason for Walmart's success is localisation. We carry local products from local suppliers that appeal to local tastes, needs and fashions." If Walmart were our local neighbourhood store, carrying only locally-produced items, it would be different in every region of every country – it would not be a supercentre. It would be a separate shop for different things – a sari shop, a bangle shop, a shop for electrical goods, a shop for vegetables. In fact, the Walmart model is based on the opposite principles, the reality identified by the *Walmart Effect*.[18]

By being the biggest buyer in most commodities, Walmart determines the fate of producers – whether they will continue to produce and what price they will sell their products at. Sherrie Ford, a factory owner and long-time manufacturing management expert says: "Every time you see the Walmart smiley face, whistling and knocking down the prices, somewhere there is a factory worker being kicked in the stomach."[19] Blue jeans made in China on the basis of super-exploited labour is not localisation, it is the worst form of globalisation.

Walmart is presenting itself as an ally of the small retailers:

> The joint venture will sell quality merchandise directly to retailers – big and small, including 'mom and pop' or kirana stores. The purpose is to establish an efficient supply chain linking farmers and small manufacturers who have limited infrastructure or distribution strength.

One would imagine that there are no wholesale markets or mandis in India which get farmers' produce to the retailers. Our trade network is more sophisticated, more complex, more efficient than any system that Walmart can introduce as a giant wholesaler. In the mandis the retailer can choose to buy from hundreds of traders; with Walmart farmers will have only one buyer and consumers will have only one seller. A study in the US shows that in the first year of a Walmart store opening, fifty people who had retail jobs in the county (locality) had lost their jobs. Three retailers closed within two years of Walmart's arrival, four within five years. Another study found that Walmart took away 15-30 per cent sales from other supermarkets.[20]

Another myth offered by Walmart is to "provide quality jobs to India's unskilled workforce, promising thousands of jobs" in a sector that already employs several millions. It also claims to "help develop local suppliers", but the reality is that it buys products from 60 countries around the world. This is not local supply. Indeed, Walmart pushes down prices so low that local producers *cannot* supply. Nancy Ridlen, the owner of Ridlen Adhesives reports, "Walmart said; 'We don't want to pay 50 cents for these glue sticks. We'll pay 45 cents. Either you take it or we'll go elsewhere.'"[21]

This is what has happened to every product, from locks to lawn mowers, shirts to jeans, and every producer who was destroyed had been tempted by Walmart's large volumes. Jim Wier, who said "No" to Walmart says: "They had the lure of volume. Once they get hooked on the volume, it's like getting hooked on cocaine. You've created a monster for yourself."[22]

World Bank and corporate retail in food

The World Bank is pushing India to focus on fruits and vegetables for export at the cost of food staples for local consumption. Thus, while the supply chain for local markets is highly evolved and sophisticated, it is perceived as deficient in the context of exports. The Bank has called this a "logistical tax". Three factors explain India's high logistical tax: (*a*) geography, which is important but not decisive; (*b*) poor transport and storage infrastructure, as well as policies that have led to the uneven utilisation of existing infrastructure and the slow creation of new infrastructure; and (*c*) high marketing costs due to the fragmentation of the supply chain. The Bank has identified laws such as the Essential Commodities Act (1955), the Agricultural Produce and Marketing Act (APMA, 1972), and the Prevention of Black Marketing and Maintenance of Supplies of Essential Commodities Act (1980), which have defended the rights of farmers to a just price and the rights of the poor to a fair price for food, as having

> ... prevented the free mobility of agricultural produce and thus segmented the Indian domestic market into many smaller markets. The government has also imposed restrictions on foreign investment in the retail of agricultural commodities, and on both foreign and domestic private investment in wholesale. These restrictions have collectively discouraged and/or prevented the private sector from undertaking large-scale investment in agricultural storage, marketing or processing activities – an example of horizontal fragmentation preventing desirable vertical integration. The result is that today there is no large, organized, efficient pan-Indian supply chain in the agricultural sector, including in horticulture.[23]

The attack on India's "geography" shows how the World Bank would like to wish away India's diversity and geography, thereby destroying our food sovereignty. Thus, instead of buying apples grown in Himachal, the Bank says it would be cheaper for Chennai to import them. This was exactly the argument used to justify wheat imports, which however, turned out to be twice as costly as domestic wheat. Navdanya has filed a case in the Supreme Court against wheat imports.

Indian laws created for food sovereignty and food security have created a decentralised and democratic framework for food distribution and marketing, which is defined as "horizontal fragmentation" by the World Bank; monopoly control by a single corporate player is defined as "vertical integration". It continues:

> The heterogeneity has persisted because low productivity regions have been shielded from competition by policy restrictions on, and the high transport costs of, the internal movement of agricultural produce.

The World Bank would like to see fossil fuel costs reduced and subsidised commodities destroy local diversified production, as we have seen in Vidarbha in Maharashtra and Wynad in Kerala. It would like to encourage monocultures of export-oriented crops, a strategy that requires identification of crops and regions that are inherently uncompetitive, where farmers would be forced to switch to alternative crops or alternative occupations in the post-liberalisation period. The creation of agricultural export zones is part of this design.

India is one of the largest and lowest-cost producers of high value agricultural commodities and yet it has a minuscule share in global trade. It produces nearly 11 per cent of all vegetables and 15 per cent of all fruits in the world. The unit values of its exports (free on board, FOB) are nearly half the corresponding world unit values, yet its share in the global export of vegetables is only 1.7 per cent and in fruits, a meagre 0.5 per cent. For the World Bank, fruits and vegetables are meant just for export to rich countries. "What impedes exports?" is its main question, not "What feeds the poor in India?" The World Bank analysis is disastrous from every perspective.

- It is disastrous for farmers who are being asked to give up their occupations.
- It is disastrous for the poor who are being denied their right to food, with a singular focus on exports.
- It is disastrous for the environment because it recommends the destruction of India's rich biodiversity and the increase in CO_2 emissions for the refrigeration of fruits and vegetables.
- It is also disastrous for communities in the North trying to create local markets to reduce their carbon footprint on the planet.

According to the World Bank, "It would clearly be efficient to allow consumers in all regions and at all times to buy from the cheapest domestic or foreign source." But what about domestic producers? What about the ecological costs of importing what can be produced locally? What about the value of local and seasonal foods for health, taste, quality? "Current high tariffs penalise the consumers in regions located far from production sources and in seasons far from the harvest season," states the Bank. This is not an issue of tariffs, but of diverse climates and seasons. Products from afar should have a higher price to cover carbon costs; unseasonal products should have a higher price to cover the costs of atmospheric pollution due to increased use of electricity for refrigeration. Local and seasonal must be rewarded in the marketplace. To reward the non-local and non-seasonal with manipulated neoliberal economies is bad for the planet, bad for consumers, bad for farmers.

Where movements call for reducing "food miles", the World Bank calls for "breaking the distance barrier". Chile exports 80 per cent of its fruits and vegetables to markets more than 1,000 kms. away. The corresponding figure for India is one per cent. This is good. India's fruits and vegetables are being eaten by Indian people and it is not contributing to carbon emissions through exporting to Europe and the US. The Bank would like to increase food miles by making "effective distance" shrink through cold chains and long-distance transport, thus "diminishing, dampening the influence of remoteness on exports". Climate change demands taking remoteness into account, to reduce both food miles and energy use in transporting fresh vegetables. Local food is an imperative in times of climate change. Protecting farmers' livelihoods and markets is an imperative in times of farmers' suicides. Ecologically for the planet, and economically for farmers, the Bank's prescriptions for India are a prescription for a suicidal economy.

On Quit India Day, August 9, 2007, a broad alliance of farmers, hawkers, traders and youth told Walmart: "Corporations! Quit Retail!"

Hundreds of thousands of traders, hawkers, farmers and workers across India protested against corporate entry in retail. The protest was organised by the National Movement for Retail Democracy, a broad alliance of farmers' unions, hawkers' groups, traders' associations, consumer forums, trade unions and various non-governmental organisations. Demonstrations took place in Delhi, Mumbai, Bangalore, Kolkata, as well as Calicut, Bhopal, Jaipur, Ranchi, Balia, Meerut, Sonepat, Nagpur, Nasik, Pune and Indore.

In Delhi, thousands protested in Chandni Chowk, a historical market, and burned effigies of Walmart, Bharti and Reliance. Mass-based organisations called on the Prime Minister and Sonia Gandhi to immediately stop the corporate entry into India. There was a strong united call to all corporations – both foreign and domestic – to "Quit Retail". The protests were timed to commemorate the start of the "Quit India" movement on August 9, 1942, with mass-based sections of society drawing parallels to the East India Company, of companies like Walmart, Bharti and Reliance.

Vandana Shiva compared the present situation with colonised India, when the British monopolised the production of salt by not allowing Indians to do so. Today, big corporations are trying to monopolise agriculture, retail and other sectors in the economy. The time has come for all of us to produce, process and eat our local food, and boycott these corporations to save our sovereignty. The very fact that the government has denied permission for Walmart to enter into retail directly, is a victory for our struggle. Praveen Khandelwal, General Secretary, Confederation of All India Traders (CAIT) said, "The livelihoods of retail traders are at stake. If big retail giants like Walmart and Reliance come into the country, small traders will be finished." Several trader and hawker leaders addressed the demonstrators.

In Mumbai, thousands of people participated in a one-day trade bandh. A mass public event was organised by the Vyapaar Rozgaar Suraksha Kriti Samiti, a joint action committee of trade associations, hawkers' groups, trade unions and others.

In Jaipur, 50 American students joined with hawkers, demanding that Walmart leave India and demanding the implementation of the National Policy on Street Vendors. Cheryl, an American studying Hindi in Jaipur, said that Walmart has had a disastrous impact on small shopkeepers and neighbourhood communities in the US, and that Indians should not allow it to operate in their country.

In Kerala, the Kerala Vyapari Vyavasayi Egono Samiti organised protest marches in over 1,000 places across the state. In Calicut, over 10,000 traders protested; they submitted a memorandum demanding that corporations keep out of retail, an immediate halt to Walmart's backdoor entry, and the repeal of the Wholesale Cash-n-Carry permission. In Kolkata, the Federation of Trade Organisations of West Bengal organised protests in all the 12 districts. Tens of thousands participated in the demonstrations in front of malls and at a protest march through the city. Demonstrations were also held throughout the state.

At a demonstration in Ranchi, Uday Shankar Ojha, who led the vegetable vendors against Reliance Fresh in May and has only recently been released from jail, demanded that Reliance Fresh and all other corporations leave the retail sector and "withdraw their sinister plans to displace millions of livelihoods".

In Bhopal, there was a state-level protest meeting in the morning at Gandhi Bhavan and traders sat on a dharna (sit-in) at Roshanara Chowk in the afternoon. A call for a Bhopal Bandh was given for August 21 to oust corporates from retail trade.

Excerpts from press releases,
Bija, Autumn 2007, Volume 45, p. 26

In 2009, Walmart was allowed entry into the wholesale market, and set up a joint venture with Bharti Enterprises.

Bharti Walmart to Double Stores in India, Eyes Top Spot in Two Years

New Delhi: Bharti Walmart Pvt. Ltd, the wholesale joint venture between the world's largest retailer and Bharti Enterprises Ltd, aims to be the top wholesaler in India, as it adds 20 stores that will sell products to retailers and other businesses in the next two years.

"In the next one or two years we do anticipate we will be in a market leadership position," said Raj Jain, chief executive of Bharti Walmart.

At the time of its India entry in 2009, the US-based Walmart had said it planned to open about a dozen wholesale stores in the country by the end of 2012.

Bharti Walmart has so far invested about $45 million (Rs. 200 crores) in India to open six Best Price modern wholesale stores – four in Punjab and one each in Kota (Rajasthan), and Bhopal (Madhya Pradesh).

Jain said the company will next open stores in Karnataka and Andhra

Pradesh in the south, where it plans to open three cash-and-carry outlets this year. It will also open stores in Chhattisgarh and Maharashtra later this year.

"We have always followed that (cluster approach) strategy and we were largely focused on Punjab, although we opened stores in other places also," said Jain. "We have covered the four big markets (in Punjab) already. My own guess is that in the years to come we can open a couple of more stores (in the state), but at this point of time we have reached where we could have reached."

At an investment of about $7.5 million per store – although depending on investments in the supply chain, spending per store would differ in different locations – Bharti Walmart would invest about $75 million in India by the end of this year to open about ten stores. Its total investment in the country could reach about $195 million by the end of 2012.

Jain said wholesale retailing is a $140 billion opportunity, out of India's estimated $350 billion annual retail business. "The opportunity is huge," he said, in a telephone interview on Thursday from Ludhiana, the native city of the Mittals of Bharti Enterprises, where the joint venture opened its fourth store in Punjab.

After years of unsuccessfully lobbying for India to open its retail market, Walmart in 2007 decided to team up with Bharti Enterprises for a wholesale venture, a business where India allows 100 per cent foreign ownership, but such ventures can sell multibrand products only to other retailers and businesses.

Meanwhile, Paris-based Carrefour SA has also opened a wholesale store in New Delhi, and Britain's Tesco Plc plans to open its first wholesale store in India later this year.

Germany's Metro AG, the first global retailer to open such stores in India in 2003, said it will rapidly expand in India, opening 50 wholesale stores in the country in the next five years.

Last year, after years of being non-committal on foreign investment in retail, India's Department of Industrial Policy and Promotion (DIPP) invited opinions from stakeholders such as large retailers and small shop-owners on whether the country should allow foreign direct investment in multibrand retail.

The government has constituted a committee to come up with a report based on the feedback DIPP received on the discussion paper.

Meanwhile, Bharti Walmart says it will continue with its wholesale business even if India opens up the retail market to foreign companies.

"We know that the debate of FDI in retail is continuing, but in the meanwhile we are opening cash-and-carry," Jain said. "And even after India's FDI opens, I don't see why we should stop opening cash-and-carry. There is a need in the hinterlands of India to improve the quality of the distribution and products, pricing and availability to the customers … the initial experience has been good so we shall continue to be on this path in addition to whatever FDI allows us to."

Abhishek Malhotra, a partner at consulting firm, Booz Allen and Co., said that for Bharti Walmart while retail in India is attractive, wholesale could be a viable business as well. "Even if they are allowed in (to invest in multibrand retail) more and more such foreign companies will continue to operate in that space," he said.

www.livemint.com May 5, 2011.

In July 2011, the Committee of Secretaries approved 51 per cent FDI in retail ventures, further pushing for Walmart's takeover of India's retail.

Re-designing the food system

Navdanya's work on biodiverse farming has shown that the more biodiversity there is on a farm, the higher its output. The polycultures of ecological agricultural systems have evolved because more output can be harvested from a given area planted with diverse crops, than from an equivalent area consisting of separate patches of monoculture. For example, in plantings of sorghum and pigeon pea mixtures, one hectare will produce the same yields as 0.94 hectares of sorghum monoculture and 0.68 hectares of pigeon pea monoculture. Thus, one hectare of polyculture produces what 1.62 hectares of monoculture can produce. This is called the land equivalent ratio (LER).

Increased land-use efficiency and higher LER have been reported for polycultures of: millet/groundnut 1.26; maize/bean 1.38; millet/sorghum 1.53; maize/pigeon pea 1.85; maize/cocoyan/sweet potato 2.08; cassava/maize/groundnut 2.51. The monocultures of the green revolution thus actually reduced food yields per acre previously achieved through mixtures of diverse crops. This falsifies the argument often made that chemically-intensive agriculture and genetic engineering will save biodiversity by releasing land from food production. In fact, since monocultures require more land, biodiversity is destroyed twice over – once on the farm, and then on the additional acreage required to produce the outputs that monoculture has displaced. Further, since chemicals kill diverse species, chemical agriculture can hardly be promoted as conserving biodiversity.[24]

Not only is the productivity measure distorted by ignoring resource inputs, it is also distorted by looking only at a single and partial output rather than the total output. A myth promoted by the one-dimensional monoculture paradigm is that biodiversity reduces yields and productivity; however, since yields and productivity are theoretically constructed terms, they change according to the context. Yield usually refers to production per unit area of a single crop; planting only one crop in the entire field as a monoculture will of course increase its yield. Planting multiple crops in a mixture will have *low yields* of individual crops, but a *high total output* of food.

The Mayan peasants in the Chiapas are characterised as unproductive because they produce only two tonnes of corn per acre, but the overall food output is 20 tonnes per acre. In the terraced fields of the high Himalaya, women peasants grow jhangora (barnyard millet), marsha (amaranth), tur (pigeon pea), urad (black gram), gahat (horse gram), soya bean (*glysine max*), bhat (*glysine soya*), rayans (rice bean), swanta (cow pea), koda (finger millet) in mixtures and rotations. The total output, even in bad years, is six times more than industrially farmed rice monocultures. A mixed organic farm in the Himalaya produces 9,000 kgs. of maize, radish, mustard greens and peas; a chemically farmed maize monoculture yields 5,000 kgs. This may be 1,000 kgs. more maize than the biodiverse system, but 4,000 kgs. less food. In terms of nutrition per acre, the biodiverse farming system is much more productive than the chemical monocultures. It provides 305 (g) of Ca and 29.3 (g) of iron compared to the monoculture.

Similarly, a biodiverse intensive system with finger millet, barnyard millet, horse gram and indigenous soya yields 1,400 kgs. of food per acre compared to a chemical rice monoculture which yields 1,200 kgs. In terms of nutrition, the former gives 338 kgs. of protein compared to 90 kgs. in the monoculture. The biodiverse intensive system gives 2,540 mgs. of carotene compared to 24 mgs. in the monoculture, and 554 mgs. of folic acid compared to 0 in the rice monoculture.[25]

Since food production, nutrition and nourishment are the main aims of agriculture, nutrition per acre is a more accurate measure of productivity than yield of a commodity in a monoculture. The nutrients produced by plants become food for humans and for soil organisms, which in turn feed the plants which feed the humans and the soils. The perennial nutrient cycle continues to be sustained and can even be intensified through biodiversity and ecological intensification.

Industrial agriculture productivity is high only in the restricted context of a 'part of a part' of the system, whether it be the forest or the farm. For example, 'high-yield' plantations pick one tree species among thousands, for yields of one part of the tree (e.g., woodpulp), whereas traditional forestry practices use many parts of many forest species.

'High-yield' green revolution cropping patterns select one crop among hundreds, such as wheat, for the use of just one part, the grain. These high partial yields do not translate into high total yields, because everything else in the farm system goes to waste. Traditional farming systems are based on mixed and rotational cropping systems of cereals, pulses and oilseeds with different varieties of each crop; no realistic assessments are ever made of the yield of diverse crop outputs in the mixed and rotational systems.

Productivity is quite different, however, when it is measured in the context of diversity which shows that small farmers can feed the world. In Brazil, the productivity of a biodiverse farm of up to ten hectares was $85 per hectare, while the productivity of a 500 ha.

one-crop farm was $2 per ha. In India, a farm of up to five acres had a productivity of Rs.735 per acre, while a 35 acre farm had a productivity of Rs. 346 per acre. Productivity in ecological farming practices is high if we calculate that it is based on internal inputs with very few external inputs. While the green revolution has been projected as having increased productivity in the absolute sense, when resource utilisation is taken into account, it has been found to be counter-productive and resource-inefficient.

What does all this evidence mean in terms of "feeding the world"? Data show that, everywhere in the world, biodiverse small farms produce more agricultural output per unit area than large farms. Even in the US, small farms of 27 acres or less have ten times greater dollar output per acre than larger ones. It is therefore time to switch from measuring monoculture yields to assessing biodiversity outputs in farming systems.

A UN report submitted to the General Assembly on December 20, 2010, by the Special Rapporteur on the Right to Food, Olivier de Schutter, confirms that ecological agriculture produces more food. "Resource-conserving, low-external-input techniques have a proven potential to significantly improve yields. Ecological interventions on 12.6 million farms increased crop yields of 79 per cent (p. 8)." The UNCTAD-UNEP study, "Organic Agriculture and Food Security in Africa" (2008), found that ecological methods increase crop yields by 116 per cent for all of Africa and 128 per cent for East Africa.

References

[1] Mayank Bharadwaj, "India's 09/10 Edible Oil Imports to Jump 46 Per Cent", March 16, 2010, Reuters.

[2] Organic Consumers' Association, "Massive Government Subsidies for GE Soybean" http://www.organicconsumers.org

[3] Victor Davis Hensen, "Pruning Farm Subsidies: US Needs Drastic Reset of Its Agricultural Policy," Ohio, *The Morning Journal*, February 17, 2011.

[4] "Helping Farmers", *Deccan Herald*, November 22, 2004.

[5] Sonu Jain, "Centre to States: Reform, Only Then You Can Get Money to Improve Farmers' Market", *Indian Express*, October 21, 2004.

[6] Rajiv Shah, "State Opposes Corporate Sector Entry in Agriculture Marketing," *Times of India*, November 21, 2004.

[7] Quoted in Vandana Shiva, "The Great Grain Robbery by Agribusiness MNCs", Research Foundation for Science, Technology and Environment, 2005.

[8] Anil Yadav, "Babu Rashtriya Kampanyo Ke Fando Se Sawdhan", *Nai Duniya*, October 29, 2004.

[9] Rasheeda Bhagat, "Give Them Empowerment First," *Business Line*, November 19, 2004.

[10] "Partial Response to Bhopal Bandh", *The Hindu*, December 21, 2004.

[11] Yogi Agarwal, "Turn-Around Time", *Business India*, June 18, 2006.

[12] L.S. Herdenia, "Farmers, Traders Up in Arms Against M.P. Government," *Kashmir Times*, December 25, 2004.

[13] Tim Lang and M. Heasman, *Food Wars*, London: Earthscan, 2004.

[14] Thomas L. Friedman, *The World is Flat*, New York: Farrar, Straus & Giroux, 2005.

[15] Kenneth Stone, "Impact of the Walmart Phenomenon on Rural Communities". www.econ.iastate.edu/faculty/stone/10yearstudy pdf

[16] ETC Report on Oligopoly Inc. www.etcgroup.org/en/node/44

[17] Personal communication from the author.

[18-22] Charles Fishman, *The Walmart Effect*, New York: Penguin, 2006.

[23] Aaditya Mattoo, et al, "From Corruption at Home to Competing Abroad," World Bank Report, 2007.

[24] Navdanya, "Biodiversity-based Productivity: A New Paradigm for Food Security and the Environment", Delhi: 2005, 2009.

[25] Navdanya, "Health Per Acre," Delhi: 2011.

9 Beyond Growth: Making Peace with the Earth

"If we have poor measures, what we strive to do (say, increase GDP) may actually contribute to a worsening of living standards … statistical frameworks are intended to summarise what is going on in our complex society in a few easily interpretable numbers. It should have been obvious that one couldn't reduce everything to a single number, GDP."

— Joseph Stiglitz

E.J. MISHAN, another eminent economist, in his book, *The Costs of Economic Growth*, points out,

> Apparently one has but to consult it to comprehend the entire condition of society. Among the faithful … to doubt that, say, a four per cent growth rate … is better for the nation than a three per cent growth rate is near-heresy; it is tantamount to doubting that four is greater than three.[1]

Mishan referred to the obsession with measuring growth as a "mass flight from reality to statistics".

Across the world, there is a deep questioning of the growth model: the rich North has become disillusioned with a growth economy both because it has not brought satisfaction, joy and happiness, and because it is now collapsing. In the countries of the South, growth is leading to the dispossession of the poor and of their resources. The violent replacement of sustenance and subsistence societies through the imposition of growth hides ecological destruction and economic dispossession. Nature and people are rendered invisible, as "growth" replaces the well-being of the earth and of communities. Abstract constructions replace living resources and living communities, means become ends, and human ends are forgotten.

It is abstractions like these that led to the sub-prime crisis and the collapse of Wall Street in 2008. As the Group of 20 stated in its Declaration at the Summit on Financial Markets and the World Economy, November 15, 2008:

> During a period of strong global growth, growing capital flows and prolonged stability earlier this decade, market participants sought higher yields without an adequate appreciation of the risks, and failed to exercise proper due diligence. At the same time, weak underwriting standards, unsound risk management practices, increasingly complex and opaque financial products and consequent excessive leverage combined to create vulnerabilities in the system. Policy makers, regulators and supervisors in some advanced countries did not adequately appreciate and address the risks building up in financial markets, keep pace with financial innovation, or take into account the systemic reunifications of domestic regulatory services.[2]

The domination of abstract instruments, divorced from reality or regulation, resulted in the collapse of financial institutions. The five largest US investment banks had combined debts of $4 trillion. Lehman Brothers went bankrupt; Bear Stearns and Merrill Lynch were taken over by other companies, and Goldman Sachs and Morgan Stanley were bailed out by the US government. While the banks were bailed out, six million US citizens lost their jobs. The total US economy is $14 trillion in terms of GDP – $9 trillion was the debt obligation in seven of the largest financial institutions.[3]

The great Indian oligarchs

The global image of India has been undergoing drastic changes in the last few decades: from being known as an exotic land of spirituality and great culture on the one hand, and massive poverty and destitution on the other, India suddenly finds itself on the world's platform presented as one of globalisation's winners. "Shining India" became not only a national political slogan by which huge economic, political and social changes were brought about and justified, but also the country's new brand name. Dollar billionaires from India, now famous worldwide, occupy the top slots of the Forbes billionaires list. How did the great Indian oligarchs emerge? Which policies and processes facilitated their rise? India is often referred to as an "emerging economy"; Indian civilisation is, of course, too ancient to be "emerging", but what exactly has emerged from globalisation and deregulation?

With the much-hyped neoliberal model based on privatisation, liberalisation and globalisation, the avenues were finally opened for the economic rise of India's billionaires, misleadingly presented as the rise of India, the miracle growth story. In the era of globalisation, the drastic reforms of the 1990s under the aegis of the then Cambridge/Oxford-educated finance minister, Manmohan Singh, came to be seen as undisputed propellers of growth – as a double-digit GDP rate was seemingly testifying. While great wealth has indeed been accumulated, it has actually remained concentrated in the hands of a few traditionally influential families, as sectors in the public domain increasingly became private oligopolies.

Yet, more recently, a wave of scandals of enormous proportions involving politicians and some of the biggest business houses is rocking the very foundations of India's new global status. The heat has been turned up on India's wealthiest: if so far business acumen and ingenuity were praised as sole determinants of successful ventures, the public is now questioning whether this ingenuity was not also at work in lobbying for particular policies, rule-bending and favouritism. As people question how such wealth came to be, it is important to examine the connection between politics, economic policies and a lopsided pattern of growth: the inequality is, in fact, the result of a process initiated two decades ago and consistently and vehemently pushed forward by governments which profess inclusive growth.

Any structural change has distributive effects. In a country like India where political, social, economic, religious and identity-based constituencies abound, as do particular interests, it is of paramount importance to examine the distribution of benefits and losses which any initiative entails. Studies suggest that the liberalisation process of the 1990s was strongly biased in favour of the corporate business sector and local elites: already powerful sections were able to reaffirm their status and wealth, increasing economic and political clout and political connections.

The corporate business sector was pushed to the forefront of the economy, presented as innovators, dynamos of change and growth. An India of 1.2 billion people was reduced to India Inc. Public sector units had come to be seen as redundant and unnecessarily bureaucratic, when not corrupt. Privatisation was strongly argued for as the panacea to resolve all of India's structural inefficiencies and problems. International financial institutions have been systematically preaching the Liberalisation, Privatisation, Globalisation (LPG) mantra through a carrot and stick approach: the country was lured through promises of rapid growth, modernisation and increased well-being for the people, through reforms pushed through structural adjustment programmes and loan conditionalities.

At the time of the economic reforms, India was in the midst of a balance of payment crisis; accepting international institutional assistance also meant accepting their diktat. The World Bank initiated a two-year $500 million Structural Adjustment Program (SAP), from December 1991 to December 1993,[4] supported by an IMF-led stabilisation programme. The SAP involved deregulation and liberalisation with the idea of opening up India's economy to the world. Subsidies were cut substantially; trade policy was liberalised with decreased tariffs; industrial and import licencing were considerably reduced; foreign direct investment, foreign equity investment and participation in business were hugely increased. The New Industrial Policy introduced in 1991 broke the public sector's domination, and crucial economic sectors such as power, telecommunications, infrastructure, mining and banking were opened up to private investment. Manufacturing sectors including iron, steel and ship-building were also opened up for private business. All traditional common property resources, public goods and services like water, electricity, health and education were steadily enclosed and privatised. Conditions were thus created for domestic and foreign private players to enter and exploit largely uncharted territory which they would soon dominate.

If the direct beneficiary of the new policy was the business sector, the middle classes too welcomed restructuring with open arms: India had been a domestic economy with production and consumption for the Indian market. With globalisation, the country's middle and upper classes were brought under the spell of all that was foreign – they were hungry for international goods, values and lifestyles, and identified government policies as regressive. Unfortunately, the general public has often remained oblivious to the deeper impact on the socio-economic reality of India, especially for local producers, small farmers, small industry and small retail. If for some, India's opening up to the world economy simply meant being able to access foreign consumer goods, for a much larger section of society this translated into a consistent, constant and unstoppable threat to their very survival through the loot of their resources and livelihoods. This divide has often been referred to as the "India-Bharat" divide – between the privileged consuming classes, largely urban, and peasants and tribals in rural areas. This has also been accompanied by a steady shift in mentality and approach to social policy, where wealth accumulation is presented as the foremost achievement, and poverty almost as individual failure.

The neoliberal paradigm has pushed strongly for a withdrawal of government's participation in the country's economic affairs. Its new reductionist role has signified a partial abandonment of what used to be the foremost guiding policy principles in India based on a socialist ideology of equality and redistribution. While liberalisation opened up avenues for corporate profits, it closed down local economies, livelihoods, safety nets and social security for the worse off. If the socialist ideology of Gandhi and Nehru implied a strong component of social justice, the new capitalist model does away with concerns over common welfare, replacing the notion of community with that of the individual. While the rhetoric is for more market and less government regulation, what is happening in fact is deregulation for corporations, and over-regulation for citizens.

The deregulation of commerce has had far-reaching and manifold consequences; first, the focus on pro-corporate policies and a reductionist role for the state is at the cost of weaker sections of society in need of social safety nets and protection; second, as the market becomes the predominant ruling institution, rights are replaced by purchasing power, leaving the majority of the population excluded from welfare and benefit provisions or dependent on "hand-outs"; third, competition for resources on an uneven playing field translates into the privatisation of the commons; lastly, the shift in mentality that accompanies capitalist growth increasingly sees this accumulation as legitimate, justifying the means for the ends. If deregulation and privatisation expose the poor to new threats of exploitation, they also set the stage for a process known as accumulation by encroachment or dispossession, typical of capitalism, where resources are not created *ex novo*, but appropriated from pre-capitalist or state sector production, or through direct takeover of common property resources which are now privatised.[5]

This kind of growth, far from leading to poverty reduction makes for a redistribution of wealth from a large base at the bottom of society to a small elite at the top. Studies of income tax reports show clearly that, with the New Economic Policy, incomes of the top one per cent increased by about 50 per cent; of this one per cent the richest one per cent increased incomes more than three times.[6] Indeed, the LPG approach was beneficial to some, but instead of the trickle-down assumption, wealth was actually percolating up: the rich were getting richer while the poor were increasingly dispossessed and marginalised – physically, socially and politically.

The most blatant evidence of this lop-sided pattern of wealth accumulation is the creation of several Indian billionaires; practically unchallenged in the newly-opened market, a handful of well-connected firms and families soon came to control huge resources, leading to the rise of the Indian oligarchs. The Forbes list of 2011 includes 50 Indian billionaires: famously, Arcelor Mittal's owner, Lakshmi Mittal (no. 6: $31.1 billion); the Ambanis: Reliance India Ltd. and Anil Dhirubhai Ambani Group – Mukesh (9: $27 billion) and Anil (103: $8.8 billion); the Ruia family (42: $15.8 billion) with Essar Group; the Jindals (56: $13.2 billion); Gautam Adani (81: $10 billion); Sunil Mittal of Bharti-Airtel (110: $8.3 billion); Anil Agarwal of Vedanta (164: $6.4 billion). Ratan Tata of the Tata Group does not appear in the list as his wealth is predominantly held by his charitable trusts; yet the size and operations of its conglomerate qualify him for this study. That some of the billionaires are self-made while others are inheritors of wealth does not affect the argument, as it confirms the tendency of wealth to remain in the hands of those already wealthy, and also that while some groups replace others, wealth stays concentrated in oligopolies.

Arcelor Mittal

The richest man in India and the sixth richest in the world, Lakshmi Mittal is known worldwide; he happens also to be the richest man in Europe and Britain, where he resides in a luxury mansion at prestigious and posh Kensington Palace Gardens. On a street known as Billionaires' Row, the house is said to be the most expensive private residence ever bought. Lakshmi Mittal's wealth of $31.1 billion derives primarily from his company, Arcelor Mittal's business in steel. With industrial capacity in twenty countries and operations in over sixty, Arcelor Mittal is reputed as a leader in steel production on most global markets, listed on the stock exchanges of New York, Amsterdam, Paris, Brussels, Luxembourg, Barcelona, Bilbao, Madrid and Valencia.[7]

Mittal is also an independent director at Goldman Sachs; member of the board of directors of European Aeronautic Defence and Space Company; World Steel Association; Foreign Investment Council in Kazakhstan; the International Investment Council in South Africa;

the Investors' Council to the Cabinet of Ministers of Ukraine; the World Economic Forum's International Business Council; the World Steel Association's Executive Committee; the Presidential International Advisory Board of Mozambique; and the International Iron and Steel Institute's Executive Committee, as well as board council member of the Prime Minister of India's Global Advisory Council of Overseas Indians.

Starting with the family's steel business, Lakshmi Mittal ventured out with the acquisition of a rundown steel mill in Indonesia, initiating his rise as a steel magnate through a process of consistent consolidation – acquiring steel-making units in large parts of Europe, US, Canada and Africa. More recently, Arcelor Mittal's proposals for Greenfield projects are being put forward in India, Liberia, Senegal, Mauritania, Mozambique, Nigeria, Russia, Saudi Arabia and Turkey. The company also banks on vertical integration to streamline production for its steel-making operations; its control over raw materials also means it is involved in mining iron ore and coal. The consolidation and vertical integration strategies resulting in market domination raise a number of issues.

First, the consolidation trend giving it significant control over the market has resulted in a huge oligopoly with substantial economic and political weight; second, the process is based on taking advantage of weaker sectors/industries/regulations in often fragile or less developed economies, turning poor labour standards and wages into profitable business assets, as they are considered to be cost-cutting devices; third, the direct sourcing of raw materials entails a strong involvement in mining which is one of the most environmentally and socially destructive economic sectors; fourth, taking a broader perspective, the thriving of metal industries derives from and banks on an ideology of over-consumption and industrialisation as the ultimate goal of development.

The policy framework in India is similarly geared to increasing production of steel, as the country aims to become a world leader with targets of 200 million tonnes of steel production by 2020. With the New Industrial Policy implemented from 1991, the iron and steel industry was removed from the list of industries reserved for the public sector and exempted from compulsory licencing. The New Economic Policy introduced the following changes in the steel industry:

- Large-scale capacities were removed from the list of industries reserved for the public sector; licencing requirements for additional capacities were also withdrawn subject to locational restrictions.
- The private sector came to play a prominent role in the overall set-up.
- Pricing and distribution control mechanisms were discontinued.
- The iron and steel industry was included in the high priority list for foreign investment, implying automatic approval for foreign equity participation up to 50 per cent, subject to foreign exchange and other stipulations governing such investments in general.
- Quantitative import restrictions were largely removed, export restrictions were withdrawn.

The regulatory framework thus allowed private domestic and foreign participation and streamlined other policies to follow suit. In the case of metal industries, for example, the New Mineral Policy, 2008, came into being with considerable deregulation and emphasis on facilitating private players into mining. The consequences of such favourable treatment are borne massively by local communities: mineral-rich Central India is now gripped by violent land wars and conflicts, as mining and steel companies divert forests and grab agricultural land to set up their facilities, leaving behind a trail of displacement, pollution and destruction. Arcelor Mittal, too, found itself involved in controversy as it set out to mine iron ore and set up steel plants in Jharkhand, Orissa and Chhattisgarh, where it encountered strong local opposition. Similarly, the promise of investment and technology has promoted privatisation of public units and, in 2008, Arcelor Mittal proposed to the government the setting up of a joint venture taking over centrally-owned coal mines held by Coal India Ltd.

As public sector units are privatised and small mills and plants taken over, industry becomes more and more concentrated and monopolistic; further privatisation is advocated by financial advisers and institutions on grounds of economies of scale. (In the case of steel, it is worth noting that POSCO was originally born and run successfully as a public enterprise; the company was privatised under IMF diktat as South Korea received institutional stabilisation loans.)

Privatisation, consolidation and vertical integration are the pillars on which huge steel empires are built in the absence of competition, or where competitors are too weak to survive.

The Reliance empire

The Reliance brand name is associated with a multitude of ventures – petrochemicals, plastic, retail, SEZ, oil & gas, electricity, finance, telecommunications – and Dhirubhai Ambani, the original founder, is held in high esteem as a man with a dream and an aspiration. Exemplifying a rags to riches tale, he is lionised as a symbol of change, of emancipation, and of success.

While Dhirubhai Ambani did indeed create an empire from scratch, he was also backed by the right connections. It is widely accepted that doing business in the licence raj era implied keeping good relations with the bureaucracy and politicians; even after the economy was liberalised and competition grew, connections in the right place were an important competitive advantage. Starting out by working at a petrol station, Dhirubhai went on to become the owner of India's largest refinery at Jamnagar in Gujarat. His break came with the purchase of a spinning mill near Ahmedabad to begin a textile company named Vimal, and he managed to raise funds from society at large rather than from institutions, initiating what is known as the *equity cult*. As the company became more successful, Ambani set out to create an industrial manufacturing complex.

Dhirubhai's Reliance was favoured particularly during Rajiv Gandhi's regime, even before formal liberalisation, as India's earlier priority in the textile sector – the khadi cotton, handspun, handwoven and handloom inspired by Gandhi – was let down through policies favouring synthetic and machine-made cloth.

The company began major diversifications around the 1980s and 1990s, the reform decades. The Rajiv Gandhi government had already initiated a set of reforms, amongst which were reducing income and corporate taxes as incentives to the private sector; reducing the list of items reserved for small-scale sectors; and deregulating several sectors including telecommunications and cement. In the decade that followed, the Narasimha Rao government pushed these reforms forward with much greater impetus, focussing particularly on industrial growth. The system of central licencing was dismantled and private companies were allowed to do business in sectors previously under the sole control of the state. Foreign participation was encouraged, imports were facilitated through a more liberal trade policy and, more importantly, the Monopolies and Restrictive Trade Practices Act was relaxed, encouraging private actors to enter previously closed markets.[8]

It is against this backdrop that the Ambani family's spectacular rise is assessed: as the economy was deregulated and liberalised the Reliance group, backed by an already familiar brand name and by the necessary economic and political clout, consolidated its business, both by diversification and aggressive expansion. Through a process of backward integration, Reliance diversified into raw materials for its textile and polyester operations, and further back into oil and chemicals. In the following years, the company through its two arms (RIL and ADAG) entered into telecommunications, petrochemicals, power, life sciences, finance, infrastructure, retail, SEZ development, entertainment and so on. In time Reliance took over Indian Petrochemicals Limited, which now controls over three-fourths of the country's petrochemical market.

A major player in the oil and gas sector, RIL was the biggest gainer of liberalisation at the time: in 1994 the Oil and Natural Gas Commission was publicly held; following privatisation in 1997-98 the government introduced the New Exploration Licensing Policy

(NELP) granting access to private players on the basis of competitive bidding – RIL was allotted the largest number of blocks after ONGC. Most recently, the Comptroller and Auditor General reported that the oil ministry and the Directorate General of Hydrocarbons (DGH) had been favouring Reliance, causing losses to the exchequer, aside from other huge benefits granted to the company by bending rules to accommodate them.[9]

As RIL's oil volume pumped from Andhra Pradesh decreased, Mukesh Ambani embarked on a partnership with British oil giant, British Petroleum: after the clearance in July 2011 the oil ministry hailed the BP-RIL deal as India's biggest FDI to date, at $7.2 billion. The synergy between companies in the West eager to enter the Indian market and domestic ones, lured by technology and investment, is increasingly visible as business becomes more and more transnational and detached from the original country's local reality. In another joint venture, RIL has partnered with Australian UXA for uranium mining; simultaneously, the company is lobbying for deregulation of this sector to allow private companies to access it, while also arguing for Indian firms to be granted incentives for the same, overseas.

The telecommunications sector was privatised around 1994 with the introduction of a National Telecom Policy. Licences for telecom spectrum were to be allotted through open competitive bidding as a means to increase fairness and accountability, but what took place was the opposite. The Reliance Telecommunications arm is currently being investigated in the country's biggest scam over 2G spectrum allocations. If the final outcome of such investigations cannot be predicted, considering the climate of lax implementation and fraudulent or absent regulatory compliance in the country, the way such events unfold is enough to raise some questions. Mukesh Ambani complained to the prime minister in this regard, as these questions are denting his reputation.

The Reliance brand's activities with regard to retail and real estate development are some of the starkest examples of how this state-corporate nexus is promoting accumulation by the rich. Through its supermarket chain, Reliance Fresh, the company has brought about a negative revolution for India's small retail sector the way Walmart did in the United States. Currently, the company is earmarking plots of agricultural land for future food production; this constitutes the last step in the privatisation of the commons, wherein food becomes a private commodity and no longer an intrinsic right. In Andhra Pradesh's Kakinada SEZ, the company has earmarked 200 acres for jatropha plantations for biofuels.

The process of forcible or coercive land acquisition for the Reliance Power SEZ in Dadri and for the multi-product one in Haryana, are other examples of the bias in favour of corporate interests. For the sake of Anil Ambani's Reliance Power SEZ at Dadri, police forces brutally fired on protestors, assaulted locals and destroyed villages as they resisted the acquisition of 2,500 acres of fertile land.[10] It must be noted that legislation such as the Electricity Act (2003) and the Energy Conservation Act (2001) introduced liberal conditions and deregulation in order to favour private sector participation: a specific mention is made of the need to revise the land acquisition process in order to facilitate power generating industries. Reliance is thus gaining massively through different avenues: aside from being the leading power distributor in Mumbai and Delhi, its Sasan project has been registered with the UN Clean Development Mechanisms, opening up profits of over Rs 2,000 crores from the sale of certified emission reduction credits (*Reliance Power Press Release*, February 3, 2011).

Essar Group

Liberalisation similarly favoured the fortunes of another family: the Essar Group, set up in 1969 by the brothers, Shashi and Ravi Ruia, who established a varied business empire comprising steel, mining, oil, power and telecommunications that pushed the brothers into the world's billionaires list.

Born into a business family, the Ruias started off as a construction company. With deregulation during the 1980s, the shipping and drilling sector were opened up for private business, and through the 1990s a number of other sectors were liberalised, including power, telecommunications, mining, ports, roads and banking. The Essar Group took advantage of this and diversified into steel, oil, gas and telecommunications. Its steel manufacturing facilities are located in India, Indonesia, Canada and North America, and its retailing and processing activities cover India, Indonesia, the UAE and UK.

As part of backward integration to its steel-making ventures, Essar is involved in mining operations in India, Indonesia, US, Mozambique and Brazil, focussing on iron ore for a total reserve of 1.6 billion tonnes, and coal for a total of 450 million tonnes.[11] Growing domestic demand from the steel industry led to a boom in metal prices; minerals are increasingly highly valued on the international market, in view of growing scarcity at a time when industrialisation and urbanisation are still significant factors pushing demand. While developed economies' mineral and metal consumption has suffered the effects of the global recession with smelters and plants closing down, developing and emerging economies are scaling up capacity, production and consumption. (This trend – arguably also favoured by carbon trading approaches to climate-change control – is based on a model of "outsourcing of pollution", where environmentally damaging industries and activities are increasingly being shut down in the West and imported by the East.)

Some of the richest regions or countries in mineral and natural resources are also amongst the most impoverished, often torn by armed conflict if not outright civil war. In India, too, as the government went ahead with its privatisation programme, Essar was granted a prospecting licence in Dantewada, Chhattisgarh, a region most affected by violent resource wars. Similarly, for Essar Steel's plant in Dhurli, Dantewada, 600 ha. of land were forcefully acquired at the cost of locals' livelihoods, human rights and democracy.[12] Interestingly, the Salwa Judum was launched on the same day as the MoUs for Tata Steel and Essar Steel were signed.

This trend of plunder and profit in natural resources such as oil and minerals, means that public utilities become private sector domains allowing for private wealth accumulation. As an example of the latter, Essar and Tata control a great part of the Sabri river in Chhattisgarh for their industrial operations.[13]

Jindal Steel & Power

Started in 1952 by O. P. Jindal, a farmer's son, to trade in steel pipes, he moved into manufacturing them and opened his first factory near Kolkata. Similar to other billionaire family companies, the Jindal group, too, moved into backward integration. While steel remained their primary focus, the company went on to diversify and create a wide portfolio ranging from mining operations to power, infrastructure and telecommunications, making it one of India's biggest private conglomerates. After the founder's demise, the group's businesses are managed by his widow, Savitri Jindal, and their four sons: Prithvi Raj, Sajjan, Ratan and Navin, in a complex cross-ownership pattern. Each brother has the largest holding of the division he manages while owning shares in the others' businesses as well.[14]

Politicians, bureaucrats and business houses in India are a closely-knit clique with interchangeable roles in many cases. Savitri Jindal, India's richest woman, is also a Congress MLA and was minister of state for revenue, disaster management, rehabilitation and housing in Haryana; Navin Jindal is a standing Member of Parliament; O.P. Jindal was also active in politics, winning a seat in the Haryana state assembly in 1991 and in the Lok Sabha in 1996; at the time of his death he was also power minister in Haryana.

The Jindal Group, too, has resorted to forceful land acquisition for its mining and industrial operations. In November 2009, a bomb exploded on a convoy of the then West Bengal chief minister and union steel minister, Ram Vilas Paswan, as they were returning after inaugurating the Jindal steel plant at Salboni. The police, in the guise of anti-Naxal operations, unleashed brutal repression on boys and young villagers who were labelled as Maoists, and three innocent tribals were killed.

In another case of expropriation of the commons, there were wide protests in Orissa as Jindal Steel and Power Limited acquired forest and community land for a 12.5 million tonnes per annum steel plant without providing compensation.[15] The locals claim that what the government calls state property is actually a community-managed resource – this constitutes the central issue in the mode of accumulation by dispossession. The death of an adivasi woman after a hunger strike protesting JSPL's takeover of water from the river Kelo for its plant, in Raigarh,[16] or distraught farmers turned into casual labourers by displacement near the Rabo village, are all byproducts of privatisation and of the broader trend that allows industries a free run as far as resources and regulations are concerned: dams by private companies have come up aplenty despite government objections. On April 20, 2012, the National Green Tribunal set aside the environmental clearance granted to the four MTPA coal mining project of Jindal Steel, and a four MTPA coal washery in Raigarh district. It called the public hearing on the project a "farce".[17]

Jindal Steel is another company that is profiting through the more covert route of the Clean Development Mechanism (CDM); it is building one of the world's largest CDMs in Chhattisgarh, a sponge-iron plant spread over 320 ha., polluting groundwater and the air and contaminating crops. Through such projects, companies claim benefits, sometimes even in contravention of the CDM policy itself. In July 2011, the Karnataka Lokayukta (Ombudsman) found Jindal Steel guilty of trading in illegally mined iron ore.

Adani Group

Gautam Adani started out as a diamond trader, but went on to accumulate a huge fortune by building infrastructure (ports), through real estate development, power generation, oil, and trading in agricultural commodities. His break came when his brother purchased a plastic unit in Ahmedabad for him to run. Importing PVC as raw material for the business, the group's profits soared substantially only after the liberalisation of India's economy: as tariffs were slashed and barriers to trade removed, import/export became a thriving business. Banking on the favourable environment, Adani was successful in building his empire, admittedly through his ability to adapt his business to the local economic and political climate: Adani Enterprises, Adani Power and Mundra Port and Special Economic Zone have grown in sectors which significantly benefited from deregulation.

The Mundra SEZ, the largest in India, spread over 10,000 ha. of land, caused the destruction of a rich mangrove ecosystem along the coasts of the Kutch Gulf, with severe consequences for water availability, fishing activities and local livelihoods. The National Fishworkers' Forum leader framed the problem as one of mal-industrialisation:

> Hazardous units manufacturing petrochemicals, pesticides and agrochemicals have mushroomed along the Gujarat coast. Refineries and private ports have compounded the misery of people living in these areas. Our survey shows that the worst culprits are the Adani Group, which is building a port at Mundra; Sanghi Cement in Sanghipur (Saurashtra); and Atul Agrochemicals in Bharuch.[18]

The SEZ and captive port have been developed in the prohibited coastal zone with the company presenting misleading evidence of its plans to obtain the necessary clearances. Moreover, the regulatory scenario works to the advantage of big business houses: the Coastal Regulation Zone (CRZ) notification prohibiting development in coastal areas was amended in 2002, then again in 2011 by the MoEF, allowing for industrial development in fragile coastal ecosystems; this was accompanied by a telling remark by the then environment minister, Jairam Ramesh, that India "must get used" to such industrial plants being located in coastal areas.

Adani is also profiting from mining; his company has mining interests across Australia, Africa and Asia. In India, Adani operates two coal mines in Chhattisgarh and one in Orissa; it is also the country's largest importer of coal. Once again, the claim that introducing competitive bidding to allow for private competition and transparency was proven to be false, as the Punjab State Electricity Board is accused of having favoured Adani, disregarding the actual bidders' entitlements for the import of 22 lakh metric tonnes of coal for its power plants, resulting in a Rs 100 crores loss to the exchequer.[19]

Adani has been assigned a contract for setting up a 1,320 MW coal-based thermal power plant on agricultural land in Chhindwara, for which the Pench river will be diverted. Farmers have been protesting against the displacement caused by the dam and the power project. On May 24, 2011, Dr. Sunilam and Aradhana Bhargava of Kisan Sangarsh Samiti were attacked by the henchmen of Adani Power; their car was smashed, Dr. Sunilam suffered a head injury and both his arms were broken. A press statement issued by the People's Union for Democratic Rights (PUDR) states,

> The attack by Adani Power Limited's armed goons is yet another instance of how powerful corporate houses are resorting to organised violence, perpetrated through their private mafias, to silence those who come in the way of their interests, and break people's attempts to organise on issues of land, water, forests.[20]

Bharti Airtel

Sunil Mittal founded Bharti Enterprises in 1976; Bharti Airtel, his flagship company, is the largest telephone operator in India and now stands fifth in world telecom, with businesses spread across nineteen countries. Starting out as a bicycle-parts maker, Mittal moved to Bombay and began importing different items, entering the international trade arena. He says it was at this point that he learnt how to navigate the Indian regulatory environment as the economic scenario began changing substantially. As the barriers came down, his company's fortunes turned. The telecom sector had so far been restricted in terms of manufacturing capacity, importing and exporting, but now it was wide open. As Mittal said in an interview, "From controlling what you could do [snaps fingers] it was gone in one day."[21] Today, Bharti Airtel is expanding beyond borders: focussing on Africa, it is striking deals with local providers and acquiring assets in over sixteen African countries.

While Mittal is a leader in the telecom sector, he is also involved in retail through a controversial partnership with US giant, Walmart.

Tata

Tata is not only a household name in India, but also one of the country's most renowned brand names abroad where it is considered something of a symbol of renascent India. According to the Reputation Institute, it is the second most trusted brand in India and the eleventh most reputable in the world. Ratan Tata, fifth generation chairman of the country's biggest private conglomerate, is also one of the most respected and trusted tycoons, although unlike the other billionaires, he does not appear in the Forbes list.

Ratan Tata was appointed chairman of Tata Sons in 1991, and under him the company began its international operations; it went on to become the giant that it is with 96 companies and operations spread across 56 countries. Of these, the steel business remains the country's largest, along with automotive and outsourcing concerns. Post-liberalisation, the company shed a number of sectors, aiming at achieving global competitiveness and domestic leadership – Tata is said to have foreseen and strategically managed the economic restructuring to its advantage. Through streamlining and rationalising operations and initiating mergers and acquisitions on an international scale, the group not only sustained the reforms of the 1990s, it also emerged as a leading conglomerate, producing everything from salt to luxury cars and service delivery. Admirers attribute such success to Tata's ability to deliver goods and services tailored to the needs of the broad public.

This, together with numerous charitable initiatives, including a "better than the rest" rehabilitation policy, has granted the company an aura of trust and benevolence. While to many, Tata stands for admirable business acumen benefitting the company and consumers, to another set of people it has meant exactly the opposite: loss of land, loss of livelihood and loss of life. The Tata Group has been involved more or less directly in environmental issues as well as in social conflicts deriving from industrial operations. Tata Steel in particular, has been at the centre of numerous controversies – in Orissa, the Dhamara port, operated through a joint venture between Tata Steel and Larsen & Toubro, was in violation of the Forest Conservation Act, yet was allowed to operate despite huge protests.

As the government deregulated mining and mineral processing, the company eyed uranium mines in a fertile agricultural zone in Tamil Nadu, encountering opposition from the local population that resisted land dispossession, livelihood destruction and environmental degradation. Similarly, in Orissa and Jharkhand, land acquisition for Tata steel plants led to the killing of innocent adivasis and the injuring of many women and children. The most well-known instance of forceful land acquisition was in Singur, West Bengal. A state famous for its land reforms, aimed at empowering landless labourers and small farmers, embarked on a path of intensive industrialisation making way for private investment. As part of this ambitious plan, it acquired land for the manufacture of India's cheapest car, the Nano. A project that was presented as a milestone for the country's common man, the world's cheapest car at Rs 1 lakh, actually translated into violent repression as police forces brutally put down resistance. The company was forced to relocate.

When recently the state's new chief minister, Mamata Banerjee (who had led the resistance), came to power, she passed a Land Bill for returning the seized land to the original owners. Tata challenged the move in court, labelling it unconstitutional, lamenting the takeover at night without prior notice and consent. Yet this is exactly what farmers face when state governments grab land for corporations. Tata was also involved in a land-grab in Kalinganagar, Orissa, where thirteen tribals were killed; in Gopalpur, protests forced Tata to halt the Gopalpur steel plant.

Nevertheless, the Tata name remains practically stain-free, as the company's charitable initiatives have also given it a considerable degree of respect. The general public tends to overlook such violent instances as an act of the state alone – and once they are placed in a context of "industrialisation and development", even forcible actions are accepted as a necessary evil. Such regressive thinking leads to the acceptance of dispossession, as long as a top-down option is presented as the "modern alternative". Tata Steel vice-president H.H. Nerukar's words on the rehabilitation of adivasis go a long way in illustrating this attitude:

> Tata Steel has improved the standard of living. There are many special initiatives for tribal development. In spite of doing this, tribals have not reached where they ought to have, even in Jamshedpur. Tribals have to be looked after much more. These people haven't seen anything positive in life, so we'll give them training. It will be a residential course. We'll take them and give them 10 days of attitude training. We'll get them to quit their habits.[22]

Vedanta

Anil Agarwal, the twelfth richest Indian in the Forbes list, was born into a business family that made aluminium conductors. He built his metal empire by acquiring previously government-owned assets: in 2001 Agarwal's company, Sterlite, acquired 51 per cent ownership of the publicly owned Bharat Aluminium Company (BALCO), the first to produce aluminium in India at a throwaway price. The takeover itself was widely protested; even the chief minister of Chhattisgarh, Ajit Jogi, supported the striking BALCO workers. The case was brought to the Supreme Court as violating the laws of the land envisioned in the Fifth Schedule of the Indian Constitution, whereby tribal land cannot be transferred to private owners. Jogi also levelled serious allegations of corruption against political figures, while protesting the Centre's bypassing of the state government. The bureaucratic apparatus remained unfazed and justified the deal on financial grounds. The PSU was allegedly worth Rs 3,000 crores, whereas the deal with Agarwal totalled Rs 551 crores;[23] at the same time, Agarwal also entered into an MoU with the Orissa government for the supply of iron ore to its newly acquired plant. As BALCO had been publicly owned the land for the plant was acquired by the government at a mere Rs 20 per acre, only to be transferred to a private company, generating profits only for its shareholders.

Similarly, the government's proposal to divest from the National Aluminium Company Limited (NALCO) was greeted with huge protests from the public, trade unions and political parties; Vedanta's Sterlite and Hindalco were among the top bidders. Acquiring NALCO would make Agarwal India's largest player in aluminium and copper. He also bought majority shares in Hindustan Zinc Limited (HZL) and in the Madras Aluminium Company, and has proposed that he buy out the remaining 49 per cent government stake in BALCO and HZL. Sterlite also owns 51 per cent of Sesa Goa, India's largest iron ore producer and exporter: the deal raised allegations of severe financial irregularities and was under investigation by the Serious Fraud Investigation Office. Other questions were raised about the NALCO divestment. While divestment is usually advocated for loss-making PSUs, these buy-outs came under intense scrutiny as the companies were running more than successfully and, arguably, were sold for a song. In return, managing the ex-PSUs would allow Agarwal a huge turnover first, because of market domination, and second, free access to the heavily sought after raw materials: iron ore, bauxite and other minerals.

In 2003, the listing of Agarwal's Sterlite-controlled Vedanta Resources on the London Stock Exchange made it the first Indian company listed on international markets, and proved to be a turning point for Agarwal's wealth creation. Unlike others who managed to maintain a good name despite serious malpractice allegations, Agarwal's ill repute grew along with his business plans. Even more ominous was Vedanta and its chairman's attempt at mining bauxite from the hills of Niyamgiri, home to the living god of the Dongria Kondh, one of India's protected indigenous primitive tribal groups who reside amidst the lush vegetation that covers the mountain.

The Dongria Kondh don't require a legal framework to determine their access to and use of resources, as principles of sustainability, equity and community guide their lifestyle. The institutional system based on individual rights not only does not protect the customary values of indigenous people, it also threatens the implementation of any rights at all. Despite specific legislations such as the Provisions for Extension of Scheduled Areas and the Forest Rights Act (2006), the government has repeatedly failed to implement them. The Niyamgiri battle is probably the most revealing, as it clearly uncovers the connection between privatisation, accumulation by dispossession, and the infringement of rights and regulations in the broader context of the state as an agent of forced industrialisation. A closer look at the means through which such wealth has been created forces the question: is it really being created or has it merely been redistributed from the weaker to the more powerful?

What does this mean for citizenship? For development? The government professes inclusive growth: yet what does this mean for the majority of India's agricultural communities, fisherfolk, landless labourers, adivasis and tribals? If we account for those who have lost their land, their sustenance, their homes and even their lives in this battle between two opposing paradigms, surely the growth story takes a hit; if we account for the thousands of hectares of land diverted to industry and hence removed from food production, that's another hit; if we start factoring in even only the financial cost of food imports, of healthcare provision for the effects of lifestyle diseases added to those of poverty and hunger, and of hazardous polluters and chemicals-led diseases, and further add the cost of internal conflict, it is fairly evident that the end result will look very different from India's growth miracle. And when we start accounting for the same in social and environmental terms, we realise that our future is at stake.

While it is worrisome enough that India's growth is following such a lopsided pattern, it is even more worrying to see how the few powerful at the top are becoming increasingly denationalised – removed from the reality of their countries, while collaborating with international counterparts across the world. Not only multinational corporations, even domestic ones are increasingly rootless as business pushes them into partnerships and joint ventures, mergers and acquisitions, all over the world. Foreign companies eye the dynamic

Indian market, both in terms of a demand for goods and services and, importantly, to gain access to India's natural resource wealth; Indian companies are following their lead, either to avoid domestic regulation where it still exists, or to repeat the same plunder and profit model abroad, often in weaker economies or fragile states.

During 2010-11, Shashi Ruia of Essar invested $1.2 billion abroad and $200 million in India; Mukesh Ambani's domestic investments were $2.7 billion while investments abroad were $8 billion; Ratan Tata invested $200 million in India and $3 billion abroad; Anil Ambani invested $400 million in India and $3 billion abroad; Sunil Mittal invested $2 billion in India and $16 billion abroad.[24] The disregard for national priorities is being translated into the creation of a group of global oligarchs increasingly removed from the ground reality of society. The super rich create gated islands of luxury beyond the reach of common people, while at the same time ensuring that their wealth is on display for others to admire and gape at. Mukesh Ambani's 27-storey residence called Antilla, in Mumbai, the capital of slums, symbolises this dichotomy, as do SEZs.

But there are other economies and sectors that we should be aware of. Closely related to the concept of people's sustenance economy is what Hilkka Pietila has termed the "free" or informal economy in industrialised societies. This consists of the non-monetary core of the economy and society and includes unpaid work for one's own and family needs; community activities; mutual help and co-operation within the neighbourhood; and so on. In addition, there is the "protected sector" consisting of production for domestic markets, which is protected and guided by official means. This sector covers food, construction, services, administration, health, schools, culture, and so on. Finally Pietila describes the familiar free-trade economy, or what she calls the "fettered" economy, which consists of large-scale production for export, and production to compete with imports. The terms in this economy are dictated by the world market, dependency, vulnerability, compulsive competitiveness and so forth.[25] In 1980, for example, the proportion of time and money that went into running each category of the Finnish economy is shown in the Table below.

		Time	*Money*
		%	%
A.	The free economy	54	35
	(informal economy)		
B.	Protected sector	36	46
C.	The fettered economy	10	19

In patriarchal economies, B and C are considered to be the primary economy, and A, the "free" or informal economy, is perceived as secondary. In fact, as Marilyn Waring has documented, national accounts and GNP figures actually exclude the informal economy which is seen as lying outside the "production boundary".[26] But what most economists and politicians call the free or informal economy is in reality, for many women, the fettered economy, because when the fettered economy becomes 'poor' – that is, runs into deficit – it is the free or informal economy (which is made up predominantly of women's work) that pays to restore it to health. In times of structural adjustment and austerity programmes, cuts in public expenditure generally fall most heavily on the poor, and on women. In many cases, government efforts to reduce the level of a country's fiscal deficit are implemented by making substantial cuts in social and economic development expenditure – hence real wages and consumption decrease considerably.

The trade metaphor *vs* nature's economy

As the 'trade' metaphor has come to replace the metaphor of 'home', economic value itself has undergone a shift. Value, which means 'worth', is redefined as 'exchange and trade', so unless something is traded it has no economic value. And 'home', as the root and metaphor for the economy, is substituted by the metaphor of 'trade', which is seen as the source of economic value. The 'trade' metaphor has also rendered nature's economy valueless; the marginalisation of both women's work and nature's work are linked to how 'home' is now perceived as a place where nothing of economic value is produced.

This shift in the understanding of economic value is central to the ecological crisis and is reflected in the change in the meaning of the term 'resource'. 'Resource' originally implied life; its root is the Latin verb *surgere*, which evoked the image of a spring that continually rises from the ground. Like a spring, a resource renews again and again, even if it has been repeatedly used and consumed. The concept thus highlighted nature's power of regeneration and called attention to her prodigious creativity. With the advent of industrialisation and colonialism, however, a conceptual break occurred. 'Natural resources' became those elements of nature which were required as inputs for industrial production and colonial trade. In this view, nature was clearly stripped of her creative power and turned into a container of raw material waiting to be transformed into inputs for commodity production. Resources are now merely any material or conditions existing in nature which may be subjected to 'economic exploitation'. With the capacity of regeneration gone, the attitude of 'give and take' has also lost its ground; it is now simply human inventiveness and industry which impart value to nature, and it is only when capital and technology have been brought in that nature will find her destiny.

An ecological and feminist agenda for trade needs to be evolved based on the ecological limits and social criteria that economic activity must adhere to, if it is to respect the environmental principle of sustainability and the ethical principle of justice. This requires that the full ecological and social costs of economic activity and trade be made visible and taken into account. Globalisation that erases ecological and social costs is inconsistent with the need to minimise environmental destruction and human suffering. Localisation – based on stronger democratic decision-making at local levels, building up to national and global levels – is an imperative for conservation as well as democracy. Through the expanded decision-making roles of marginalised groups, including tribals, peasants and women at local levels, certain criteria can be evolved to distinguish between economic activities that need to be locally controlled, and those that can be globalised.

Globalisation has undermined the capacity of local communities and citizens to influence policies that affect their lives. Localisation and decentralisation do not imply dictatorships or isolation – they are based on the principle of subsidiarity, and help to discriminate between the different aspects of social and economic life. They establish appropriate forms of governance for each activity, to ensure the protection of people and the environment.

Most work in the world is done by women. More significantly, most of the work that I call the sustenance economy, is called the subsistence economy by Maria Mies, Veronika Bennholdt-Thomson and Claudia van Werlhof.[27] Genevieve Vaughan calls it the "gift economy",[28] and Riane Eisler calls it the "caring economy".[29] As Ronnie Lessem and Alexander Schieffer observe,

> If the fathers of capitalist theory had chosen a mother rather than a single bourgeois male as the smallest economic unit for their theoretical constructions, they would not have been able to formulate the axiom of the selfish nature of human beings in the way they did.[30]

On such false assumptions of capitalist patriarchy does the entire edifice of the dominant economic paradigm rest. A change in paradigm has become a survival imperative.

Beyond "free-market democracy"

Freedom in our times has been purveyed as "free-market democracy", but as we have seen, free-markets mean freedom for corporations to exploit whom and what they want, where they want, how they want.

The distancing of instruments of growth from reality must create bubbles – the housing bubble, the food bubble, the land bubble. Just as the illusion of growth and the fiction of finance has made the economy volatile and unpredictable, the fiction of the corporation as a legal person has replaced citizens and made society unstable and non-sustainable. Corporations have been assigned legal personhood, and corporate rights are now displacing the rights of the earth, and the rights of people to the earth's resources. Though corporations are not natural persons, they are recognised as such in law. A legal construction thus acquires human rights and is able to quash the human rights of people and the natural rights of all beings. Moreover, corporations are able to constantly expand their "human rights"; they are able to transform biodiversity into "intellectual property" by shaping laws; they can own water and rivers; they can own the air, the skies and the carbon in the atmosphere. They can even own and trade in nature's ecological services through the green economy.

Democracy is supposed to be by the people, of the people, for the people. On January 21, 2010, the US Supreme Court legalised democracy as being of the corporations, by the corporations, for the corporations, by ruling that, "it is a violation of corporations' civil liberties to limit their influence over the political process". Rushkoff says:

> Even though they are artificial entities with greater access to capital, infinite longevity and no interest in or connection to humanity, we now guarantee them the right of free speech ... freedom of speech was intended as a way for human beings to guarantee their ability to speak out against largely systemic and structural repression. A corporation has that same guarantee.[31]

In effect, the *Citizen United v. Federal Election Commission* case allows corporations to hijack democracy, it allows them to consolidate the corporate state which privatises every aspect of life and transforms it into a commodity to maximise profits. Recognising that we are part of the earth, and earth citizenship is our highest humanity, Tagore wrote,

> Now the problem before us is of one single country, which is the Earth, where the races as individuals must find both their freedom of self-expression and their bond of federation. Mankind must realise a unity wider in range, deeper in sentiment, stronger in power than ever before.

The limitless hunger of industrial capitalism and imperialism was seen by Tagore as a prolific weed:

It is carnivorous and cannibalistic in its tendencies, it feeds upon the resources of other people and tries to swallow their whole future ... Before this political civilisation came to its power and opened its hungry jaws wide enough to gulp down entire continents of the earth, we had wars, pillages, changes of monarchy and consequent miseries, but never such a sight of fearful and hopeless voracity, such wholesale feeding of nation upon nation, such huge machines for turning great portions of the earth into mincemeat.[32]

The voices of the 99 per cent

In the US, the Occupy Movement is called the movement of the 99 per cent. The fact that they were supported by actions around the world when they were going to be evicted, shows that everywhere people are fed up with the current system. They are fed up with the power of corporations, they are fed up with the destruction of democracy and people's rights. They refuse to give their consent to the bailout of banks by squeezing people of their livelihoods. The contest, as the 99 per cent describe it, is between life and economic interests, between people and corporations, between democracy and economic dictatorship.

Their organising style is based on the deepest and the most direct democracy. Those from the dominant system are puzzled; they call the movements leaderless because they are unable to understand that in the squares, everyone is a leader, respecting the leadership of everyone else. This is self-organisation. This is how life works. This is how democracy works. This is what Gandhi called Swaraj. Those used to hierarchy and domination do not understand horizontal organising and decision-making. Gandhi described the principle of horizontal organising as the difference between circles and pyramids:

Life will not be a pyramid with the apex sustained by the bottom, but it will be an oceanic circle whose centre will be the individual always ready to perish for the village, the latter ready to perish for the circle of villages, till at last the whole becomes one life composed of individuals, never aggressive in their arrogance, but ever humble, sharing the majesty of the oceanic circle of which they are integral units. Therefore, the outermost circumference will not wield power to crush the inner circle, but will give strength to all within and will derive its own strength from it.[33]

The general assemblies in the squares of Spain are living examples of these "ever expanding, never ascending" oceanic circles. When everyone has to be included in decision-making, consensus is the only way; this is how indigenous cultures have practised democracy throughout history. When corporate rule displaces democracy, participation is replaced by representation and the people's representatives mutate into corporate representatives who represent money power. The new movements of the future are movements of the excluded who have been deprived of every right, political, economic and social. They have nothing to lose but their disposability and dispensability.

In spite of being the victims of brutal injustice and exclusion, non-violence is a deep commitment of these new movements, and "Occupy" is in fact a reclaiming of the commons. The park is the physical commons in every town. Today, the parks are places for announcing to Wall Street, to banks, to governments, that the 99 per cent is withdrawing its consent from the present disorder which has pushed millions to homelessness, joblessness and hunger.

Consumerism lubricates the war against the earth. Since corporate exploitation violates all limits, it is based on debt. The first is the ecological debt to the earth and to societies which have been ravaged for resource exploitation; the second is the debt into which countries are trapped as multilateral financial institutions give loans to commercialise every sector of the economy. Both nature's economy and the sustenance economy are destroyed. Self-provisioning gives way to borrowing, production is replaced by consumption. This is what has happened to India's agriculture. First India was indebted by borrowing for the green revolution in 1965-66, then the debt thus created imposed structural adjustment as the "reforms" of 1991, combined with the imposition of WTO rules in 1995. The third is the consumer debt in rich countries. In 2010, US consumer debt outstandings stood at $2.4 trillion; consumers pay nearly 12 per cent of their income to service debts. Americans own 1.5 billion credit cards, which amounts to nine credit cards per person, and were expected to have a $6,500 billion credit card debt that year.[34]

"Enoughness" has become vital to the experience of a freedom that is inclusive of the freedom of all beings and all people.

"Enoughness" is the basis of earth democracy and earth citizenship.

"Enoughness" creates the conditions of peace, both peace with nature and peace between people. Greed drives resource conflicts, wars with the earth, and wars against people.

"Enoughness" is based on caring for the earth and society. This caring creates the imperative of sharing, of recovering the commons. And a culture of sharing is a culture of peace.

On November, 2010, a historic case was filed by an international coalition of defenders of nature's rights at the Constitutional Court of Ecuador against British Petroleum and its crimes against nature. Ecuador recognises the rights of nature in its current constitution, adopted in 2008, which provides the fundamental basis for this legal case with regard to the massive environmental disaster caused when BP's Deepwater Horizon rig exploded on April 20, 2010. The company constantly prevaricated about the scale of the disaster and topped this up by using unusually high amounts of toxic chemical dispersants to cover up the spill. The BP oil spill was the largest marine oil spill in the history of the petroleum industry, almost twenty times greater than the Exxon Valdez oil spill. The oil flowed for three months, releasing 4.9 million barrels of oil before the spill was capped on July 15, 2010.

It caused major damage to marine and coastal ecosystems and devastated the Gulf's fishing and tourism industries. In Louisiana, 510 kms. of shoreline were polluted. In October 2011, the Office of Protected Resources of the National Marine Fisheries Services of the US found that dolphins and whales continued to die at twice the normal rate. More than 8,332 species, including 1,200 fish, 200 birds, 1,400 molluscs, 1,500 crustaceans, four sea turtles, and 29 marine mammals were impacted. By November 2010, 6,814 dead animals, including 6,104 birds, 609 sea turtles, 100 dolphins, had been culled. This was clearly an ecocide, and its impact went beyond the Gulf of Mexico.

In June 2010, BP set up a $20 billion fund to compensate the millions of people whose lives and livelihoods had been destroyed by the spill. The defenders of nature are not seeking financial compensation since the harm done to it cannot be compensated for monetarily. Some of the key demands in the Ecuador case are that BP should release all data and information on the ecological destruction caused by the oil spill, and that it should also refrain from extracting as much oil underground as it spilt in the Gulf of Mexico. Ecuador has also decided to keep the oil underground in the Yasuni National Park to protect the Amazon forest. Besides this, the activists have called for supporting the Yasuni ITT proposal of the Ecuadorean government to leave the oil in that sensitive ecosystem underground. They also urged the US government to extend the moratorium on offshore oil drilling.

The case against BP was unique because it recognised the rights of nature; it was unique because it was based not on commercial and moral demands, but the ethical demand for ecological responsibility. And because we are all members of the earth community which knows no national borders, an international group of activists filed the case jointly. It included:

- Nnimmo Bassey (Friends of the Earth, Nigeria, and Coordinator of Oilwatch International and 2010 Laureate of the Right Livelihood Award)
- Delfín Tenesaca (President of ECUARUNARI, indigenous Andean-Ecuadorean organisation)
- Blanca Chancoso (Ecuadorean indigenous leader)
- Líder Góngora (representative of the ancestral people of mangroves)

- Alberto Acosta (ex-President of the Constitutional Assembly of Ecuador)
- Ana Luiz Valdéz (representative of social movements from Chiapas, Mexico)
- Diana Murcia (Colombian human rights lawyer)
- Cecilia Chérrez (President of Acción Ecológica, Ecuador)
- Vandana Shiva (eco-feminist and winner of the 1993 Right Livelihood Award)

Bolivia is also working to incorporate the rights of the earth into its Constitution. On Earth Day, 2010, the President of Bolivia, Juan Evo Morales Ayma organised a conference on Rights of Mother Earth; the idea was to start a process for adopting a Universal Declaration of the Rights of Mother Earth on the lines of the Universal Declaration of Human Rights. Without earth rights, there can be no human rights; it is time to strengthen human rights by deepening the recognition that humans depend on the earth, that the earth provides us sustenance, that the earth comes first.

Making peace with the earth

Humanity stands at a precipice. We have to make a choice. Will we continue to obey the market laws of corporate greed or Gaia's laws for maintenance of the earth's ecosystems and the diversity of her beings? The laws for maximising corporate profits are based on:

1. Privatising the earth
2. Enclosing the commons
3. Externalising the costs of ecological destruction
4. Creating corporate economies of death and destruction
5. Destroying democracy
6. Destroying cultural diversity

The laws for protecting the rights of Mother Earth are based on:

1. Respecting the integrity of the earth's ecosystems and ecological process
2. Recovery of the commons

3.   Internalising ecological costs
4.   Creating living economies
5.   Creating living democracies
6.   Creating living cultures

The transition from corporate control of the earth's resources to earth democracy has become an imperative for the survival of democracy, human freedom and the human species. This transition includes the following:

1.   A shift in our worldview from the Cartesian-mechanistic paradigm that defines the earth as dead matter to recognising that she is alive and vibrant, the source of all abundance and all life, that we are a part of the earth, not apart from her, that we are her children, not her masters and owners.

2.   A shift in the perception and presumption of the earth, her ecosystems and resources, and all her beings as the property of corporations, to the recognition that the earth's resources are our commons, to be cared for and shared.

3.   A shift from reductionist, fragmented knowledge that sees the earth and our bodies as separate and divided, to the awareness that everything is connected, and life is relationship.

4.   A shift from measuring and maximising Gross Domestic Product to experiencing joy, happiness, fulfilment and maximising Gross National Happiness.

5.   A shift from the freedom of corporations to freedom for all life on earth.

6.   A shift from a preoccupation with competition to a dedication to cooperation.

7.   A shift from corporate globalisation to economic localisation based on minimising the exploitation of natural resources while maximising the creativity of dignified, meaningful livelihoods and work.

8.   A shift from the culture of limitless consumption and consumerism to cultures of conservation, caring and compassion, from cultures of death to cultures of life.

9. A shift from hierarchical monocultures, systems of exclusion and domination, to inclusive cultures based on diversity, with the recognition that

Earth Rights are Human Rights
Earth Rights are Women's Rights
Earth Rights are Indigenous Rights
Earth Rights are the Rights of Children, Youth and Future Generations.

References

[1] E. J. Mishan, *The Costs of Economic Growth,* London: Staples Press,1967, pp. xviii-xix.
[2] Declaration of G-20, Whitehouse.gov
[3] Ref: http://www.treasurydirect.gov/govt/reports
[4] The World Bank Independent Evaluation Group: Structural Adjustment in India http://lnweb90.worldbank.org/ed oeddoclib.nsf/b57456d58aba40e585256ad400736404/0586cc45a 28a2749852567f5005d8c89?OpenDocument
[5] Prabhat Patnaik, "The Economics of the New Phase of Imperialism," www.macroscan.org/anl/aug05/pdf/Economics New-Phase-pdf
[6] Parthapritam Pal and Jayati Ghosh, "Inequality in India: A Survey of Recent Trends," DESA Working Paper no. 45, July 2007.
[7] See the Arcelor Mittal and BBC websites for details of the company's holdings worldwide.
[8] Stuart Corbridge and John Harris, *Reinventing India*, London: Polity Press, 2000.
[9] "CAG says Govt. Favoured Reliance", *The Statesman,* June 13, 2011.
[10] Navdanya, *The Great Indian Land-Grab*, op. cit., 2011.
[11] Essar Company Profile, www.essar.com
[12] "Essar Gets Bailadila Prospecting Lease", *Down to Earth*, April 15, 2007.
[13] "Water Wars", *Tehelka,* January 29, 2011.
[14] "Jindal vs. Jindal…or Jindal Plus Jindal?" *Business Today*, October 9, 2010.
[15] "Villagers Protest Forest Acquisition", *Down to Earth*, January 31, 2011.
[16] "Water Wars", *Tehelka,* January 29, 2011.
[17] "Green Tribunal Says No to Jindal Steel", *The Hindu*, April 20, 2012.

18 "Fishworkers' Campaign Draws Attention to the Sale of Marine Waters", *Down to Earth*, June 15, 2008.

19 "Power of Black Gold", *Tehelka*, September 10, 2011.

20 http://sanhati.com/articles3610

21 Bharti group's Sunil Mittal on "Lessons of Entrepreneurship and Leadership," available at http://knowledge.wharton.upenn.edu/india/article.cfm?articleid=4306

22 Vandana Shiva and Ajsar Jafri, "Stronger Than Steel: People's Movements Against Globalisation and the Gopalpur Steel Plant," Delhi: RFSTE, 1998.

23 http://www.alacrastore.com/mergers-acquisitions/sterlite_industries_India_Limited-1080728

24 "Flight of Capital", *India Today*, August 1, 2011.

25 Hilkka Pietila , "The Triangle of the Human Economy: Household, Cultivation, Industrial Production", in *Ecological Economics*, February 20, 1997, pp. 113-28.

26 Marilyn Waring, *If Women Counted: A New Feminist Economics,* San Francisco: Harper & Row, 1988.

27 Maria Mies and Veronika Bennholdt-Thomson, *The Subsistence Perspective*, London: Zed Books, 1999.

28 Genevieve Vaughan, *For: Giving – A Feminist Criticism of Exchange*, Texas: Plain View Press, 1997.

29 Riane Eisler, *The Real Wealth of Nations*, San Francisco: Berrett Koehler Publishers, 2007.

30 Ronnie Lessem & Alexander Schieffer, *Integral Economies*, Farnham: Ashgate/Gower, 2010.

31 Doug Rushkoff, "Corporations as Über Citizens", Rushkoff.com, January 22, 2010.

32 Quoted in Sisir Kumar Das (ed.), *The English Language Writings of Rabindranath Tagore*, op. cit.

33 Quoted in R.Kothari, *Towards New Horizons*, Ahmedabad: Navjivan Press, 1974.

34 http://www.money-zine.com/financialplanning/debt.consolidation/consumer-debtstatistics